# SNOWSHOE ROUTES

*washington*

# SNOWSHOE ROUTES

*washington*

Second Edition

DAN A. NELSON

THE MOUNTAINEERS BOOKS

Published by
The Mountaineers Books
1001 SW Klickitat Way, Suite 201
Seattle, WA 98134

First edition, 1998. Second edition, 2003.

Published simultaneously in Great Britain by Cordee, 3a DeMontfort Street, Leicester, England, LE1 7HD

Manufactured in the United States of America

Project Editor: Margaret Sullivan
Editor: Julie Van Pelt
Cover and Book Design: The Mountaineers Books
Layout Artist: Jennifer LaRock Shontz
Mapmakers: Jerry Painter and Jennifer LaRock Shontz
All photographs by the author unless otherwise noted.

Cover photograph: *Couple snowshoeing, Mount Baker National Forest, WA*
    © Don Mason/Corbis
Frontispiece: *Snowshoers and skiers share the route into Cowlitz Park, Mount Rainier National Park*

*Library of Congress Cataloging-in-Publication Data*
Nelson, Dan A.
  Snowshoe routes, Washington / Dan Nelson.— 2nd ed.
      p. cm. — (Snowshoe routes series)
Includes index.
  ISBN 0-89886-884-X (pbk.)
  1. Snowshoes and snowshoeing—Washington (State)—Guidebooks. 2.
Trails—Washington (State)—Guidebooks. 3. Washington
(State)—Guidebooks. I. Title: Snowshoe routes. II. Title. III. Series.

GV853.N45 2003
796.92'09797—dc21
                              2003011273

# Contents

-------------------

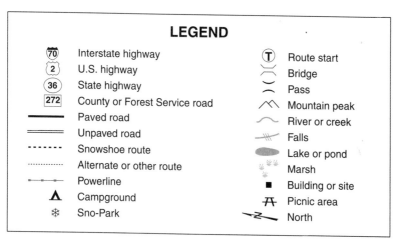

# LEGEND

| | |
|---|---|
| 70 | Interstate highway |
| 2 | U.S. highway |
| 36 | State highway |
| 272 | County or Forest Service road |
| | Paved road |
| | Unpaved road |
| | Snowshoe route |
| | Alternate or other route |
| | Powerline |
| Λ | Campground |
| ❋ | Sno-Park |

| | |
|---|---|
| T | Route start |
| | Bridge |
| | Pass |
| | Mountain peak |
| | River or creek |
| | Falls |
| | Lake or pond |
| | Marsh |
| ■ | Building or site |
| ⊼ | Picnic area |
| | North |

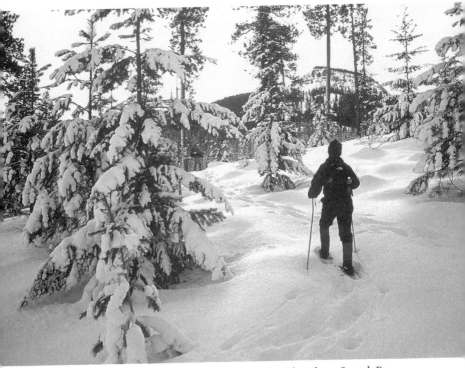

*Making tracks through the open forest on the ridge above Swauk Pass*

# Preface

In the mid-1990s, snowshoeing took off. This age-old activity began to boom as a winter sport. As the new millennium dawned, the sport kept growing. In the Pacific Northwest today, snowshoeing is rivaling cross-country skiing in numbers of enthusiasts.

Part of the reason for that is the tremendous popularity of hiking in the Pacific Northwest. Summer hikers are loath to give up their favorite pastime simply because the seasons change. So, come winter, hikers have two options—step onto a pair of cross-country skis, or strap on snowshoes. In the past, skis have been the preferred choice for backcountry enthusiasts. But not everyone wants to take the time, or make the considerable effort, needed to master the art of cross-country skiing in mountain country. Snowshoeing has become a popular alternative.

Following years of slow growth and relative obscurity as a recreational pursuit, snowshoeing began to boom in the early 1990s. Since 1990, the number of people enjoying a winter hike on snowshoes has increased by more than 500 percent. Probably the main reason for this trend is the ease with which beginners can become accomplished snowshoers. Anyone who knows how to walk, knows how to use snowshoes—just strap them on and walk, it's as simple as that. Another reason snowshoes are increasingly popular is that hikers can get to the same areas in winter that they hike to in summer. They can move easily through thick forests and up steep slopes. Skis, on the other hand, are more difficult to maneuver on forest trails, and uphill slopes pose tougher challenges for novice skiers (although the downhill run is undeniably more fun on skis).

Although hikers can travel many of the same trails on snowshoes that they can in the summer, more often than not the trailheads for those trails are inaccessible by car. Fortunately, the surge in interest in cross-country skiing in the 1970s prompted the state of Washington to build and maintain a series of Sno-Parks throughout the state. These facilities are merely parking

11

lots that are kept cleared of snow, and access roads that are kept plowed during the winter. More than 110 Sno-Parks are maintained for winter recreationists, with no fewer than fifty devoted solely to nonmotorized recreationists.

Cross-country skiers and snowmobilers have utilized these Sno-Parks for two and a half decades now. Many of the facilities also feature groomed ski trails, groomed snowmobile trails, and a few even have tracks set for skiers who prefer that mode of skiing.

While the skinny skis and screaming snowmobiles crowd the groomed roads and wide trails leading out of these parking areas, snowshoers can take advantage of the solitude found on the forest trails that angle away from the roads. These snow-laden paths are impossible—if not illegal—for snowmobilers to negotiate and too difficult for the majority of skiers to attempt. But a hiker wearing a pair of modern snowshoes can climb the snowy trail as easily as a hiker can trudge up switchbacks in summer. In fact, snowshoers have a decided advantage over their summer colleagues simply because they can often walk right over the top of many difficult obstacles—thick brush, fallen logs, treacherous talus fields, and so forth. A heavy blanket of snow can level the most difficult field so that in winter, hikers feel like they are hiking through an open meadow, whereas in summer, hikers may find the same area to be an impassable slope of slide alder.

Unfortunately, that blanket of snow can also make finding a specific trail next to impossible. That's where this book comes in. I have put together 100 of my favorite winter hikes around Washington and present them here as a means of helping other hikers find the beauty of the winter backcountry without the hassle of trying to pick and choose a route. Of course, the routes I describe here are not as easy to follow as a snow-free summer trail, nor should snowshoers think they have to follow my exact footprints. Part of the mystique and wonder of snowshoe hiking is the ability to explore anywhere—a route is limited only by a snowshoer's physical and mental limits, tempered with a heavy dose of common sense and avalanche awareness.

# Introduction

Snowshoes are the earliest known means of making travel on snow easier. The best archeological evidence suggests these early "foot extenders" originated in central Asia about 4000 B.C. Further evidence shows that without this mode of winter transportation, aboriginal people would not have been able to journey to what is now North America via the Bering Strait. Snowshoes are a natural for modern-day winter trekking, as more and more people are coming to realize. With a little planning and preparation, you can embrace the beauties of the backcountry year-round.

*One of the joys of snowshoeing is 'reading the signs' of passing wildlife, such as these fox tracks*

Definite benefits are derived by supplementing warm-weather hiking with snowshoeing come winter. In addition to the readily apparent payoffs of summer hiking—escape from the mechanized, hectic world, if only for a short time; strenuous, healthy workouts in beautiful surroundings; the thrill of accomplishment after hiking a long trail or climbing a steep peak; communion with the natural world—winter wilderness rambling offers its own rewards. The landscape is more serene, covered in a sound-absorbing carpet of snow. No irritating swarms of bugs gnaw on your exposed skin, and far fewer humans compete for a spot in the quiet wilderness.

Of course, there are other winter recreation considerations, most notably the weather—the cold weather. This factor influences all the benefits—and dangers—of exploring a snow-shrouded wilderness.

The lower temperatures of winter make snow recreation more intense than its warmer-season counterparts. The planning and preparation of a trip takes more time and thought. More equipment and clothing are needed for winter camping. The discomforts of a poorly planned trip are more acute. But the pleasures of a good outing are more profound.

## STEPPING OUT INTO THE SNOW

The most visible change from summer to winter is your method of locomotion. When the snow flies, it is no longer possible to merely lace up your sturdy boots and head up the trail—try doing that after a deep pack of Cascade concrete has filtered down on the hills, and you'll find yourself exhausted in the first 100 yards. That's where snowshoes come in. Snowshoes are the easiest way to get acquainted with winter wilderness. The basics of snowshoeing are simple—it's just like walking, but with bigger feet. Of course, there is a bit more to it than that, but essentially, any other techniques are simply variations of walking strides.

Snowshoes themselves come in a variety of forms. Traditional shoes are made with wooden frames and rawhide laces for decking. These range in shape from round "bear paws" to long, tapered "Yukons," which feature a lot of surface area and extended tails that drag in the snow to help keep the shoes pointed forward. You can still find wooden shoes, although the lace decking is usually made with strips of neoprene rubber these days, but the best bet for any general-use winter hiking is the "modern" design. This is essentially a narrow bear paw. It features an aluminum or rigid plastic oval frame with a solid decking of synthetic fabric. Several shoes are now available that are made from extruded plastic. Some of these solid plastic shoes are lightweight, affordable, and for the most part, very effective. Regardless of the type, make sure the shoes have ice spikes—called crampons, or cleats—under the fore-foot and heel plates.

The size of your snowshoes depends on a number of factors, primarily your weight (including the weight of your pack) and the kind of snow in which you'll be trekking. In the Cascades, the general rule is to plan on heavy, wet snow. Most people under 180 pounds can wear snowshoes in the 8-by-25-inch category. Larger folks, or hikers who will be carrying heavy packs, should consider shoes in the 9-by-30-inch range. Big guys with very heavy packs can go up to a 9-by-36-inch shoe.

If you plan to snowshoe in the Rocky Mountains, or in areas where the snow is generally lighter and fluffier, you'll need to move up a step in shoe size. Before buying a pair of snowshoes, it is a good idea to rent several different pairs to get a feel for which model you prefer and which size is best for you.

## FOOTWEAR

Unlike cross-country skiing, there are no specific boots that must be worn with snowshoes. Regular hiking boots, mountaineering boots, heavily insulated "pac" boots, or even cross-country ski boots can be worn with the easy-to-use bindings found on most quality snowshoes. Ideally, you want boots that provide the type of ankle and foot support found in regular hiking boots, but which also keep your feet warm and dry.

Many hiking boot companies have begun to work with snowshoe makers to design insulated hiking boots specifically for snowshoe trekking. The best option now is to use all-leather hiking boots that are large enough to comfortably allow you to wear a thick layer or two of insulated socks, and then cover the boots with waterproof gaiters. Just don't pack too much wool into your boots, because too tight of a fit will make your feet feel even colder than if there were no insulation.

## CLOTHING

In addition to snowshoes, you'll need to carry several layers of bulky clothing in your pack for winter excursions. Avoid anything made with cotton. Instead, you'll need multiple layers of synthetic or wool clothing.

By layering your clothing, you can easily make adjustments when you start to heat up (and you will heat up, as walking in snowshoes is a better aerobic workout than walking on a dry trail) or cool down—just add or subtract a layer or two. Working from the skin out, start with a good base layer of silk or synthetic (polypropylene, Capilene, Thermastat, etc.) long

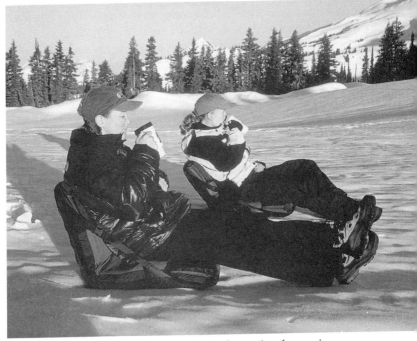

*Snow campers make use of their sleeping pads to enjoy the sunrise*

johns. These will form a thin insulating layer next to your skin, but more importantly, they will pull moisture away from your body. Without that wicking action, the moisture could end up freezing on your skin, causing almost instant hypothermia.

Over the base layer, add a thin insulating layer, like a wool or synthetic fleece sweater and pants. On very cold days, or if you generally get cold easily, cover this layer with a thicker insulating layer—a fleece jacket or vest. When the wind is blowing or moisture is in the air, top off the whole outfit with a sturdy waterproof parka and pants. This layer will cut the wind and prevent any external water from soaking through.

The idea behind building an insulation shell in layers is that you can then easily adjust your clothing to the conditions. When getting started each day, take into consideration not only the weather but also the type of snowshoeing you'll be doing. A lot of climbing early on means you'll be working hard, and if you have too many layers, you'll quickly work up a sweat. To avoid that, adjust the layers to the point where you can just feel a chill as you start out, knowing that within a few steps you'll be warmed up enough to be comfortable, but not overheated.

## OTHER GEAR

Every time you venture more than a few yards away from the road on a snowshoe outing, you should be prepared to spend the night under the stars (or under the clouds, as may be more likely). Winter storms can whip up in a hurry, catching you by surprise. What was an easy-to-follow trail during a calm, clear day can disappear into a confusing world of white in a windswept snowstorm. Therefore, every member of the party should have a pack loaded with The Mountaineers Ten Essentials, as well as a few other items that aren't necessarily essential but are good to have on hand in a winter emergency.

### The Ten Essentials: A Systems Approach

1. Navigation (map and compass). Carry a compass and a topographic map of the area you plan to be in, and know how to use them.
2. Sun protection (sunglasses and sunscreen). While necessary for most high-alpine travel, sunglasses are absolutely essential for snow. Snow blindness (sunburn of the eyes) can render you immobile and helpless.
3. Insulation (extra clothing). This means more clothing than you would wear during the worst weather of the planned outing. If you get injured or lost, you won't be moving around generating heat, so you'll need to be able to bundle up. (See Clothing above.)
4. Illumination (headlamp or flashlight). If caught after dark, you'll need it to follow the trail. If forced to spend the night, you'll need it to set up emergency camp, gather wood, etc. Carry extra batteries and bulb.
5. First-aid supplies. Nothing elaborate is needed—especially if you are unfamiliar with some of the uses. Make sure you have adhesive bandages, gauze bandages, pain-relief medicine, etc. A Red Cross first-aid training course is recommended.
6. Fire (firestarter and matches/lighter). An emergency campfire provides warmth, but it also has a calming effect on most people. Without it, the night is cold, dark, and intimidating. With it, the night is held at arm's length. A candle or tube of firestarting ribbon is essential for starting a fire with wet wood. Pack matches in a waterproof container and/or buy the waterproof/windproof variety. Book matches are useless in wind or wet weather, and disposable lighters are unreliable.
7. Repair kit and tools (including knife). There are a multitude of uses for a knife; some come easily to mind (whittling kindling for a fire; first-aid applications), while others won't become apparent until you find you don't have a knife handy. A multitool is an even better option because the pliers can be used to repair damaged snowshoes. My repair kit contains

a 20-foot length of nylon cord, a small roll of duct tape, some 1-inch webbing and extra webbing buckles (to replace any that might break on snowshoe bindings), and a small tube of fast-bonding glue.

8. Nutrition (extra food). Pack enough so that you'll have leftovers after an uneventful trip. (Those leftovers will keep you fed and fueled during an emergency.)

9. Hydration (extra water).

10. Emergency shelter. (See Camping below.)

In addition to these essentials, I add my emergency survival kit, which holds a small metal mirror, an emergency Mylar "blanket," a plastic whistle, and a tiny signal smoke canister—all useful for signaling to search groups, whether they are on the ground or in the air.

Other items you might want to carry with you on your snowshoe outings include a small compactable snow shovel and ice saw. Both tools are extremely useful when setting up a camp in the snow. Many snowshoers find ski poles very helpful, especially when climbing or descending hills, and some campers prefer to pull their gear on a sled rather than pack it on their backs.

*A snow camp on Mazama Ridge offers glorious views of Mount Rainier*

## SNOWSHOEING TECHNIQUE

As I stated at the outset, if you can walk, you can walk on snowshoes. Generally, that is true; however, a few special techniques can help in tricky situations. Heading up and down hills, for instance, can be a problem unless you alter your hiking technique to accommodate the snowshoes.

To climb a hill, kick your toe into the hillside to dig the forefoot cleats into the snow, and then step down, putting weight on the toe so that the cleats get a good, solid bite into the slope. To go back down the hill, lean forward slightly and plant your whole foot solidly on the surface of the snow. This engages the entire surface of the snowshoe on the slope, and by leaning forward, you distribute your weight evenly on all the cleats. If, however, you lean back and keep your weight more on your heels (as you generally would do when hiking), you'll disengage the cleats on the front half of the snowshoe and slide forward.

Also, if you find you need to back up, the first thing you'll notice is the back of the snowshoe drags under your foot and trips you up. Counter this by using your trekking poles to push down on the front of the snowshoe, forcing the back to lift as you lift your foot. This is also the easiest way to turn around on snowshoes.

Perhaps the biggest difference between walking and walking on snowshoes is the distance between your feet. With snowshoes, you'll need to walk a bit straddle-legged so that the shoes don't overlap or hit your legs as you stride.

## CAMPING

There is nothing like spending a night in a snowy wilderness setting. The cold, clear sky and quiet forest are unlike anything you'll experience in the summer. But winter camping has different requirements than camping in the other three seasons. In terms of gear, you'll need a cold-weather sleeping bag (something rated to 0 degrees at least, or an insulation liner for your three-season bag) and a four-season tent. Here in the wet Northwest, the best bet for sleeping bags are those with synthetic fill, or insulation layers. Synthetic fills are (relatively) inexpensive, work even when wet, and have evolved to be nearly as efficient and compressible as goose down. Goose down is a wonderful insulator and compresses well to fit into a stuffed backpack, but if it gets wet, it is no good at all. Down is also expensive, and if you add a waterproof shell to a down bag (a necessity in Washington's climate), you drive the price through the roof.

For shelter, you can build snow caves, stay in backcountry huts (found on some maintained ski-trail networks), or pitch a tent. The tent is the best

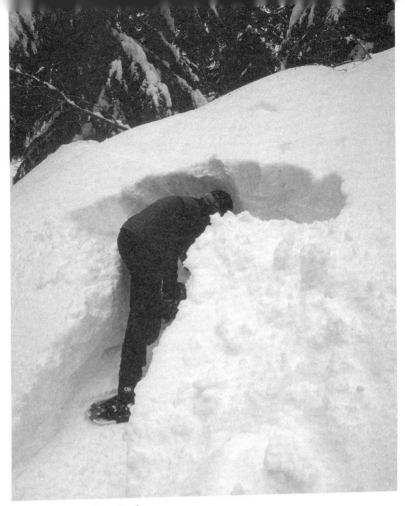

*Snow cave near Deer Park*

option, but it must be sturdy enough to withstand potentially violent winter winds and heavy snowfall. Most backpacking tents are sold as three-season tents and don't have the stability needed to stand up to the extreme abuses of winter. Four-season tents are built sturdier, with more poles, steeper walls (to shed snow), and heavier flies. All that extra engineering is necessary to make them snow-safe, but it also drives up their price. Fortunately, four-season tents can be rented, so you won't have to invest in a new fabric home if you camp only a few times a year.

When setting out on a winter backpacking trip, keep in mind the short daylight hours of winter and the longer amount of time you will need to set up camp. Plan carefully, and err on the side of caution—it is better to cut a trip short than to push on to a planned destination after darkness has fallen.

Setting up a winter camp is much different than setting up a summer camp. You'll want to do it when you still have plenty of daylight! Remember that the cold weather will slow you down, and you will be setting up your tent wearing mittens or gloves. But before the tent goes up, clear a place for it. Brush off loose snow and/or stomp down a flat pad for the tent floor. If time allows, build a "wind wall" on the windward side of the tent. Do this by packing snow into a thick, semicircular wall up to 4 feet high. This wall deflects the worst of the night's wind around the tent, keeping the tent warmer and more secure.

While you are setting up camp, "make" water by melting snow. This can take a long time (and burn a lot of stove fuel, so pack extra).

Once your basic camp is set up, if you still have daylight left, you can spiff up the place by building a "kitchen." Excavate a trough roughly 2 feet wide and 2 feet deep. Cut seats into one wall of the trough and a "table" into the other. Step into the trough, and you can then sit down to do your cooking and eating.

## DETECTING AVALANCHE DANGER

Winter recreation has some risks inherent to the season. Cold temperatures and wet conditions are the obvious ones, and proper clothing and preparation are essential to help you deal with the cold and wet. But as harsh as the weather conditions can be, it's the snow that poses one of the biggest threats to winter recreationists, especially in the mountains. The danger of avalanche is found anywhere there is a slope with snow on it. Sometimes the danger is minimal, sometimes a slide is inevitable, and frequently you won't be able to tell the difference by looking at the hillside. Knowledge of current snow conditions, recent weather patterns, and future weather forecasts are all necessary to help you understand and evaluate the avalanche danger on a given day, in a given area.

*Ice crystal on Granite Mountain*

*Snow load falling off tree*

One of the best resources available to winter recreationists is the Northwest Weather and Avalanche Center, which keeps detailed records on weather and snow patterns and conditions and makes its findings available to the public via a recorded message line. Every time you plan to venture out into the snowy mountains, you should first dial the Avalanche Center or check their website (see Appendix A, Contact Information) to get the avalanche danger report for your area of interest. Or failing that, purchase and use a weather radio. These radios tune in special FM frequencies not normally found on home radios. These frequencies, 162.4 to 162.55 megahertz, are reserved for use by the National Oceanic and Atmospheric Administration (NOAA), so they can broadcast ongoing weather reports and conditions. Frequent mountain weather reports, which include avalanche condition reports, are broadcast on the Northwest weather radio.

In addition, you should learn to recognize the clues of avalanche danger. All avalanches start with unstable snow—snow that isn't bonded to the hillside. Avalanches are of two primary types: slab avalanches occur when large solid sections of snow break away at once, and loose snow avalanches occur when unattached snow crystals slide down a slope, dislodging more and more snow as they go.

A quick study of the slope ahead of you can reveal clues to avalanche potential. First, estimate the steepness of the slope. Avalanches are most common on a slope of 30 to 45 degrees, but they can and do release on slopes as gentle as 25 degrees or as steep as 65 or more degrees. Second, take note of the profile of the slope. A slope with a convex profile—that is, it bulges out a bit—is more likely to slide than a concave slope. Third, look at the exposure of the slope. A north-facing slope may be slower to stabilize than other slopes because it doesn't receive as much direct sunlight, and therefore the snow doesn't settle and compact as quickly. A leeward slope tends to become wind-loaded with unstable snow more often than a windward slope, since a windward slope generally has less snow, and what is there is more compacted by the wind. Wind is a major contributor to avalanche hazards, and the higher and more prolonged the wind, the greater the threat of avalanche.

Other visible clues to avalanche danger include the following:

- Sticky snow, which indicates the surface snow is warmer than the snow below.
- Evidence of recent avalanches. If you see a slope that has apparently slid in the last 24 hours or so (rough, disturbed surface of slope, large snowballs or piles of loose or clumped snow at slope base), consider it a good indication that snow conditions are unstable.
- Hollow drumming or "whomping" sounds coming from the snow underfoot indicate slab conditions, and a high potential for release.
- Rime ice on trees. This build-up of ice and frost suggests there were high winds during a recent storm, and therefore chances are good that leeward slopes are highly wind-loaded and likely to slide.
- Broken limbs and/or snow plastered to the uphill side of trees shows past avalanche occurrence. A slope that slides once will slide again after the next storm.

Understanding and recognizing these signs isn't all there is to know about avoiding avalanche danger. This discussion simply serves as a brief primer on the subject. More detailed information is readily available in a number of excellent books, including *The ABCs of Avalanche Safety* by Sue Ferguson and E. R. LaChapelle (The Mountaineers Books).

## FINDING A DESTINATION

This book details 100 winter hiking routes in Washington. That is by no stretch a complete inventory of the possible snowshoe outing destinations. The goal of this book is to show some of the better areas to explore and to encourage backcountry enthusiasts to get out in the cold months and enjoy the beauty of the snowbound mountains.

There are hundreds, if not thousands, of routes available for snowshoe trekkers in this state. The best way to find them is to utilize your library of hiking guidebooks, your inventory of topographic maps, and your growing knowledge of what makes a good winter hike. Plan a snowshoe hike using these tools, as well as current information on snow and weather conditions.

If you are new to snowshoe hiking, start slow. Pick a short hike for your

*Looking up the Muir Snowfield to Mount Rainier's summit*

first outing to get a feel for the sport and your abilities. And above all, be flexible. You may find a trip in these pages that sounds like a perfect outing for you. But if the weather is unfavorable, or avalanche dangers are high in that region, make another choice. You can always hike your first choice another time. Better to explore a different location than to risk getting caught in an avalanche's path.

Exercise good judgment and basic common sense, take advantage of the knowledgeable rangers and avalanche forecasters, and learn to evaluate avalanche potentials and determine snow conditions and you will have a good outing. Like all outdoor adventures, winter hiking has its dangers, but planning and precaution can mitigate most of them. Be prepared, and you will be safe.

## SNO-PARKS

Most of the hikes in this book originate from state Sno-Parks. These facilities are parking areas maintained throughout the winter exclusively for winter recreationists. Many are open for multiuse by skiers, snowmobilers, dog mushers, snowshoers, and sledders, although nearly half are set aside for nonmotorized sports. Even if a Sno-Park is open to snowmobilers, there is no reason to pass it by. Typically, snowmobilers will stick to the groomed roads and trails leading away from the Sno-Park, leaving plenty of untracked areas for snowshoers to explore.

Permits are required to park in these facilities, and the permit fees are used to keep parking spaces plowed, bathrooms clean and maintained, and ski and snowmobile trails groomed and maintained. Washington State Sno-Park permits are available by the day, by the week, or for an entire season, and thanks to a cooperative recreation program, the Washington permit is also accepted in Oregon and Idaho (and permits from those states are accepted here). Sno-park permits are available at U.S. Forest Service ranger stations, outdoor retailers, and online from Washington State Parks (see Appendix A, Contact Information).

## USING THIS BOOK

The route descriptions in this guide are self-explanatory. But keep a few things in mind as you browse through the book, looking for that perfect outing.

### Rating the Trails

The rating system for the hikes is subjective, and not everyone will agree with every rating. The individual ratings are based on the following guidelines:

**Easiest:** No previous snowshoe experience is required. These are great trails for first-timers who want to get a feel for the sport. Generally, elevation gain and loss is small and avalanche dangers are minimal at all times. These are good routes for groups with children or when campers are pulling loads of gear on sleds.

**More difficult:** Some previous snowshoe experience is helpful, and some winter survival skills are recommended (i.e., basic knowledge of avalanche slope evaluation, emergency shelter construction, etc.). A bit more climbing is required, as these trails feature more elevation gain, but for the most part, elevation gain is less than 1000 feet or, if more, the slope is gradual and relatively stable at all times. Routes may include forest trails, narrow logging roads, or moderate-slope climbing.

**Most difficult:** Hikers should have good experience and familiarity with snowshoes. These routes feature sections that will need to be evaluated for avalanche safety every time. The trails climb considerably and may include climbing to ridge tops. Traverses across forested or open slopes may be required. An ability to self-arrest with an ice ax or trekking pole is recommended.

**Backcountry:** These routes follow topography rather than trails or roads, so skill with a map and compass is essential. A variety of conditions may be encountered along backcountry routes, including steep elevation gains and losses. These routes require complete competence in winter survival skills, avalanche and snow condition evaluation, and some basic mountaineering skills.

*Snowshoer picks a path along route to Diamond Head*

## Round Trip

Because snow levels vary so widely from year to year—and month to month—round-trip distances listed here are not absolute. Some of the routes begin at formal Sno-Park areas, and are therefore fairly consistent in their trip mileage, but others begin wherever the snow line is encountered, so the distances can increase or decrease by several miles based on snow accumulation. The starting points for the mileage are calculated from the average base point.

## Hiking Time

Everyone moves at different speeds, but a general rule of thumb is to estimate that when walking on snowshoes, you'll be moving 30 to 50 percent slower than you would walking on a bare trail. So if you generally hike at a rate of 3 miles per hour, figure you'll be doing 1.5 to 2 miles per hour on snowshoes.

And that slower rate, combined with short winter days, means you should plan on doing fewer miles than you would if you were hiking bare trails in the summer. In fact, you should plan to cut your hiking mileage by the same 30 to 50 percent. For example, if you generally take summer day hikes of 10 to 15 miles, plan to take snowshoe hikes of 6 to 10 miles.

## Elevation Gain

Starting from the base starting point, this number is the accumulated total elevation gain from the trail's start to its high point. The total will vary if snow levels force you to start above or below the starting point listed.

## High Point

This is the elevation of the highest point on the route, not necessarily the end point.

## Best Season

There is only one accurate answer to the question, "When is the best time to snowshoe each route?" That answer is, "It depends." But since that's not too useful, I have put myself on the line and offered an estimate of when you'll find the best conditions for each route. Bear in mind, though, that first answer. The best time to snowshoe any given route is when the snow is stable, yet deep and fluffy; when the weather is clear and calm; and when the route is free of avalanche danger. While a trail may be great one December, it could be bare of snow the next. I have snowshoed some trails in June that I had hiked the previous June with no snow in sight. So, again, I have estimated a range for the "average" year and ask that you be open-minded with your interpretation of that range.

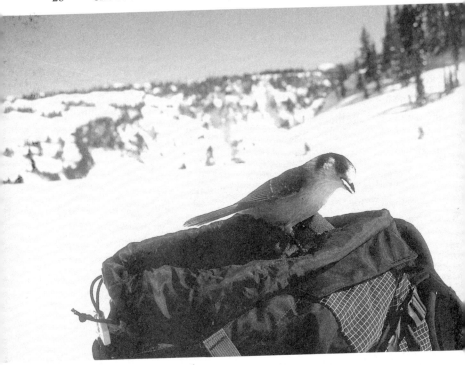

*Camp robber near Snow Lake*

## Maps

Not enough can be said about the importance of carrying and using good topographic maps on every outing. Winter hiking isn't like summer hiking—the trail isn't always visible. In fact, more often than not, the "trail" doesn't exist anywhere but on the map. It is your responsibility to make sure that you are on course.

The maps in this book are not designed to be used for routefinding. They are intended as locator maps to assist you in visualizing the hike and to help you locate the route on a topographic map.

To help you find the maps you need, I have also listed the Green Trails and/or Custom Correct maps covering the hiking area. Green Trails and Custom Correct maps are commercially produced. While many snowshoers may have and use U.S. Geological Survey (USGS) maps—they are available for the entire state—I have found the commercially produced maps, when available, are more beneficial to recreationists because they are revised regularly, with updated trail and road information. USGS maps are not up-dated regularly. Many of the Washington maps haven't been revised for more than twenty years, so the roads and trails listed on them may be outdated, although the geographic information is still highly accurate.

Custom Correct offers detailed topographic maps for the Olympic Peninsula. The maps are not based on a grid system like USGS maps, but instead are designed to cover entire river valleys and/or trail networks. As such, the Custom Correct maps have a lot of overlap, but their strength is the fact that for any given hike, only one map is needed. Green Trails maps, on the other hand, are based on a grid system covering the Olympic Peninsula and the entire Cascade Range through northern Oregon.

### Who to Contact

In addition to calling the Northwest Weather and Avalanche Center hotline, it is a good idea to contact the local land manager to get current information on the specific area you plan to visit. To make it easier for you to do that, I have included the name of the agency in charge of the land traversed by each route. Addresses and phone numbers are provided in Appendix A, Contact Information.

## A NOTE ABOUT SAFETY

Safety is an important concern in all outdoor activities. No guidebook can alert you to every hazard or anticipate the limitations of every reader. Therefore, the descriptions of roads, trails, routes, and natural features in this book are not representations that a particular place or excursion will be safe for your party. When you follow any of the routes described in this book, you assume responsibility for your own safety. Under normal conditions, such excursions require the usual attention to traffic, road and trail conditions, weather, terrain, the capabilities of your party, and other factors. Keeping informed on current conditions and exercising common sense are the keys to a safe, enjoyable outing.

*The Mountaineers Books*

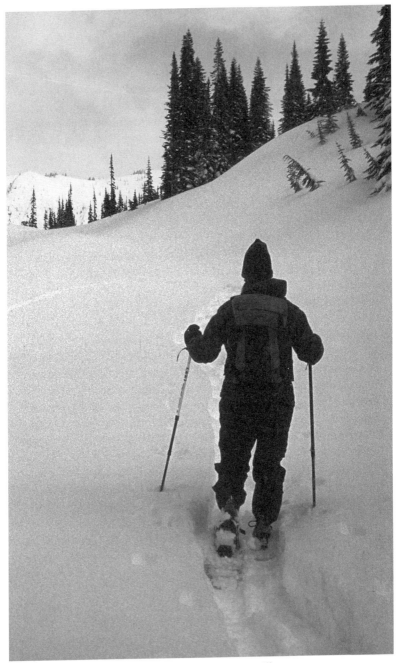

*Snowshoer hiking along road to ridge, Hurricane Hill route*

# --1--

# Hurricane Hill

| | |
|---:|:---|
| **Rating:** | Easiest to more difficult |
| **Round trip:** | 6 miles |
| **Hiking time:** | 4 hours |
| **Elevation gain:** | 800 feet |
| **High point:** | 5760 feet |
| **Best season:** | Late December through early March |
| **Maps:** | Green Trails: Mount Olympus No. 134, Mount Angeles No. 135; Custom Correct: Hurricane Ridge |
| **Who to Contact:** | Olympic National Park |

*See map on page 33.*

Hurricane Ridge is the preeminent destination for folks who want to see the beauty of Olympic National Park any time of the year. When winter rolls in and the broad, sweeping meadows of the ridge are blanketed in snow, and the high jagged peaks of Bailey Range are swaddled in white, the area is unbelievably beautiful. All the best—and some of the worst—aspects of snowshoeing are found here. Wide, wonderful panoramic views; alpine meadows of rolling snowdrifts; frosted evergreens and dark, brooding forests; and occasionally, frigid, scouring winds that blind all visitors with white-out conditions.

Hurricane Ridge, and the snowshoe hike to Hurricane Hill, offers the best views in the park of majestic Mount Olympus. The peak so captivated early explorers with its beauty that the mountain was deemed worthy of being home to the gods.

To get there, from Port Angeles drive 17 miles up Hurricane Ridge Road to the Hurricane Ridge Visitor Center. Park near the lodge, and sign in with the rangers at the center.

Heading west from the lodge, snowshoe along the roadway as it rolls around the flank of the Hurricane Ridge meadows. The road soon enters forest and drops gently with the ridge for nearly a mile. The trail levels out along a high saddle, passing a broad picnic area near the end of the road. A brief climb from the picnic area takes you to the end of the road at 1.5 miles. At this point the real snowshoeing work begins. If you are just looking for a quiet stroll, turn back here and explore the trailside meadows on your return trip; but if you are looking for more of a challenge, continue toward Hurricane Hill.

Following the general path of the small hikers' trail west from the end of

*Looking south toward Mount Olympus from Hurricane Hill*

the road, snowshoe steeply up an exposed ridgeline to the top of Hurricane Hill. The trail stays on the west side of the ridge, passing under two tricky avalanche chutes. Snowshoers will do better to merely stick to the narrow (sometimes, knife-edged) ridge crest all the way to the top. If the snow is heavily crusted or icy, even snowshoes with heavy cleats will not be enough to ensure safe footing, so come prepared to turn around before reaching the true summit of Hurricane Hill.

Even if the top isn't reached, the views are spectacular all along the trail. To the north, the Strait of Juan de Fuca is a dark blue ribbon between the Olympic foothills and the far shore of Canada's Vancouver Island. Northeast, the San Juan Islands are seen cradled in the calm, blue waters of upper Puget Sound, with Mount Baker rearing its icy head beyond. To the east, Mount Angeles and McCarthy Peak jut up at the far side of the Olympic Mountains. To the south, Mount Olympus reigns supreme, dominating the impressive Bailey Range.

There is beauty to behold in every direction. But there is also the possibility of danger. Weather on Hurricane Ridge is unpredictable and prone to rapid changes. Come prepared for a variety of conditions—sunny days can quickly fade into heavy fog and frigid temperatures. Calm weather can give way, in just minutes, to heavy winds and white-out conditions. Be ready for extreme conditions, and be willing to turn back the moment the weather starts to turn foul.

--2--

# Mount Angeles

**Rating:** Backcountry
**Round trip:** 6 miles
**Hiking time:** 6 hours
**Elevation gain:** 600 feet
**High point:** 5900 feet
**Best season:** Late December through early March
**Maps:** Green Trails: Mount Angeles No. 135; Custom Correct: Hurricane Ridge
**Who to Contact:** Olympic National Park

Although little elevation gain occurs along this route, a lot of work is necessary for snowshoers planning to play here. The trail starts high and stays high as it skirts steep ridges and traverses around the flanks of towering mountains. But with the hard work comes ample rewards. Stunning views of Elk Mountain, Maiden Peak, Blue Mountain, and the deep Cox Creek valley lie off to the southeast. Above, Mount Angeles and Rocky Peak loom large. And all around the trail are picturesque scenes of winter loveliness—open meadows, frosted evergreens cradled by rolling snowdrifts, and icicles hanging like crystal fingers off rocky ledges on the mountain face.

To get there, from Port Angeles drive 17 miles up Hurricane Ridge Road

*Snowy meadow and forest along the route to Heather Park*

to the Hurricane Ridge Visitor Center. Park near the lodge, and sign in with the rangers at the center.

From the visitor center, snowshoe right around the downhill ski area and turn north to climb to the ridge crest above the rope-tow. Snowshoe out along the ridge crest with Mount Angeles towering dead ahead. The trail is fairly level as it pierces small stands of forest and crosses open meadows. At 1.8 miles, the route rolls under the nose of Sunrise Ridge, which stretches off to the left. The trail stays high on the narrow ridge as it passes Sunrise and crosses above a wide, open basin on the left. This pretty, forested alpine valley nestles between Sunrise Ridge and Mount Angeles. On the east side of the trail, the slope drops steeply to the Cox Creek valley. The road to Hurricane Ridge is occasionally seen directly below the trail.

At 2.7 miles, the trail curves right across the steep flank of Mount Angeles. Continue north, leaving the trail route, and climb a 0.25 mile to the top of a wide bench on the southern flank of the mountain. Here, at 5900 feet, enjoy views of the mountain while avoiding the avalanche-prone east side of Mount Angeles—the area to which the trail leads.

Plenty of opportunities are available for scrambling around the flanks of the mountain, but you will find that the slopes are steep and avalanche danger is high throughout the area when the snow isn't completely stable. Make good use of the Northwest Weather and Avalanche Center, and the avalanche information posted at the Hurricane Ridge Visitor Center, before venturing out on this trail.

-- ? --

# Eagle Point

**Rating:** Most difficult
**Round trip:** 9 miles
**Hiking time:** 7 hours to 2 days
**Elevation gain:** Up to 2500 feet
**High point:** 5500 feet
**Best season:** Late December through early March
**Maps:** Green Trails: Mount Angeles No. 135; Custom Correct: Hurricane Ridge
**Who to Contact:** Olympic National Park

With the sweeping line of white mountains that ends at glacier-capped Mount Olympus stretching before them, snowshoers will wonder why they ever bothered visiting this area in the summer. The hike begins with a short, steep descent, and then wanders over fairly level terrain—just a few rolling hills— as the trail stretches east under the flank of jagged Steeple Rock and Eagle Point. Snowshoers will find great views of the distant peaks of the Bailey Range, and look down into the dark Lillian River valley.

To get there, from Port Angeles drive 17 miles up Hurricane Ridge Road to the Hurricane Ridge Visitor Center. Sign in at the center (required for all users), and then drive back down the road 0.5 mile to the trailhead parking area near the first bend in the road.

Start the hike from the last switchback on Hurricane Ridge Road. You will need to hike a few hundred yards back from the parking area, and then drop off the road end, descending a steep hill for about 100 yards before reaching the fairly level, wide trail leading off to the east. You'll be in high

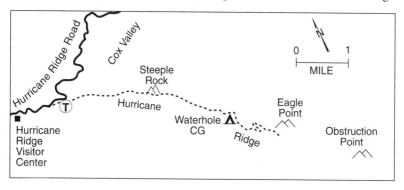

subalpine forest with frequent breaks with views south to Mount Olympus and the Lillian River valley and northwest to Mount Angeles.

The trail skirts along a windswept sidehill meadow on the flank of Steeple Rock. Be careful here, as the fierce winds can load up avalanche chutes and create hazardous conditions occasionally. But if the winds are calm and the weather is clear, this is also the best place to find truly grand views of the entire Bailey Range of the Olympic Mountains. Steeple Rock is passed at just under 2 miles from the parking area.

In another 1.5 miles, you'll pass a broad, sheltered forest clearing known as Waterhole Camp. This is a great place to camp, or just to stop and catch your breath, taking in the scenery. Snowshoers looking for a gentle outing (or if the snow is icy) can pitch their tents here. For a more strenuous trek, push on past Waterhole to reach the flank of Eagle Point, a 6247-foot summit towering over the trail.

This last leg is treacherous in inclement weather, so pay attention to weather reports and current conditions. If a storm threatens, make camp at Waterhole and save the ascent to Obstruction Point for another time, or do it the next morning as a pre-breakfast blood-warmer if the air is clear and calm.

*Snowshoer climbing slope below Cathedral Peak toward Eagle Point*

This route makes a fine outing for novice winter campers. The trail is level enough that carrying winter camping gear isn't too difficult, and the distance is short enough to be doable but not long enough to get you out into a true wilderness camp.

--4--

# Klahhane Ridge

|  |  |
|---|---|
| **Rating:** | More difficult |
| **Round trip:** | 4 miles |
| **Hiking time:** | 6 hours |
| **Elevation gain:** | 1500 feet |
| **High point:** | 6080 feet |
| **Best season:** | January through early March |
| **Maps:** | Green Trails: Mount Angeles No. 135; Custom Correct: Hurricane Ridge |
| **Who to Contact:** | Olympic National Park |

Klahhane Ridge towers over the Hurricane Ridge Road, providing outstanding views of Mount Angeles and the long sweep of Hurricane Ridge. The trail climbs steeply, but once the work is done, snowshoers can trek along the long ridge stretched between Mount Angeles and Rocky Peak.

To get there, from Port Angeles drive 15 miles up Hurricane Ridge Road to the broad plowed area signed as the Third Peak Parking Area. (This parking lot is about 2.5 miles from Hurricane Ridge Visitor Center.) Hike about 0.25 mile up the road (heading toward Hurricane Ridge) to a hairpin turn in the road. The route begins in a creek basin on the north side of the road.

During warm summer months, the trail switchbacks back and forth steeply up this narrow drainage, covering more than 1.6 miles before attending the ridge top. With a thick blanket of snow, however, snowshoers can kick step a more direct route to the top, cutting the climbing distance to about a mile. The downside is that though the route is just a mile long, it climbs more than

*Descending corniced slope along Klahhane Ridge*

1400 feet in elevation. You can either gasp your way through a straight ascent, or sweat yourself through a more moderate-angled and less grueling, but longer, route up.

For the best views and clearest route, stay on the right flank of the creek basin and angle east toward the Klahhane Saddle. Once in the saddle, you can turn left and stomp through the wind-stacked snowdrifts along the ridge to the flank of Mount Angeles. Or, for a more leisurely and more scenic trek, turn right and stroll east along the ridge. Be aware that several sections of ridgeline can be heavily corniced—big overhanging drifts of snow—so you need to stay to the center of those sections to avoid collapsing a cornice and starting an avalanche.

From this open ridge, you can peer south across the Cox River valley to Hurricane Ridge. The rocky spire of Steeple Rock is due south, and the high summit of Obstruction Point anchors the east end of Hurricane Ridge. Follow the ridge east as far as you care to, then retrace your steps, taking care to descend slowly and carefully.

## --5--

# Blue Mountain/Deer Park

|  |  |
|---|---|
| **Rating:** | More difficult |
| **Round trip:** | Up to 14 miles |
| **Hiking time:** | 6 hours to 2 days |
| **Elevation gain:** | 2500 feet |
| **High point:** | 6000 feet |
| **Best season:** | January through early March |
| **Maps:** | Green Trails: Mount Angeles No. 135; Custom Correct: Hurricane Ridge |
| **Who to Contact:** | Olympic National Park |

This route offers a glorious exploration in natural history as well as a bit of human history. The natural history comes in the form of deep, old forest and an abundance of wildlife. Snow trekkers can wander amongst cedars and firs, luxuriating in the snow-flocked beards of moss that drape the trees. Martens and fishers (or at least their tracks) can often be seen scampering between the trees. Bobcats and cougars also roam these woods and hillsides, as do black-tail deer and the odd mountain goat.

The human history of Deer Park Road is less obvious. The road, which

*Snowshoers should practice digging a snow cave once in a while*

climbs to the Blue Mountain summit, once led to a rope-tow ski area. The tow rig now resides on Hurricane Hill, but skiers still frequent this road so be prepared to share the route—don't stomp on the ski tracks, and be cautious rounding curves since skiers like to blast down the slope on their return run.

To get there, from Sequim, drive west on U.S. Highway 101 toward Port Angeles. At the very edge of Port Angeles—you'll see a movie multiplex theater on the left—turn left (south) onto Deer Park Road. Follow this 9 miles to the Olympic National Park Boundary. The road may be gated here (elevation 2000 feet). If the gate is open, continue up the road another 2.8 miles to a second gate at 3500 feet (or as far as the snow allows). If the first gate is closed, park there (do not block the gate) and start your trek. If the road is snow free, you'll need to hike to the snow line before donning your snowshoes.

From the second gate (the most likely starting point), the road wanders east and south, climbing 5 miles along the long ridge on the north flank of Blue Mountain. The road rolls through shadowy, gray-green forests for the first few miles before breaking out into occasional clearings and hillside meadows. Snowshoers can branch off to the east though the larger of these clearings to climb to the ridge crest if they want broad views without going all the way to the top.

Those who want to push on to the end of the road, though, can continue south along the roadway to find the sweeping meadows of Deer Park (5300 feet) at about 5 miles from the second gate. Great camps can be found along the edges of the meadows. For an extended adventure, push up through the open expanses of Deer Park, edging east, before turning north and climbing the southern flank of Blue Mountain, reaching the summit ridge about 7 miles from the second gate. Be alert to avalanche conditions and if there is any chance of slides, stay clear of the mountain's flanks—hold to the road near the lower reaches of Deer Park.

--6--

# Mount Townsend

**Rating:** Most difficult
**Round trip:** 10 to 13.5 miles
**Hiking time:** 7 hours to 2 days
**Elevation gain:** Up to 2500 feet
**High point:** 5500 feet
**Best season:** Late December through early March
**Maps:** Green Trails: Tyler Peak No. 136; Custom Correct: Buckhorn Wilderness
**Who to Contact:** Olympic National Forest, Hood Canal Ranger District

Starting with a road walk, this snowshoe trek leads through steep clearcuts, virgin forest, and up to some near-vertical alpine meadows, but throughout it all, one aspect is constant: incredible, staggering views. The vistas from the road and trail along this route include sweeping views of Mount Rainier, upper Puget Sound, lower Hood Canal, and all of the eastern Olympic peaks. Snowshoers can scatter out and explore untouched snow in meadows and forests well off the trail, or they can stick to the assigned path and make a nice, quiet day hike of it. Or they can do both and spend a night or two and explore the possibilities of the slopes of Mount Townsend. The mountain itself is more of a long ridge. The summit stretches north to south and, although it's difficult to get to the top thanks to a slew of avalanche chutes, there is no shortage of scenic overlooks on which snowshoers can pause and admire the long mountaintop.

To get there, from Quilcene drive north on U.S. Highway 101 for 1.5 miles to Lords Lake Road on the left (west). Continue up Lords Lake Road for 3 miles before turning left (south) onto Forest Road 2909 and driving 3.5 miles. At a wide road junction, turn left (the sharpest left of two possible left turns) onto FR 27 and follow it through a loop curve to the west. Continue west on FR 27 to the point where the snow is deep enough to impede your progress, generally near the head of the Little Quilcene River valley at 3000 feet.

To find the best snowshoeing options, cross the Little Quilcene River via the FR 27 bridge and snowshoe up the road as it climbs steeply up through broad meadows (clearcuts), traverses around to the south side of the valley, and rolls south to a low saddle at 2 miles (3700 feet). The pretty views of the first leg of the trek are supplemented here with stunning panoramas sweeping from Mount Townsend over the Quilcene River valley, east to Puget Sound, and beyond to Mount Rainier.

The road drops from the saddle, rolls south around the nose of the ridge and, at 3.5 miles, encounters a small side road on the right. Follow this narrow, brushy road southwest for 1 mile to intercept the Mount Townsend Trail at 4.5 miles. This forested hiking path climbs steeply from its trailhead for 0.25 mile before turning west on a long, climbing traverse to the base of the steep walls of the upper reaches of Mount Townsend.

Stop your climb before breaking out of the trees near the 4500-foot level if there is even a whisper of a chance of avalanche. If the snow is extremely stable, continue to snowshoe up the trail to reach the ridge crest (5500 feet) at 6 miles.

When the avalanche danger is moderate or higher, a better alternative for winter camping is to turn left when you encounter the Mount Townsend Trail and descend along it for 0.5 mile to reach, at mile 5 from your car, one of the small, three-sided shelters that were so common in the Olympic Mountains in the middle half of this century.

Return the way you came or, to complete a loop, hike another 0.5 mile down the trail from the shelter to a trailhead on FR 27. Turn left on the road, and hike 1.5 miles up it as it curves northwest to reach the point where the spur road took off to join the upper trail.

*Snowshoer looking toward Mount Townsend*

--7--

# Lena Lake/Valley of Silent Men

| | |
|---:|:---|
| **Rating:** | Backcountry |
| **Round trip:** | Up to 10 miles |
| **Hiking time:** | 6 hours |
| **Elevation gain:** | 2000 feet |
| **High point:** | 2800 feet |
| **Best season:** | Mid-January through late February |
| **Maps:** | Green Trails: The Brothers No. 168; Custom Correct: The Brothers–Mount Anderson |
| **Who to Contact:** | Olympic National Forest, Hood Canal Ranger District |

*Mossy tree aong the trail to Lower Lena Lake*

This is an unusual snowshoe outing in that, except in periods of heavy snow, the lower section of the trail may require hikers to strap their snowshoes to their backs while they hike a mile or two up to the snow. The Lower Lena Lake Trail doesn't offer panoramic vistas, but there is a pretty forest surrounding the route, with a nice creek basin to cross and the beautiful lake to enjoy. Beyond the lake, a short excursion to the Valley of Silent Men leads snowshoers into a cathedral-like forest of massive trees, flanking a clear, tumbling stream in a narrow valley. The ancient trees sport drooping beards of emerald green lichens and mosses, and the stream is lined with a lacy network of ice.

To get there, from Hoodsport drive 13 miles north on U.S. Highway 101 to a junction with Hamma Hamma Road (Forest Road 25). Turn left (west) onto Hamma Hamma Road, and continue west 8 miles to the Lena Lake trailhead parking area on either side of the road. The trail is on the right (north) side of the road.

In heavy snow years, a thin layer of snow may be found at the trailhead (800 feet), but generally you will have to leave your 'shoes on your packs and start up the trail in your boots. The trail climbs steeply, though, and shortly after crossing Lena Creek at 1.5 miles, the snow deepens. When it is too deep, or too slick, to hike in boots, strap on the snowshoes and continue.

The trail tapers into a gentle climb at 1.6 miles and a quiet, serene forest surrounds the route. At 3 miles, the trail rolls along the west side of Lower Lena Lake (2050 feet). Follow the lakeshore north, and turn right to cross the first inlet stream at the north end of the lake. Head east along the second inlet, East Fork Lena Creek, as it climbs into the lush ancient forest of the Valley of Silent Men. Trail signs indicate this is the climbers' route to The Brothers, but generally you won't be going that far. Snowshoe up the bottom of the valley, following the trail corridor as it weaves through the trees, for up to 1.5 miles from the lake before turning back.

The valley makes a great place to stop for a leisurely picnic. Sit and enjoy the quiet music of the stream tumbling over icy rocks. Listen to the songs of the birds flitting through the branches of the trees above: gray jays, as always, dominate the air when there is any chance they can beg—or steal—a meal from hikers. Relax in the soothing peace that covers all visitors to these cathedral forests, which are made all the more peaceful by the quiet of winter.

## -- 8 --

## Coal Pass

|  |  |
|---|---|
| **Rating:** | More difficult |
| **Round trip:** | 10 miles |
| **Hiking time:** | 6 hours |
| **Elevation gain:** | 2400 feet |
| **High point:** | 4500 feet |
| **Best season:** | January through early March |
| **Map:** | Green Trails: Mount Baker No. 13 |
| **Who to Contact:** | Mount Baker–Snoqualmie National Forest, Mount Baker Ranger District |

*See map on page 49.*

For those snowshoers who like to just get out and walk for miles without worrying about the intricacies of routefinding in deep snow, the Coal Pass trek is a great option. The route follows a wide roadbed as it climbs from the forested Glacier Creek valley to the open views in Coal Pass. The road weaves through many forest clearings and crosses several creek basins before reaching its end at the 4500-foot pass separating the twin peaks of Lookout Mountain. From the pass, views to the southeast sweep over Mount Baker's northwest flank, from Chowder Ridge to Lincoln and Colfax Peaks, with the sprawling ice of Coleman and Roosevelt Glaciers in between.

To get there, from Bellingham drive east on State Route 542 (Mount Baker Highway) to the town of Glacier and continue another 0.7 mile, passing the U.S. Forest Service Public Service Center, before turning right (south) onto Forest Road 39 (Glacier Creek Road). Drive to the snow line, usually found near a road junction with FR 3940 (gated) just past Coal Creek, about 5.2 miles from Mount Baker Highway.

Strap on your snowshoes, and start the trek by following FR 39. Snow-mobilers and skiers also use this road, so stick to the side to avoid being run down by motorists and to avoid tromping on the carefully laid tracks of skiers. The road climbs along Lookout Creek before crossing the creek and traversing south above the deep cut of Glacier Creek Gorge. In 2 miles, go right at the fork onto FR 36. (The left fork leads to Route 9, Coleman Glacier.)

The road traverses through young second-growth forest, clearcuts, and steep alder slopes before banking to the left and crossing the upper Lookout Creek basin near the 4500-foot level, 2 miles from the start of FR 36. Across Lookout Creek basin, the road loops north, and then flips through a wide switchback to reach another road junction. Stay right (on FR 3610), and climb steeply through a short series of switchbacks and a 0.5-mile-long traverse to reach Coal Pass, just a touch over 5 miles from the Coal Creek parking area.

Soak up the views from the pass, enjoy a leisurely lunch, and then decide whether to head back or extend the outing. For more adventures, leave Coal Pass and climb to the left (south), ascending the main peak of Lookout Mountain (5021 feet). There is no formal trail, but climbing through the trees and

*Tributary creek which drains into Coal Creek.*

meadows is easy with snowshoes. Pick the path of least resistance. The best bet is to climb steeply, but angle just a bit to the left on the ascent to avoid the steepest pitches. The summit is about 0.5 mile from the pass. To cut the return trip mileage, drop to the east from the summit to rejoin the road about 0.5 mile down from the pass.

## --9--

## Coleman Glacier

Rating: Backcountry
Round trip: 9 miles
Hiking time: 1 to 2 days
Elevation gain: 4500 feet
High point: 6000 feet
Best season: January through February
Map: Green Trails: Mount Baker No. 13
Who to Contact: Mount Baker–Snoqualmie National Forest, Mount Baker Ranger District
*See map on page 49.*

Starting with an easy stroll along a wide trail in a narrow creek valley, this trek offers a taste of all the best winter has to offer. The trail climbs away from the valley bottom after a few miles and presents two choices: a modest climb along a wide road to a high promontory with great views of Mount Baker, or a longer, more strenuous climb along the narrow, forested path on Heliotrope Ridge. Both provide wonderful views, and a good stretch of the legs in deep snows, but snowshoers must share the road with skiers and snowmobilers, while the Heliotrope Ridge Trail is quiet and usually untracked. But this also means the trail is considerably more difficult to follow than the wide roadbed. Novice snowshoers will find plenty of excitement and enjoyment on the Mount Baker view trek, while more experienced backcountry snowshoers will find the Heliotrope Ridge Trail puts their skills to good use.

To get there, from Bellingham drive east on State Route 542 (Mount Baker Highway) to the town of Glacier and continue another 0.7 mile, passing the U.S. Forest Service Public Service Center before turning right (south) onto Forest Road 39 (Glacier Creek Road). Drive to the snow line, usually found near a road junction with FR 3940 (gated) just past Coal Creek, about 5.2 miles from Mount Baker Highway.

Beginning at the snow line, follow FR 39 upvalley. Snowmobilers and skiers also use this road, so stick to the side to avoid being run over by motorists and to avoid tromping on the carefully laid tracks of skiers. The road climbs through thick, young forest for the first 0.5 mile before crossing Lookout Creek and leveling out somewhat. A few small clearcuts offer modest views and the first opportunity to step off the track and practice some deep-snow travel techniques.

In 2 miles the track forks. Stay to the left on FR 39 (the right fork leads to Route 8, Coal Pass), and in about 0.5 mile the road curves sharply to the right. The Heliotrope Ridge trailhead is found at this corner. Turn left into the forest, and follow the trail corridor east, crossing Grouse Creek almost immediately and climbing through the shadowy woods. The trail may be difficult to find in places, so follow the widest corridor between the dark tree trunks. The route climbs steadily for 0.5 mile before tapering into a long, ascending traverse along Heliotrope Ridge's north side.

About 1.5 miles after leaving the road, cross the upper reaches of Kulshan Creek. This is the best place to establish camp if you plan to spend the night. The trees offer shelter from the wind and weather, while the views are found less than 0.5 mile away. To get to those views, turn right on the west side of the Kulshan Creek draw, and climb uphill to break out of the trees and enjoy views of Coleman Glacier and upper Heliotrope Ridge.

For a less strenuous outing, stick to FR 39 at the trailhead and climb to the right along the roadway for another 1.5 miles. The road ends at a high viewpoint above clearcut meadows. The view of Mount Baker's northwest side, with its sprawling Coleman and Roosevelt Glaciers, is unmatched. Enjoy the view over lunch, and then if you want a change of pace, abandon the road as you start the return trip. Point the tips of your snowshoes toward Mount Baker, and drop downhill, angling slightly to the right, through the meadows and trees for a little off-trail snowshoeing before rejoining the road in 0.25 mile or so.

# --10--

# White Salmon Creek

| | |
|---:|:---|
| **Rating:** | Easiest |
| **Round trip:** | Up to 10 miles |
| **Hiking time:** | 6 hours |
| **Elevation gain:** | 300 feet |
| **High point:** | 2400 feet |
| **Best season:** | December through early March |
| **Map:** | Green Trails: Mount Shuksan No. 14 |
| **Who to Contact:** | Mount Baker–Snoqualmie National Forest, Mount Baker Ranger District |

Bring the whole family to this beautiful river valley. The wide track, with plenty of open meadows and forest glades for exploring, offers great snowshoeing for folks of all abilities. The scenery will, likewise, appeal to all. The views begin with the glorious winter landscape around the trail—picture dark, shadowy evergreens flocked with heavy white snow set beside a clear mountain river—but soon all eyes are drawn to the vista beyond. This is a narrow valley, and the mountains flanking it soar straight up into the sky. From Goat Mountain to Mount Sefrit and the Nooksack Ridge, the peaks form a ragged skyline far above the valley floor.

When venturing out this way, be sure to call the district ranger first to get a current snow report. This is a fairly low-elevation trail, and although some years 3 or 4 feet of snow may be along the trail, mild winters can find the track snow-free for much of its length. Of course, one of the conveniences of snowshoes is that regular hiking boots can be worn when walking on them. That means, when the snow is thin, just stash the snowshoes and take a winter hike.

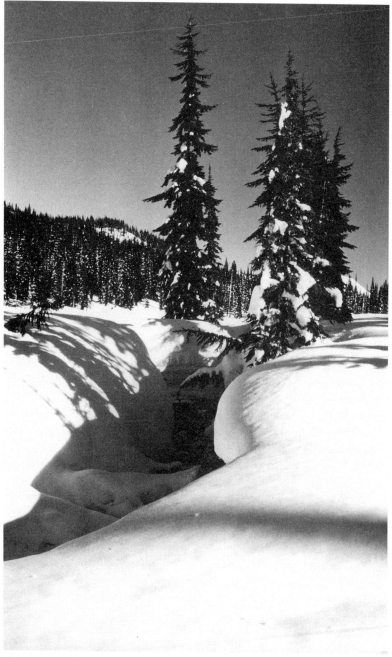

*Open water along White Salmon Creek*

To get there, from Bellingham drive east on State Route 542 (Mount Baker Highway) to the town of Glacier. Continue another 12.5 miles past Glacier, and turn left into the Salmon Ridge Sno-Park, which is found just past the North Fork Nooksack River Bridge.

From the Sno-Park, you can simply ramble out into the open glades along the Nooksack River, but to get in a full day of snowshoeing, head out along Forest Road 3070 as it parallels the picturesque river upstream. As you hike up the valley, be sure to stay off the groomed ski tracks. Volunteers groom this trail for cross-country skiers, and there is no faster way to irritate skiers than by tromping their tracks into a series of deep snowshoe depressions. But plenty of room is available for all, and in several areas you can take off through open meadows to get well clear of the ski tracks and be off on your own.

Angle off to the left in the first mile or so to get down to the river for some water views. But stay back from the edge because weak snow may be overhanging the water. As you move up the valley, veer to the right to climb onto the foot of the valley wall and enter the dark cedar and hemlock forest. At 2 miles, turn sharply to the right (south) and climb a small bench for good, open views of Goat Mountain to the north.

Then traverse around the lower edge of the bench and enter the White Salmon Creek basin. Pick a path through the trees to the edge of the creek. For an extended outing, push on upstream and continue until the trees get too tight or your legs get too tired. To keep the trek modest, turn downstream and follow the White Salmon for 0.25 mile back to the main track, which ends where the White Salmon empties into the Nooksack.

# --11--
# Artist Point

|  |  |
|---|---|
| **Rating:** | More difficult |
| **Round trip:** | Up to 5.5 miles |
| **Hiking time:** | 4 hours |
| **Elevation gain:** | 1200 feet |
| **High point:** | 5200 feet |
| **Best season:** | December through April |
| **Map:** | Green Trails: Mount Shuksan No. 14 |
| **Who to Contact:** | Mount Baker–Snoqualmie National Forest, Mount Baker Ranger District |

Artist Point may have earned its name because of the oft-captured image of the broad meadows filled with summer wildflowers, backed by the towering rock summit of Mount Shuksan and glacier-crowned Mount Baker. But many feel the area is even more beautiful and worthy of reproduction on film or

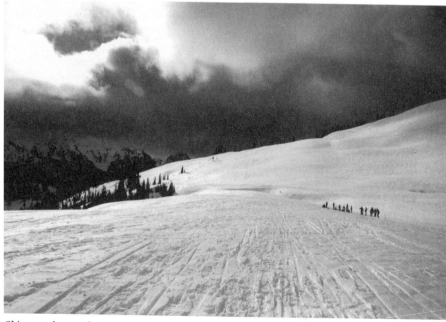

*Skiers and snowshoers on the meadows near Artist Point*

canvas when shrouded with snow. The actual namesake of this trail is a high viewpoint between the two great peaks. All around the point are ancient forests, and come winter, the deep green trees are cloaked in shrouds of white as wind-driven snow and hoarfrost cling to the evergreen limbs. On overcast days, the area becomes a world of black and white, with many shades of gray. But on clear, calm days, the world is blue and white: white snow, white peaks, blue-tinted evergreens, and sapphire blue skies.

To get there, from Bellingham drive east on State Route 542 (Mount Baker Highway) to the road end, about 55 miles, at the upper parking lot of the Mount Baker Ski Area.

To start the trip, leave the south (upper) end of the ski area parking lot and edge along the flank of the downhill area along the access road leading to Austin Pass, or choose the steeper, straight-up route followed by the summer hiking trail. Just past the ski runs, the route turns upward and you begin a long, steady climb to the pass. Stay off to the right of the road to avoid cross-country skiers who are heading for the deep, backcountry bowls beyond Artist Point. The track covers 500 feet of elevation gain from the parking area to 4700-foot Austin Pass, but that gain is easily accomplished on snowshoes—it's the side-stepping cross-country skiers who will be sweating this section.

From Austin Pass, the road sweeps out to the left in a long switchback. Keep right, and climb the open meadows ahead to cut across the neck of this loop, rejoining the road in a few hundred yards at the road end at the lower end of Kulshan Ridge, just past the 2-mile mark. A final 0.25 mile of hiking to the left along this ridge gets you to the impossibly beautiful views at Artist Point.

Soak in the views of Mount Shuksan to the east, Mount Baker to the west, and to the southwest Coleman Pinnacle towers seemingly just beyond reach. Backcountry telemark skiers are often seen playing in the steep, deep snow bowls along Ptarmigan Ridge, which stretches between Artist Point and Coleman Pinnacle. This ridge is filled with dangerous avalanche chutes, so before deciding to trek out along it, be sure of the current avalanche conditions.

A better option for an extended trek from Artist Point is to the left (east) along the more stable snow of Kulshan Ridge. A half mile of hiking along the deep snow on the ridge crest leads to Huntoon Point, a high knob on the upper end of Kulshan. From this lofty observation point, look out over the expanse of the Mount Baker Wilderness to the west and south, the North Cascades National Park (which encompasses Mount Shuksan) to the east, and the ragged line of Shuksan Arm——reaching out from Shuksan—to the north.

## --*12*--
# Middle Fork Nooksack River

**Rating:** Backcountry
**Round trip:** 7 miles
**Hiking time:** 5 hours
**Elevation gain:** 900 feet
**High point:** 3000 feet
**Best season:** December through early February
**Map:** Green Trails: Hamilton No. 45
**Who to Contact:** Mount Baker–Snoqualmie National Forest, Mount Baker Ranger District

The most difficult part of this snowshoe hike is getting to the snow. But once the network of roads has been safely navigated, the fun can begin in earnest. This is a largely untouched winter wilderness setting, and finding solitude amid such staggering beauty is remarkable. The trail follows the Middle Fork Nooksack River upstream in the very shadow of majestic Mount Baker. When tired of viewing that big volcano, glance right and soak in the beauty of Loomis Mountain.

On the return trip, Mount Baker is at your back, but the twin towers of Sisters Mountain loom ahead. In the midst of all this mountain scenery live an array of wild creatures for snowshoers to quietly observe. Snowshoe hares, ptarmigans—large grouselike birds that turn snowy white come winter—martens, weasels, foxes, and blacktail deer thrive in this valley. Of course, with all those prey-animals living here, predators are close at hand. Bobcats, lynx (one of the last population of lynx in Washington), cougars, coyotes, and possibly even wolves roam these woods. These critters pose little danger to healthy, adult humans, and any encounter with them should be counted as a blessing.

To get there, from Bellingham drive east on State Route 542 (Mount Baker Highway) for 18 miles before turning right onto Mosquito Lake Road (about 2 miles north of the junction of Mount Baker Highway and State Route 9 at Deming). Drive 5 miles east on Mosquito Lake Road, and then turn left (east) onto Forest Road 38. Continue 11 miles east on FR 38 to a junction with a small spur road (elevation 2000 feet) on the right, signed as the access to Elbow Lake Trail. Depending on snow levels, park here, or in light snow years continue up the main road another 1.5 miles to a switchback. The Middle Fork Nooksack trailhead is found at the apex of this switchback corner.

Most years, the snow is at or below the Elbow Lake trailhead parking area. From the Elbow Lake trailhead, hike the 1.5 miles up FR 38 to the Middle Fork Nooksack trailhead. Relax and enjoy the scenery along this road, which is nearly level and well graded. Mount Baker dominates the northeast horizon, and the wide bed of the Middle Fork Nooksack River is a constant source of entertainment to your right. The river weaves in and out of gravel bars and small forested islands, and the snow-lined banks provide a crisp edge to the tumbling waters of the river.

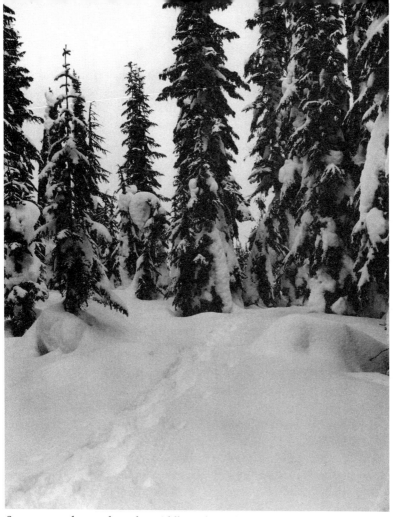

*Snow-covered trees along the Middle Fork Nooksack route*

At the first hairpin turn in the road, go straight to find the trail at the point of the switchback. The trail continues to follow the river upstream, while the road climbs the hill away from the river. The trail is narrow, and if the snow isn't deep, there may be a few downed trees to scramble over. This trail is seldom maintained, and fallen trees are nearly always present. However, the trees are more a hindrance to skiers than snowshoers, and they help to ensure solitude on this beautiful trail.

The next 1 mile of trail parallels the river, and the views remain largely unchanged: where the forest is open, Mount Baker, Loomis Mountain, and Park Butte dominate the skyline; where the forest canopy closes in, the beautiful old-growth forest and sparkling river will captivate you.

At about 3 miles (3200 feet), the trail begins to climb toward Mazama Park on the southwest flank of Mount Baker. The trail, though, is difficult to follow as it traverses several avalanche slopes and dips into areas of dense forest. Better to just enjoy the views, and turn back when the trail turns vertical.

## --13--
## Schriebers Meadow

**Rating:** More difficult
**Round trip:** 11 to 14+ miles
**Hiking time:** 1 to 2 days
**Elevation gain:** 1200 feet
**High point:** 5200 feet
**Best season:** January through March
**Maps:** Green Trails: Hamilton No. 45, Lake Shannon No. 46
**Who to Contact:** Mount Baker–Snoqualmie National Forest, Mount Baker Ranger District

Depending on the starting snow elevation, this may be a wonderful day hike in wide meadows or a long, overnight trek through forests before reaching those alpine clearings. Regardless, this route is a jewel for winter enthusiasts. Expect to share the road and trail with cross-country skiers and probably a few snowmobilers, although midweek or after mid-January (after the typical holiday rush to the hills) finds the setting tranquil and uncrowded. But even if others are along the route, there is plenty of wild country and beautiful scenery for all to share. The great white cone of Mount Baker looms over the trail to the north, while the broad, undulating snowfields of Schriebers Meadow beckon one and all out into the untracked expanses for a moment of wintry solitude.

To get there, from Sedro-Woolley drive east on U.S. Highway 20 (North Cascades Highway) for 14 miles before turning left (north) onto Forest Road 11 (Baker Lake Road). Drive north on FR 11 for 12.5 miles, and then turn left onto FR 12. Continue on FR 12 for 3.5 miles to the Sno-Park at the junction with FR 13. If snow conditions permit, turn right and drive up FR 13 to the snow line (typically about 3 more miles, near the 2500- to 3000-foot elevation).

If the snow is heavy, park at the Sno-Park and begin a 5-mile trek along the wide, forested corridor of FR 13. This leads up a pair of switchbacks before tapering in a long, climbing traverse along the hillside above Sulphur Creek. The road ends at a broad parking area marking the trailhead for the Schriebers Meadow–Park Butte Trail. This road section provides a good stretch for the legs without an excessive workout, leaving you with plenty of energy for snowshoeing through the wondrous meadows above.

At the road end, the route jumps onto the narrow trail, crossing Sulphur Creek before climbing in a short 0.25 mile to the lower edge of Schriebers Meadow. This world of white is a paradise of winter recreation. Skiers are sure to be found slashing down the slopes flanking the meadows, and on busy Saturdays in January, expect to hear the whine of a few snowmobiles, too. To find solitude, angle off into the untracked reaches of the meadows. To the south, climb up a moderate slope for 0.25 mile or so to reach a basin with three or four ice-covered alpine tarns. Here the views of Mount Baker are at

*Foggy forest at the edge of Schriebers Meadow*

their ultimate best, and good campsites are found in this area, too. Just pick a spot big enough for a tent on the leeward side of the hill, with a glade of trees flanking your site for added shelter from storms in February.

Another alternative is to push on for a longer snowshoe trek to Survey Point, by crossing the flat meadows to the northwest and then starting a gradual climb between two long rocky ridges. These ridges are lateral moraines—rock piles that were pushed aside by flowing glaciers. Climb this wide trough, and in about 1.5 miles from the end of the road, cross the upper reaches of Rocky Creek. Use care here because the many seemingly solid snow bridges may be weak and unsafe, especially late in the season or after periods of unusually warm weather. After you cross the creek, the climbing is steep and steady for another 0.5 mile. Then bear left (west), and traverse a long, open slope to reach the top of the ridge of the left-hand moraine for stunning views of Mount Baker, the sprawling white blanket of Schriebers Meadow, and the high peaks of Park and Black Buttes to the west.

--*14*--
# Sauk Mountain

Rating: Backcountry
Round trip: 11 miles
Hiking time: 8 hours
Elevation gain: 3500 feet
High point: 5500 feet
Best season: Late December through early February
Maps: Green Trails: Darrington No. 78, Lake Shannon No. 46
Who to Contact: Mount Baker–Snoqualmie National Forest,
Darrington Ranger District

Although this snowshoe trek makes use of a road for much of the route's length, the way is steep, generally icy, and the upper section follows narrow, avalanche-prone hiking trails. But when conditions are good, the physical exertion needed to tromp up this steep-sloped peak is richly rewarded with stunning views of the jagged crests of a multitude of North Cascade peaks. Glacier Peak dominates the horizon to the southeast, but the landscape closer at hand is just as lovely. Because of the frequent, frigid winds, the vegetation of exposed meadows on the upper slopes of Sauk is usually glazed with frilly ice lacing. Hoarfrost, formed by wind-driven moisture and cold air temperatures, creates delicate icy ornamentation on limbs, leaves, and—when they stand still too long—snowshoers.

To get there, from Sedro-Woolley drive east on U.S. Highway 20 (North Cascades Highway) to the town of Concrete. Continue east another 6.5 miles, and turn left (north) onto Sauk Mountain Road (Forest Road 1030). If you pass Rockport State Park, you have gone too far. (Turn around, and drive 200 yards west of the park to find the Sauk Mountain Road junction.) Drive north on Sauk Mountain Road to the snow line—generally about 1.5 miles up the road, near a junction at the 1400-foot level.

After turning around and parking well off the main road, continue up the roadway on snowshoes. The road repeatedly switchbacks as it climbs relentlessly for another mile through open clearcut meadows and thin patches of second-growth forest. The road continues to climb, now in heavy second-growth timber, until, near the 4-mile mark, views reveal stunning peeks down into the perpetually mist-laden Sauk River valley and southwest toward Glacier Peak.

*Small drift on the upper flank of Sauk Mountain*

Keep hiking along the windswept road as it rolls along the flank of Sauk Mountain to a final switchback corner at about 4.5 miles. Here Puget Sound comes into view. From this point, near 3600-feet, the road climbs back toward the west to a point directly below the summit of the mountain. This stretch crosses several avalanche chutes and should be attempted only when avalanche danger can be confirmed as minimal.

On days when the snow is stable, push on the last mile to the end of the road and the start of the summer hiking trail to the summit of Sauk. The summit should be approached only by advanced winter mountaineers because the upper slopes are icy, steep, and prone to rock- and snowslides.

When avalanche dangers are moderate or higher, turn around at the last switchback, or to add a couple of miles to the outing, bear northwest on a small spur road that leads out onto Jackman Ridge. This partially logged ridge is largely unremarkable, but the trail along its crest is mostly level for its 1-mile length, and some excellent views of the upper Puget Sound basin are found along the way.

## --15--

## Iron Mountain

**Rating:** Backcountry
**Round trip:** 9 miles
**Hiking time:** 8 hours
**Elevation gain:** 1800 feet
**High point:** 4000 feet
**Best season:** January through early March
**Map:** Green Trails: Oso No. 77
**Who to Contact:** Mount Baker–Snoqualmie National Forest, Darrington Ranger District

This area won't be looked at twice by wilderness seekers in summer months, but when blanketed in snow, the narrow logging roads and gentle slopes are magically transformed into a pristine wilderness. There are no awesome views of scores of high peaks over beautiful wilderness rivers, but the scenery is lovely and very enjoyable. Just trekking through a quiet forest blanketed in a heavy quilt of snow is reward enough for this snowshoer.

Snowshoers with excellent routefinding skills can cut cross-country through forest and meadow to climb high onto the flanks of Iron Mountain. Meanwhile, less experienced winter travelers can stick to the roadway for several miles. Bear in mind that snowmobilers frequent the roads in the area on weekends, so weekdays may be the best time to visit. Also, although snowshoers hiking cross-country will find the climb to Iron Mountain quiet and snowmobile-free, snow machines may be encountered near the summit because a long, looping road leads nearly to the top of the mountain.

To get there, from Sedro-Woolley drive south on State Route 9 across the Skagit River Bridge and immediately turn left (east) onto South Skagit Highway. Drive east along the South Skagit Highway as it parallels the river upstream. In about 12 miles, turn right (south) onto Forest Road 17 and follow it south as it climbs the Cumberland Creek valley. Drive to the snow line, usually at least 5 miles up the road, near the 2000-foot level.

*Forest clearing on the cross-country route to Iron Mountain*

Start up the road as it climbs gradually but steadily for the next 2.5 miles. The route slices across a few small clearcuts and pierces some dense, second-growth forest before reaching a junction with FR 1770 on the left. Snowshoe up this short spur road as it curves north and then turns back to the east. After a mile on this road, 3.5 miles from the start, the road curves back to the north. Leave the road here, and climb through the young forest, angling up the slope. There is no trail here, so simply pick the path of least resistance while always going up and slightly to the left (north). The forest here is mixed, with some young second-growth among thinner, old forests and open meadows.

About a mile of snowshoeing from the end of the road, after gaining about 450 feet in elevation, cross the wide path of FR 1775 at the top of the ridge. This road meanders for several miles along the ridge crest. Turn left and follow it north as it approaches the high peak of Iron Mountain. About a mile up the ridge, 5.5 miles from the start of the hike, the road forks. The left fork slants out along the southwest side of the mountain; the right fork, the main road, curves around the eastern flank of the peak. There is no easy approach to the summit proper, but this junction is a good turnaround point.

Enjoy the views from the ridge, including some nice views west toward Puget Sound, before heading back.

Time and distance can be saved with some effort by dropping off the road and heading west through the forest immediately. This means dropping down the slope at a steeper angle than where it was climbed, but the main route, FR 17, is directly downhill from FR 1775. No matter where you drop off, just head straight downhill, being careful to avoid rocky promontories and tight thickets of brush, to catch FR 17.

## --*16*--
# Segelsen Ridge

|  |  |
|---|---|
| **Rating:** | Easiest to more difficult |
| **Round trip:** | 6 to 21 miles |
| **Hiking time:** | 6 hours to 2 days |
| **Elevation gain:** | 2500 feet |
| **High point:** | 4516 feet |
| **Best season:** | January through February |
| **Map:** | Green Trails: Darrington No. 78 |
| **Who to Contact:** | Mount Baker–Snoqualmie National Forest, Darrington Ranger District |

This is a low-elevation route, so the best time to strap on snowshoes for a walk on Segelsen Ridge is in midwinter when the snow is at its deepest. Although better snow is oftentimes found elsewhere, this popular ridge hike offers great views without a long drive on mountain roads. The ridge is long and winding, so even on the busiest of winter weekends, there is plenty of country for all comers. In the course of a day (or for those looking to cover all of the ridge country, a long weekend), the recreationists quickly disperse along the trail. On the long downhill sections, skiers flit past trudging snowshoers; on the equally long ascents, skiers waddle up the roads spraddle-legged, stomping herringbone patterns in the snow, while snowshoers gracefully hike past them.

To get there, from Arlington drive east on State Route 530 (Mountain Loop Highway) for 24.5 miles. Near the Whitehorse Mercantile, turn left (north) onto Swede Heaven Road. Continue 2 miles north, and then bear right onto Forest Road 18 and drive to the snow line. Most years that is at least 3 miles up FR 18 at the South Finney Creek Sno-Park (elevation

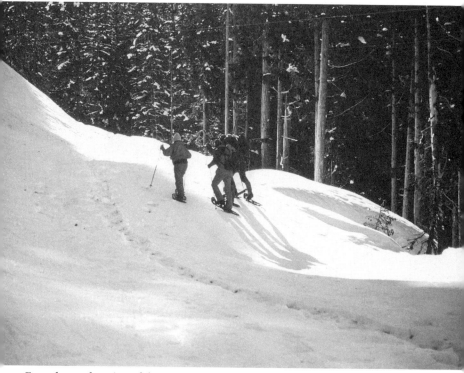

*Even the road section of the route offers snowdrifts to climb*

1200 feet), but sometimes it is more like 6.5 miles, just past the 2000-foot-elevation point at Cascade Creek. Hiking mileage in this description begins at the Sno-Park.

Whether on a day hike or a long overnight trip, start snowshoeing up FR 18, and at 1.5 miles above the Sno-Park, the first choice presents itself. Straight ahead lies the main road and the long ridge route it leads to. To the left is a narrow old road winding steeply up through young second-growth and some small clearcuts to the crest of a 2685-foot unnamed knob. When the snow is deep, this road offers a chance to get away from the crowds, as well as providing a good workout, nice views, and a full day of snowshoeing.

The climb to the knob's summit and back to your car covers about 6 miles. Those choosing this lesser-used trail will find that the narrow jeep road divides a mile after leaving FR 18. Stay left, and traverse around the knob, staying just below the summit. The road soon loops back to the right (north) and climbs the western flank of the hill. To reach the true summit, leave the roadway about 1.5 miles from FR 18 and climb the moderately steep forested slope to the crown of the hill. Push on to the southern edge of the summit crown for some nice views over the Stillaguamish River valley to Whitehorse Mountain beyond.

For a more extended outing, ignore this side trip and instead press on up FR 18 as it banks to the left, crosses the Cascade Creek valley, and continues to climb north toward the snout of Segelsen Ridge. The views along this stretch of the trek are limited, but the occasional clearcut slope allows some peeks up the valley to the long ridge and down the valley to Whitehorse Mountain.

At 5 miles, the road takes a hard switchback to the left and rolls around the snout of Segelsen Ridge before entering the final climbing traverse toward the ridge crest. The fastest way to the top of the ridge is via a small access road, FR 1855, found some 6.5 miles from the Sno-Park. Turn right, and climb the narrow, winding FR 1855 toward the crest. This road switches back about 0.5 mile above FR 18, and then slants steeply upward for another mile or so.

At about 2 miles above FR 18, leave the roadbed and climb a tiny two-track trail for 0.25 mile along an ascending traverse before abandoning all tracks and climbing cross-country, up through trees, about 400 yards to the southern summit of the ridge crest (elevation 4516 feet).

To extend the trip even more, return to the spur FR 1855 and continue up-slope to the uneven crest of Segelsen Ridge. Head north along this ridge line for another 2 miles, all the while enjoying the stunning views of the surrounding countryside of open meadows, as well as the distant vistas sweeping over Whitehorse Mountain, Round Mountain, and Stillaguamish Valley.

--17--

# Rat Trap Pass

                **Rating:** More difficult
           **Round trip:** 7.5 miles
          **Hiking time:** 6 hours
       **Elevation gain:** 1900 feet
          **High point:** 3500 feet
         **Best season:** December through February
                   **Map:** Green Trails: Sloan Peak No. 111
      **Who to Contact:** Mount Baker–Snoqualmie National Forest,
                          Darrington Ranger District
                          *See map on page 70.*

This little pass bridges the gap between the Crystal Creek valley to the south and the Straight Creek valley to the north. Come summer, the area is a bleak little saddle scarred by clearcuts and a narrow dusty road. But dump several feet of snow on the pass to mask the ugly logging scars, and Rat Trap Pass becomes a stunning little alpine world. High, rocky cliffs cradle snow-filled meadows and picturesque little groves of juvenile fir and hemlock. The climb to the pass is pretty enough to make the journey enjoyable, if not overly remarkable, but it's the destination that makes this snowshoe hike one to remember. By mid-December, Rat Trap Pass offers snowshoers a wide world of snowy exploration. Climb through open fields of snow to find secluded little playgrounds blocked off from other pass visitors by the rolling landscape and remnant stands of forest. Enjoy a midday repast with stunning views of the wintry landscape all around. White Chuck Mountain towers over the pass to the west, while the eastern skyline is punctuated by the craggy tops of Circle Peak and Meadow Mountain.

To get there, from Darrington drive southeast on State Route 530

(Mountain Loop Highway) for 9 miles before turning left (east) onto Forest Road 23 (White Chuck River Road). Continue east on FR 23 for 5 miles before crossing the White Chuck River. Drive another 0.3 mile after the river crossing to the junction with FR 27 and turn left. Park in the broad area near the road junction, or drive north along FR 27 to the snow line.

From the road junction, hike up the road, staying clear of the ever-present ski tracks, as it climbs north up a secondary valley above the White Chuck River. In less than a mile, the route crosses Crystal Creek and climbs in another 0.5 mile to the first clearing. Here, look southwest for an open view of the snow-crowned monolith of Glacier Peak. Stick to the roadway for another 2 miles, passing Crystal Creek Road (FR 2710)—see Route 18, Crystal Lake— at 2.5 miles from the parking area, to gain the lower reaches of the meadows surrounding Rat Trap Pass. Along this stretch, the route climbs a long traverse with periodic open views of White Chuck Mountain in front of you on the left.

Once at the meadows of the pass, angle off to the left for the best views and thinnest crowds. A small road cuts up the moderate slope, but pick a destination on the opposite side of the snowy fields and angle toward it. Climb the slopes, slicing through the few stands of mature forest and around the jumble of juvenile trees scattered here and there until reaching a suitable spot for lunch. Your picnic spot may be just beyond the main trail leading into the pass, halfway up the hillside on the western wall of the pass, or at the farthest, along the narrow draw that holds the frozen waters of Straight Creek at the far northern edge of the Rat Trap Pass meadows.

*Heading down from Rat Trap Pass*

## --18--

# Crystal Lake

**Rating:** Backcountry
**Round trip:** 13.5 miles
**Hiking time:** 1 to 2 days
**Elevation gain:** 2800 feet
**High point:** 4485 feet
**Best season:** January through February
**Map:** Green Trails: Sloan Peak No. 111
**Who to Contact:** Mount Baker–Snoqualmie National Forest, Darrington Ranger District
*See map on page 70.*

With its many open views back toward Pugh Mountain, this trail offers an exceptional weekend outing in the winter wilderness. The trail begins gently enough, climbing along a wide, moderately pitched road. It then turns up a secondary valley and crawls along a narrower, steeper road. Finally, the route becomes a narrow, winding single-track trail in a dark, old forest. This section is not for the fainthearted nor for untested navigators. The trail is often hard to find, and snowshoers have to trust their skills with map, compass, and common-sense navigation to wend their way up the valley to the pretty little alpine lake lying between Circle Peak and Meadow Mountain.

Those who expend the considerable effort to hike the trail are amply rewarded. Along the way, the views and local scenery are magnificent: from sweeping panoramas that take in Pugh and White Chuck Mountains to up-close and personal encounters with the deep gray-green forest of old fir, hemlock, and cedar wrapped in a cloak of snow and frost. Snowshoers will leave most of the ski traffic behind as they peel away from the main track to Rat Trap Pass (see Route 17) and angle up the side valley of Crystal Creek and its headwaters at Crystal Lake. With fewer folks crowding the route, wildlife is more visible—the ever-present whiskey jack whistles all along the route, while weasels, ptarmigans, and even a few sly foxes have been spotted as well.

To get there, from Darrington drive southeast on State Route 530 (Mountain Loop Highway) for 9 miles before turning left (east) onto Forest Road 23 (White Chuck River Road). Continue east on FR 23 for 5 miles before crossing the White Chuck River. Drive another 0.3 mile after the river crossing to the junction with FR 27 and turn left. Park in the broad area near the road junction, or drive north along FR 27 to the snow line.

*Lakeshore meadow*

From the road junction, hike up the road as if heading toward Rat Trap Pass. The first 2.5 miles offer some nice views of Glacier Peak, Pugh Mountain, and the White Chuck River valley from a gentle trail. At the junction of FR27 and the smaller FR 2710, go right onto FR 2710 to begin the climb up into the Crystal Creek valley. The road switches back a time or two, climbing some 500 feet in less than 0.5 mile before rolling into a long traverse up the valley. The road stays well above the creek itself, but the steep side-walls above the road provide their own problems. Snow conditions must be scrupulously checked before entering this valley because a high degree of avalanche danger can exist.

The road forks in 1.5 miles from the FR 27 junction. Stay left to remain on the north side of Crystal Creek—the right fork slants down across the valley and then rolls out into a long, looping traverse above the White Chuck River. The route to Crystal Lake becomes narrower at the fork, but it holds fairly level as it continues to traverse upvalley to the road end, nearly 1.5 miles past the last fork.

The summer trailhead of the Crystal Lake Trail is found at the road end. The trail is a faint, seldom-maintained path that is difficult enough to find in August. Come winter, the path is visible only as an often-indistinct corridor through the trees. If the trail is lost below the snow, just pick the path of least resistance through the trees, staying on the north side of the creek while climbing gradually to the 4400-foot level.

In about a mile, at 4400-feet, the creek turns right as it drops over a modest falls. At this point the trail is down close to the creek banks, but it remains on the north side of the water until right before the lake is reached—about 0.25 mile above the falls. Crystal Lake is at 4485 feet, and from its shores, Circle Peak, Meadow Mountain, and the crown of White Chuck Mountain are visible. The lake basin offers plenty of fine sites for camping. Crystal Lake is seldom frozen solid enough for safe travel across it, so stick to the shore-lines to prevent an unwanted plunge into the icy waters.

## --19--

# Kennedy Hot Springs

**Rating:** Backcountry
**Round trip:** 11 miles
**Hiking time:** 1 to 2 days
**Elevation gain:** 1050 feet
**High point:** 3330 feet
**Best season:** Late January through late February
**Maps:** Green Trails: Glacier Peak No. 112, Sloan Peak No. 111
**Who to Contact:** Mount Baker–Snoqualmie National Forest, Darrington Ranger District

It's difficult to truly appreciate a natural hot spring unless snow is on the ground. That holds doubly true for Kennedy Hot Springs. The warm pools are a nice reward for the long, cold snowshoe trek along the White Chuck River. But without the snow to make the trail tough come winter, the reward would not be as pleasant. These warm springs would be just as crowded—and therefore uninviting—as they are in the summer.

Kennedy Hot Springs gets so much public pressure in the warm months that by early August, the slow-flowing springs can't flush the litter and bacteria out fast enough. After a few months of little or no use, in late autumn the pools are clear and relatively clean again—ready once more to ease the aching muscles of the snowshoers who struggle into the steaming basin. Still, it's advised that bathers avoid dunking their heads underwater as there may be lingering bacteria that, although unable to penetrate our tough skins, could find a home in the sensitive mucus membranes of the nose and eyes. Also, be aware that traditionally, Kennedy Hot Springs is clothing optional, so be prepared for bare encounters. Likewise, if kids are present in the springs, bathers

*Snow- and ice-laden stream along the trail to Kennedy Hot Springs*

should refrain from baring all until the tykes are taken back to camp by their parents. Common sense and courtesy are key to hot springs harmony.

To get there, from Darrington drive southeast on State Route 530 (Mountain Loop Highway) for 9 miles before turning left (east) onto Forest Road 23 (White Chuck River Road). Drive 11 miles to the road end and the trailhead parking area for the White Chuck River Trail at 2300 feet. In periods of heavy snow, it may be necessary to park farther down the valley and snowshoe up the road a few miles. Most years, however, the road is drivable to the road end or to within a mile of it.

The White Chuck River Trail is narrow and follows the base of the steep north wall of the valley. There are several areas where avalanches can and do occur, so extreme caution must be used in evaluating the snow and avalanche potential. (Be sure to call the Northwest Weather and Avalanche Center hotline before leaving on this hike; see Appendix A, Contact Information.)

The trail begins with a brushy trudge through alder along the banks of the White Chuck River before slanting upslope. At about 0.5 mile from the trailhead, the route climbs the valley wall above the river and begins a 5-mile traverse of the hillside to the hot springs. Along the way, there are several creeks to cross and at least two tricky slide areas to negotiate.

The first creek crossing comes nearly 1.5 miles from the trailhead; Fire Creek is crossed at 2500 feet elevation and poses little difficulty. Shortly past the creek, near the 2-mile mark, Pumice Creek is crossed, and the first avalanche/ mudslide area is encountered. There is usually a jumble of brush, boulders, some downed trees, and an open scar of snow-free mud on the hillside that has sloughed off onto the trail. If the tangle of debris is especially thick, it is sometimes necessary to slip out of your snowshoes to avoid entangling the straps in the branches and sticks protruding from the slide material. Other times, there is enough snow to cover the mess. In these cases, hurry over the snow-laden piles because although the snow means easier travel, it also means there is potential for an avalanche.

Just 0.5 mile past this first debris field is another steep slope and slide area. This time, though, instead of the slope terminating in a jumble of debris, it runs out into the river. This is the trickiest part of the trail. If the snow is thin and well packed, it's possible to follow the narrow trail across this steep slope—careful use of an ice ax and a safety line is recommended at all times. But if the snow is deep or even a little unstable, it's better not to risk a slide down into the icy waters of the river. Instead, backtrack a few dozen yards until you can angle uphill through the trees to reach the top of a slanting bench that crosses over the slide area. Turn parallel to the trail, and traverse the slope above the slide area; then carefully angle back down through the thick trees to the trail.

Once you are back on the trail, it's fairly smooth snowshoeing the last 3 miles to the hot springs. At just past the 4-mile mark, the trail does a quick one-two through a pair of switchbacks, getting you up to the 3100-foot level for a 1.5-mile-long traverse into the Kennedy Creek basin. Cross a small side branch of the White Chuck River, another unnamed rivulet emptying into the river, and finally Kennedy Creek to reach a small ranger cabin near the springs and plenty of flat campsites nearby.

To get to the springs from the campsites, cross a narrow, snow-laden bridge over the White Chuck River and turn upriver to find the soaking pools about 20 yards beyond the bridge. Be careful around the pools, as bathers hopping out of the soothing waters drip all over the snow and rocks and the pools' edges. This water then freezes, creating a treacherous coating of ice around the springs (and frequently along the trail back to the campsites). It's a good idea to use trekking poles or ice axes when walking to and from the springs.

# --20--
# Mount Pilchuck

| | |
|---|---|
| **Rating:** | Easiest to more difficult |
| **Round trip:** | 11 miles |
| **Hiking time:** | 10 hours |
| **Elevation gain:** | 2600 feet |
| **High point:** | 4000 feet |
| **Best season:** | Late January through late February |
| **Map:** | Green Trails: Granite Falls No. 109 |
| **Who to Contact:** | Mount Pilchuck State Park |

Mount Pilchuck is a popular haven for summer hikers, but many snowshoers fail to appreciate the challenges offered by the steep, snow-laden slopes of the mountain. That's their mistake. Mount Pilchuck offers several miles of gently climbing trail that follows the winding road leading to the summer trailhead

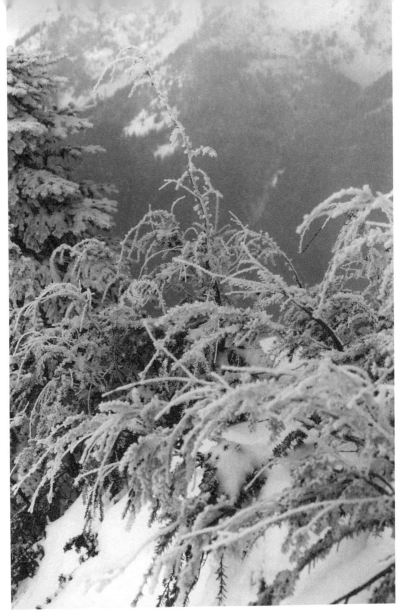

*Hoarfrost-coated tree*

parking area. Farther up the trail, adventurous snowshoers can forsake the roadway and hike up through the trees or along the wide runs of an abandoned downhill ski area. The alpine skiers swarmed here in the 1970s, but the resort failed after just a few years, leaving broad slopes for snowshoers to climb and telemark skiers to swoosh down. From the top of the runs, the

Stillaguamish River valley—including the deep, dark cut of Robe Gorge—sprawls below, while the jagged top of Pilchuck looms overhead.

To get there, from Granite Falls drive east on the Mountain Loop Highway 1 mile past the Verlot Public Service Center, and turn right (south) onto Mount Pilchuck Road (Forest Road 42). Continue up the road 1.6 miles to reach the winter closure gate. Park in the wide areas near the gate, but do not block the main road or any side access (private) roads.

The vehicle gate marks the end of all legal motorized traffic, so after snowshoeing around it, enter a world of default wilderness. The road climbs steadily but not too steeply along its first 2 miles. Off-road rambling isn't recommended in this early stage, but about 3.5 miles up the trail—just after crossing a small stream—there is an opportunity in heavy snow years to angle up through the trees to the left, cutting across the neck of a wide switchback. This will require some routefinding skills because there is no true trail. However, the trees are widely spaced enough that, if the undergrowth is buried in enough snow, you can simply climb between them.

If you prefer to keep things simple and serene, continue around on the road. At just over 4 miles, the road switches back to the left. A half mile farther up the route, the road turns back to the right, but if the snow is stable and avalanche dangers are minimal, a better option awaits. From the corner of the second switchback, head straight out toward the southeast in a climbing traverse of the snowy slope on the flank of Pilchuck. In less than 0.5 mile, the first open run of the old ski area is encountered. Climb up this wide trail, sticking to the edge near the trees to avoid a nasty confrontation (i.e., collision) with backcountry skiers practicing their telemark turns on the open slopes.

By using this steep, direct approach, the climb to the top is more of a workout, but it cuts nearly a mile off the road distance. It will also get you to the top before the crowds of skiers can kick their way up the road. That means more time at the top—the end of the road and the site of the old ski lodge—to enjoy the views alone and uninterrupted. The lodge is long gone, but the views of the Stillaguamish River valley and the high, serrated ridges above it are as beautiful as ever.

If you have a mountaineering background and advanced avalanche-recognition skills, you might consider climbing part way up the Mount Pilchuck Trail. The route is steep and difficult to find as it winds its way up through forests, rocky slopes, and dangerous avalanche chutes. This added adventure isn't for the fainthearted or the untested—summer hikers often get lost here.

## --21--
# Heather Lake

**Rating:** More difficult
**Round trip:** 4 miles
**Hiking time:** 4 hours
**Elevation gain:** 1100 feet
**High point:** 2440 feet
**Best season:** Early January to late February
**Map:** Green Trails: Granite Falls No. 109
**Who to Contact:** Mount Pilchuck State Park
*See map on page 79.*

The Heather Lake Trail can be a wonderful route for snowshoers as it climbs just 2 miles—gaining more than 1000 feet—through thick second-growth forest to arrive at a stunningly beautiful alpine lake nestled in a deep rock cirque on the north face of Mount Pilchuck. The trail is heavily traveled in the summer, but winter visitors will find the crowds thin and the forests even more beautiful when blanketed in soft white. The lake features several excellent campsites around its perimeter, each with its own charm and glorious view of Mount Pilchuck or the Stillaguamish Valley. The short distance

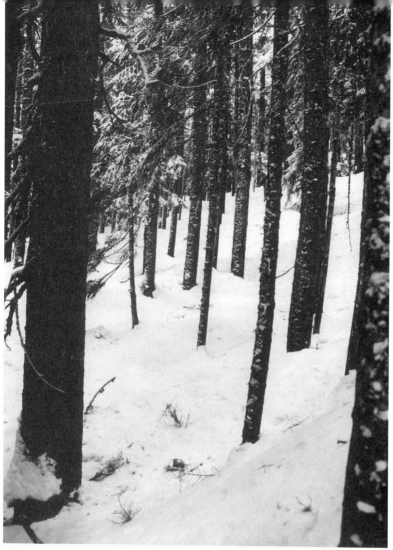
*Along the steep trail to Heather Lake*

makes this a great destination to consider for first-timers in the art of winter camping.

To get there, from Granite Falls drive east on the Mountain Loop High-way 1 mile past the Verlot Public Service Center and turn right (south) onto Mount Pilchuck Road (Forest Road 42). Continue up the road 1.6 miles to reach the winter closure gate. Park in the wide areas near the gate, but do not block the main road or any side access (private) roads.

The trail leaves the left side of the parking area near the gate and imme-diately begins climbing through the dense young forest, switching back a time or two before traversing west into the Heather Creek valley. The trail climbs steadily alongside the creek, gaining more than 1000 feet in the 2 miles to the lake. After nearly a mile of climbing, notice how the surrounding forest begins to age. Old, stout trees of massive size are mingled with the young, crowded stands of second-growth fir and hemlock. At the 1.2-mile mark, the forest is entirely old growth, with ancient hulks towering over the trail and long-dead trunks lying scattered about the forest floor. The decaying fallen trees provide just the rich nourishment seeds need to sprout and grow into young, upstart trees. In this way, the dead trees, or nurse logs, hold the roots of a new generation, closing the circle of forest life. Even buried under snow, these nurse logs are evident. Just look for the long rows of young trees, and imagine them all rooted in one long, straight log.

The trail reaches the Heather Lake basin at just above 2400 feet and breaks out of the forest and into open views of the towering summit of Mount Pilchuck beyond. The lake is at a low enough elevation that at no time should you attempt to cross its ice; the ice is seldom thick enough to support an adult, and even then, it is likely riddled with cracks and fissures, which could open and send you into a quick bout of hypothermia.

Campsites can be found around the perimeter of the lake, and the best are on the eastern shore where the slope is most gradual and the view most splendid.

## --22--

# Lake Twentytwo

Rating: Backcountry
Round trip: 5 miles
Hiking time: 4 hours
Elevation gain: 1200 feet
High point: 2440 feet
Best season: Early January to late February
Map: Green Trails: Granite Falls No. 109
Who to Contact: Mount Baker–Snoqualmie National Forest, Darrington Ranger District
*See map on page 79.*

Although the snow is frequently thin at the base of this trail, the route climbs quickly and snowshoes are needed not only for flotation but also for traction

*Icicles and small waterfall along the trail to Lake Twentytwo*

on the steep slopes. The workout is extensive, but the rewards are phenomenal. The trail follows a beautiful tumbling creek as it rushes down a narrow gorge. Along the way, the creek drops over no fewer than four pretty waterfalls, with each successive one sporting larger and more intricate ice mantles.

To get there, from Granite Falls drive east on the Mountain Loop Highway 1 mile past the Verlot Public Service Center and continue east 2 miles to the Lake Twentytwo trailhead on the right (south) side of the highway.

If the snow is thin at this low-elevation trailhead, strap your snowshoes on the back of your pack and hike up the trail until the snow deepens. The trail climbs gradually for 0.25 mile, then turns straight up the creek valley and rolls through a long series of switchbacks. Frequently, even if the snow isn't deep, snowshoes will be required simply because the beefy crampons on their base afford a sure grip on the slick trail.

The first waterfall is passed 0.5 mile up the trail, and then more are seen at 1 mile, 1.2 miles, and 1.5 miles. Just past the third waterfall, the trail levels out (relatively speaking) as it rolls west along the hillside for several hundred yards before turning back toward the creek. It passes through a couple of these longer, more moderate switchbacks before making a long, straight traverse back to the creek at the fourth falls. From there, it's a 0.25-mile climb to the lakeshore.

This trail is steeper and the lake more remote than the nearby Heather Lake route (Route 21), but it is also less visited in winter months. Some of the open slopes above the trail, especially on the upper reaches, are prone to slide in moderate to high avalanche conditions, so use caution.

## --23--

# Boardman Lake

**Rating:** More difficult
**Round trip:** 11.6 to 11.9
**Hiking time:** 1 to 2 days
**Elevation gain:** 1800 feet
**High point:** 3000 feet
**Best season:** Late December through late February
**Map:** Green Trails: Silverton No. 110
**Who to Contact:** Mount Baker–Snoqualmie National Forest, Darrington Ranger District
*See map on page 89.*

The best way to enjoy this scenic wonderland is by planning to spend the night beside the high mountain lake. By taking at least 2 days to complete the trek, the views and scenery can be enjoyed to their utmost. Making a camp at day's end also means spending several hours in this beautiful area when all the hotshot snowmobilers and speedy skiers are headed for home. Best of all, though, a 2-day trip means watching the sun set in a blaze of midwinter glory and, come morning, watching it rise anew over the orange-dappled peaks of the North Cascades.

To get there, from Granite Falls drive east on the Mountain Loop Highway 4 miles past the Verlot Public Service Center and turn right (south) into the wide area near the junction with Forest Road 4020 (Schweitzer Creek Road). Park here, and start hiking up the heavily visited Schweitzer Creek Road.

Loads of recreationists are usually on the Schweitzer Creek Road system: Skiers love it because of the scenic beauty of the area. Snowmobilers like it because of the wide roadways and loop possibilities. Snowshoers will love it because of the opportunities to share in the beauty of the area on the gentle trails before leaving the hordes behind and venturing out into the seldom-visited splendor of the narrow trail to the lakes.

*Along the shoreline of Boardman Lake*

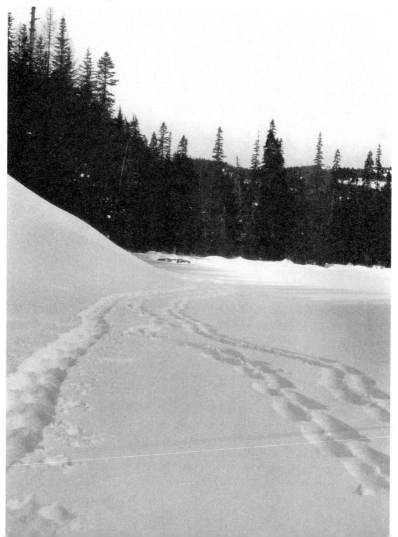

To begin the snowshoe trek, walk up the gently climbing Schweitzer Creek Road as it ascends a ridge face above its namesake creek. The road pierces the old, moss-laden forests of the valley bottom and climbs into increasingly young second-growth forest. After 2.5 miles, the scenery picks up and the views increase. The forests give way to open meadows (i.e., clearcuts) that spread like downy white quilts upon the hillside. Beyond these pillowy white meadows stretch the ragged crests of the Mountain Loop peaks: Three Fingers, Big Four, and Vesper Peak all scratch the sky on the far side of the Stillaguamish Valley to the east.

The road splits at just over 2.5 miles. Stay left on the main road as it rolls east around a small, rounded hilltop. (A right turn leads to Route 24, Bear Lake.) The route along this section pierces second-growth forests of Douglas fir, with occasional breaks of sunshine as it crosses clearcut meadows. Stay to the edges of the road along here, as snowmobilers tend to increase their speed on the long, straight stretches.

Five miles from the parking area at the base of the hill, the road sweeps right through a hairpin corner. A couple hundred yards past the apex of the turn, find the Boardman Lake trailhead on the left. This hiking trail climbs gently for just under a mile, passing Lake Evan after a mere 100 yards, before continuing on into increasingly old forest. The trail climbs steadily from Lake Evan but gains just 200 feet along the way. The trail is fairly easy to follow, even in heavy snow years, but if you lose it in the trees, simply head due south, climbing straight up the slope to reach the northern end of Boardman.

The trail crosses the lake's outlet stream immediately upon reaching the lake. This area can be a bit tricky because of the jumble of logs clogging the neck of the outlet stream. The debris allows you to keep your feet dry while crossing, but the odd angles of the many logs can make footing precarious at times. Use care when stepping over the logs, and the crossing can be accomplished without undue difficulty.

Once across, enjoy the views of the ice-covered lake and distant vistas. To the east, Mallardy Ridge lines the sky. To the north, Boardman Creek leads down into the Stillaguamish Valley, and beyond that are the high peaks of Three Fingers, Big Bear Mountain, and Liberty Mountain. To the south, Bald Mountain rises over the lake basin. Good campsites are located along the eastern shore of the lake for those planning to stay and enjoy the beautiful basin at sunset and sunrise.

To return home, head back down the narrow forest trail to its junction with the road. From there, go right to retrace your steps, or head left and make a loop of the trip. Going this way, the road descends more than a mile, crossing a clearcut and young stands of second-growth timber. About 1.25

miles from the Lake Boardman trailhead, the road banks right—a blue-diamond blaze on the trees nearby indicates a trail. Continue straight ahead along this connector trail to reach the narrow bed of FR 4021. Stay right on this new road, and follow it down 2 miles to a junction with FR 4020. Go left and walk the last 2 miles out to the junction with the Mountain Loop Highway.

## --24--
# Bear Lake

**Rating:** More difficult
**Round trip:** 10 miles
**Hiking time:** 6 hours
**Elevation gain:** 1400 feet
**High point:** 2775 feet
**Best season:** January through late February
**Map:** Green Trails: Silverton No. 110
**Who to Contact:** Mount Baker–Snoqualmie National Forest,
Darrington Ranger District
*See map on page 89.*

Oddly enough, this trail is largely ignored by skiers and snowmobilers despite its glorious wilderness-like atmosphere and stunning scenery. The trail branches off the Schweitzer Creek Road, which does draw a lot of snow traffic, and climbs gradually to a pretty little alpine lake amid young forest. The route crosses some old clearcut meadows, which provide ample opportunity for snowshoers to bask in the midwinter sun before ducking back under the green canopy of forest that shades most of the route. The bulk of the climbing is taken care of in the first few miles, leaving a leisurely hike over the last couple miles. That's as it should be because the best views, prettiest forests, and most enjoyable snow lie along the upper sections of the trail.

To get there, from Granite Falls drive east on the Mountain Loop Highway 4 miles past the Verlot Public Service Center and turn right (south) into the wide area near the junction with Forest Road 4020 (Schweitzer Creek Road). Park here, and start hiking up the heavily visited Schweitzer Creek Road.

Expect to share the route with skiers and snowmobilers for the first 2.5 miles, as it climbs the popular Schweitzer Creek Road. The road ascends a ridge line above the creek. The first 0.5 to 0.75 mile of road ambles through

*Snow layered on a downed tree, Bear Lake route*

a thick rainforest-like environment—trees heavy with moss and lichen shade the road. But as the route starts to climb the ridge, the forest changes to young second-growth and occasional small clearcuts.

At 2.5 miles, as it crosses the head of Schweitzer Creek, the road splits. This is the start of the Schweitzer Loop—one road eventually leads back to the other. Loopers are best served by going left (also the way to Route 23, Boardman Lake), but to access Bear Lake, turn right onto FR 4021 and hike across a generally flat forest and meadow area. The road curves south, providing some nice views east toward Big Four Mountain, Vesper Peak, Sperry Peak, and Little Chief.

Near the 4-mile mark, the road splits again. Most of the ski and snowmobile tracks will head off on the left fork (FR 016). FR 4021, the right fork, is the road less traveled, but it is also the road to Bear Lake. So, hooking sharply to the right, cross Black Creek and hike west up a very gentle slope. The road meanders and wanders a bit, but when the snow is heavy (covering the underbrush), straighten out the course by heading cross-country across the necks of the looping turns. Just bear west-northwest, and recross the road in a few hundred yards.

A half mile farther, at 4.5 miles, the road makes a big swing south, and then hooks abruptly northwest. Near the 5-mile mark, a small trail leads due west from the roadway. Hike along this forest path about 200 yards to find Bear Lake at 2775 feet.

# --25--
# Mallardy Ridge

|  |  |
|---|---|
| **Rating:** | More difficult |
| **Round trip:** | 10 miles |
| **Hiking time:** | 6 hours |
| **Elevation gain:** | 1900 feet |
| **High point:** | 3500 feet |
| **Best season:** | Late January through early March |
| **Map:** | Green Trails: Silverton No. 110 |
| **Who to Contact:** | Mount Baker–Snoqualmie National Forest, Darrington Ranger District |

Mallardy Ridge is one of the spectacular wild areas that is seldom enjoyed by summer hikers because there are few true trails and no protection from motorized recreationists. Come winter, the old logging roads become de facto trails as the snow drifts over and around them, turning this heavily roaded area into a wild, scenic wonderland. Follow the roads for an easy, carefree outing with the family, or go cross-country to make the journey more difficult and more adventurous. No matter how the ridge is explored, there is plenty of enjoyment for all. In addition to the simple beauty of the snowy playground immediately at hand, the views of the high, craggy peaks of the Mountain Loop region are astounding. From various points along the snowshoe trails, enjoy views of Three Fingers and White Horse Mountains to the north; Big Four, Sperry, and Vesper Peaks to the east; and Bald Mountain to the south.

To get there, from Granite Falls drive east on the Mountain Loop Highway 7.4 miles past the Verlot Public Service Center, and just before crossing the Red Bridge, turn right (south) into the wide parking area near the junction with the Mallardy Ridge Road (Forest Road 4030).

Snowshoe along the Mallardy Ridge Road as it glides through the ancient cedar forests along the valley bottom. Soon, however, the road tilts upward and begins the long, steady climb up the side of the ridge. If you are looking for a short day trip, consider taking one of the spur roads encountered along the first couple of miles, but bear in mind these side trails lead nowhere (except into pretty snow-painted forests).

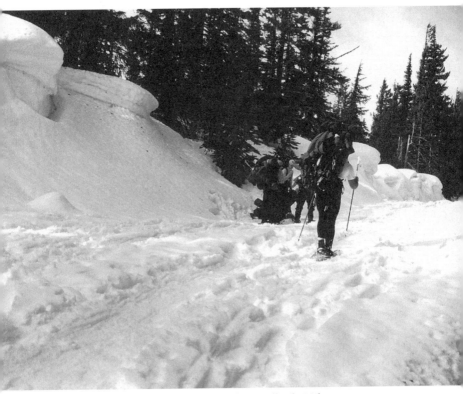

*Snowshoer heading up the long road to Mallardy Ridge*

To make the most of the trek, continue up the main road to the first major road junction at 1.5 miles. Go right onto FR 4032—the smaller and generally less well-traveled of the two options—to access Mallardy Ridge. The road rolls up and down for a mile, crossing Mallardy Creek, before the long, southbound ascent of the ridge. The crest is reached at the 5-mile mark and makes an excellent place for a leisurely lunch before turning back.

From the crest, enjoy sweeping views of Bald Mountain—seemingly just an arm's length away, just west of Boardman Creek—as well as the more mammoth hulks of Little Chief Peak to the east and Liberty Mountain to the north.

## --26--
# Marten Creek

|  |  |
|---|---|
| **Rating:** | Backcountry |
| **Round trip:** | 7.5 miles |
| **Hiking time:** | 5 hours |
| **Elevation gain:** | 1300 feet |
| **High point:** | 2800 feet |
| **Best season:** | Late December through early February |
| **Map:** | Green Trails: Silverton No. 110 |
| **Who to Contact:** | Mount Baker–Snoqualmie National Forest, Darrington Ranger District |

Marten Creek Trail is an oft-overlooked route in summer months that is virtually forgotten come winter. That is a blessing to those who know of, and take advantage of, the beauty of this secluded little forest valley. The crowds skip over this trail because there are no high, windswept ridges to explore and no deep alpine lake basins in which to camp. But there is a narrow, winding trail that is loads of fun to follow on snowshoes, a rich forest ecosystem to explore, and a host of wildlife to view and appreciate. (In low-snow years, it may be necessary to carry the snowshoes on the lower section of trail, but the upper valley is generally deep in snow by mid-December.)

To get there, from Granite Falls drive east on the Mountain Loop Highway about 9 miles past the Verlot Public Service Center, and just past Marten Creek Campground (closed in winter), turn around and park in the narrow parking area on the left (north) side of the highway at the Marten Creek trailhead.

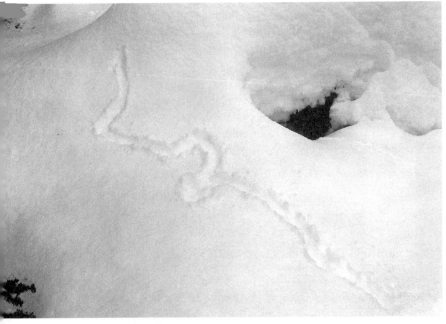

*Small mammal tracks in snow*

The trail climbs steadily from the highway, staying well above the creek itself for the first mile. The views are limited to the local forest scenery, but that is rich enough to hold anyone's attention. Of course, there's not a lot of time for gawking, as this narrow, under-maintained trail is rough and, with a blanket of snow on it, avoiding snowshoe-tearing branches and toe-grabbing logs requires undivided attention at times.

At other times, however, the trail is open and easily followed. These stretches—especially past the 1-mile mark—are where the views can be best appreciated. After the initial 1.5 miles, the trail stops climbing and rolls into a long traverse of the ridge wall above the creek, dipping at times to water level before angling back up into the open forest above. Around 2.5 miles, the trail angles left toward the head of the valley. It continues another 0.8 mile before the formal trail peters out.

It's possible, when the snow is stable, to continue up the valley for another 0.5 mile to get right under the shadow of the near-vertical headwall. Just don't get too close, as avalanches aren't the only danger here. Rockfalls are much more common than snowslides, and just as deadly. If the weather is warming, or the avalanche danger is moderate or great, don't push past the end of the formal trail.

Because the creek valley is relatively wide-bottomed with plenty of lush undergrowth for forage, it's common for deer to be found in this area. And where there are deer, there are cougars. Count yourself lucky if you see one of these big, elusive cats. Usually the only proof that mountain lions exist in these woods comes in the form of deep, clawless tracks pressed into the snow.

Big animals aren't the only inhabitants here. Grouse roost in the trees near the creek, snowshoe hares scamper through the underbrush along the trail, and at least one great horned owl glides silently between the trees looking for a midwinter meal of rabbit, vole, or marten. Yes, the creek is aptly named—martens have also been seen along this pretty trail.

## --27--

# Kelcema Lake

| | |
|---:|:---|
| **Rating:** | More difficult |
| **Round trip:** | 10 miles |
| **Hiking time:** | 6 hours |
| **Elevation gain:** | 1600 feet |
| **High point:** | 3182 feet |
| **Best season:** | January through February |
| **Map:** | Green Trails: Silverton No. 110 |
| **Who to Contact:** | Mount Baker–Snoqualmie National Forest, Darrington Ranger District |
| | *See map on page 96.* |

Explore a pretty forest valley and deep lake basin in snowmobile-free splendor since this route is maintained for nonmotorized winter recreation only. The trail is frequented by cross-country skiers, but if snowshoers just think

*The lower section of the trail to Kelcema Lake*

of skiers as fellow snowshoers who prefer long, skinny snowshoes, there is no problem sharing the trail. After all, there is plenty of wonderful country and splendid scenery here for everyone to enjoy. The route follows a small road that parallels Deer Creek on its way up the valley to the Kelcema Lake trailhead. The route climbs steadily, but at a gentle enough rate that snowshoers of all abilities will enjoy this outing. In addition to a gentle climb, the route offers beautiful old forests to explore, open clearcut meadows to play in, and high craggy ridges and peaks to admire.

To get there, from Granite Falls drive east on the Mountain Loop Highway about 12 miles past the Verlot Public Service Center to the end of the plowed road. Park in the cleared pullout area on the north side of the highway.

Find the start of Deer Creek Road (FR 4052) near the eastern edge of the parking area and start snowshoeing up the road. The lower section is frequently crowded with families sliding on inner tubes and sleds. Be careful not to trudge across their line of descent as they are more often than not plummeting downhill, out of control. Also, as a matter of courtesy, while trekking up the road try to avoid stomping down the twin grooves carved by cross-country skis.

As the road climbs through the first, thick grove of second-growth forest, the views are limited to the roadway itself. After just a mile, the road slowly banks west, following the course of the creek, and you can catch a few glimpses north of the crown of Bald Mountain. Gradually, the views increase in quantity and quality. The narrow road continues to roll upstream, as the thick second-growth forest gives way first to small clearcuts and then to older, more mature forests. Near the 2.5-mile mark, stop for a breather and you will find the increasingly pretty views before you are nothing compared to the scenery at your back. Turn around and look down the valley to see a skyline punctuated by Big Four Mountain, and Sperry, Vesper, and Little Chief Peaks.

At 3.5 miles, the trail crosses Deer Creek—stay to the center of the bridge to avoid sloughing snow—and climbs out of the valley bottom. The road gains elevation steeply for the next mile as it sweeps west before switching back to climb toward the headwaters of the creek. At 4.5 miles, the road re-crosses the creek and runs into the Kelcema Lake trailhead.

The road continues west for another 0.25 mile, and most cross-country skiers will follow it out. With wide snowshoes you have a decided advantage over skinny skis on forest trails, so turn left just after crossing the creek and climb the Kelcema Lake Trail. This narrow path weaves through old second-growth forest—with a few ancient giants left to inspire the younger trees—for 0.5 mile. The trail climbs gently along this stretch, and because the trail corridor is fairly wide, the route is easy to follow. The lake is met near the outlet stream, and some nice campsites are scattered along its shores as well as plenty of places to sit and enjoy a quiet lunch while soaking in the beauty of the region. Bald Mountain, to the south, towers over the lake basin, and Devils Peak is visible across the valley to the east.

## --28--
# Coal Creek

| | |
|---:|:---|
| **Rating:** | More difficult |
| **Round trip:** | 6 miles |
| **Hiking time:** | 4 hours |
| **Elevation gain:** | 900 feet |
| **High point:** | 2400 feet |
| **Best season:** | January through March |
| **Map:** | Green Trails: Silverton No. 110 |
| **Who to Contact:** | Mount Baker–Snoqualmie National Forest, Darrington Ranger District |

The snow-covered sections of the Mountain Loop Highway are open to any-one and everyone with the means to enjoy the snow—be it via cross-country skis, snowshoes, inner tubes, dogsleds, or snowmobiles—but the side valleys leading away from the main road are often ignored by all of these recreationists. That's a mistake that snowshoers can quietly take advantage of. The Coal Creek valley is the first large valley leading north away from the Mountain Loop Highway, and it offers outstanding opportunities to trek through untouched meadows, open stands of forest, and along clear, sparkling creeks. There is no true trail much of the way, but the wide valley allows snowshoers to pick out their own paths while enjoying the quiet basin and its surrounding natural beauty.

To get there, from Granite Falls drive east on the Mountain Loop Highway about 12 miles past the Verlot Public Service Center to the end of the plowed road. Park in the cleared pullout area on the north side of the highway.

From the parking area, follow the Mountain Loop Highway up the Stillaguamish River valley for nearly a mile. Look for the Coal Creek Campground on the right. Just past the campground, cross Coal Creek, and then bear left onto a tiny spur that leads north. This road ends in just a few hundred yards, but a faint skier and snowshoer trail—marked with blue-diamond blazes—climbs up the Coal Creek valley.

The trail pierces a stand of old second-growth forest. The blazes, sporadically placed, are sometimes difficult to see. If the next blaze is out of sight, just continue a gentle climb, going straight up the face of the thinly forested hill while staying well above the creek itself. In less than a mile, the trail encounters FR 4062. Turn left and follow it as it traverses and gently climbs

*Jay in the trees alongside the trail to Coal Lake*

the valley wall on the east side of Coal Creek. The road ends in another mile, offering picturesque views down the valley to the Stillaguamish River valley and beyond to Hall and Marble Peaks.

## --*29*--
# Big Four Ice Caves Viewpoint

|  |  |
|---:|:---|
| **Rating:** | Easiest |
| **Round trip:** | 7 miles |
| **Hiking time:** | 3.5 hours |
| **Elevation gain:** | 250 feet |
| **High point:** | 1800 feet |
| **Best season:** | January through March |
| **Map:** | Green Trails: Silverton No. 110 |
| **Who to Contact:** | Mount Baker–Snoqualmie National Forest, Darrington Ranger District |

Want a walk through a gorgeous winter wonderland without a sweaty climb up a steep trail? This route offers all the beauty and majesty found in the wintry mountains without the strenuous workout usually required to see such splendor. It is perfect for taking the family on a gentle snowshoe stroll or for introducing newbies to the joys of snowshoeing.

The trail is wide—actually, most of the "trail" is on a section of the unplowed Mountain Loop Highway—and flat, so first-timers can get the feel for walking on snowshoes without having to worry about climbing, crossing, or descending steep slopes. But despite its mild nature, this trail accesses some truly wild country. Trekking up to the base of Big Four Mountain, snowshoers can gawk in awe at the towering peak before them. The granite monolith of Big Four, with its long icicle fingers and snowy cap, captivates most visitors, but it's not the only natural wonder found here. Huge ancient trees, a clear, ice-rimmed river, and hordes of animals—big and small—are here to enjoy as well.

To get there, from Granite Falls drive east on the Mountain Loop Highway about 12 miles past the Verlot Public Service Center to the end of the plowed road. Park in the cleared pullout area on the north side of the highway.

Leave the parking area and trek up the snowbound Mountain Loop Highway as it follows the Stillaguamish River upstream. The road is lined with towering cedar and fir trees—many of which sport long, flowing beards of green. At 0.5 mile, cross the sparkling waters of Coal Creek as it rushes in from the north to empty into the Stillaguamish. Follow the road more than 2 miles until a small side road veers away to the right. This is the entrance to the Big Four Picnic Area and the trailhead for the Big Four Ice Caves Trail.

The ice caves themselves are typically blocked by early December—heavy snowfall and continual avalanches keep the caves capped tight throughout the winter—but the 1-mile trail from the picnic area is worth exploring. The trail leads to the base of Big Four and, along the way, offers outstanding views of the giant rock face of the mountain. Though it may be tempting to snowshoe right up to the jumbled pile of snow at the mouth of the ice caves, resist that temptation. That pile of snowballs is what remains of the devastating avalanches that flash down the side of the mountain after every snowstorm

*Icicles dangling off a tree branch are evidence of the freeze-and-thaw cycle typical of low elevation areas*

and after most sunny mornings. The bright sun on the rock face weakens the snow and ice, sending it crashing down on the trail below with absolutely no warning.

## --30--

## Silver Star View

|  |  |
|---|---|
| **Rating:** | More difficult |
| **Round trip:** | 4 to 20 miles |
| **Hiking time:** | 3 hours to 2 days |
| **Elevation gain:** | 700 feet |
| **High point:** | 3500 feet |
| **Best season:** | December through early March |
| **Maps:** | Green Trails: Washington Pass No. 50, Mazama No. 51 |
| **Who to Contact:** | Okanogan National Forest, Methow Valley Ranger District, Winthrop Office |

This route provides the unique opportunity to snowshoe up the middle of one of the most popular highways in the state. Come summer, State Route 20

(North Cascades Highway) is swarming with tourist traffic. But by December the road is snowbound, and it stays that way until June or July most years. That means snowshoers and cross-country skiers can play in the road without fear. Of course, there is still a danger of being run over, but the danger comes not from cars and trucks but from sliding snow. Avalanche chutes line the upper section of the highway as it approaches Washington Pass, so recreationists are well advised to stick to the lower areas and avoid the route altogether when avalanche dangers are moderate or higher.

To get there, from Winthrop drive west on SR 20 to the end of the plowed road. Park in the wide parking area.

Strap on your snowshoes, and trek up the highway, staying to the side of the road to avoid tromping on skiers' tracks and to avoid collisions with snowmobilers who occasionally zip along this route. The road parallels the Methow River upvalley, making a long, gradual curve to the left, and offers great views of the many high peaks that mark the North Cascades crest.

Snowshoeing up the first 2 miles, the view is straight ahead toward the Needles—a collage of rocky spires towering up to 8140 feet. As the road curves to the southwest, the magnificent crown of Silver Star Mountain comes into view on the left, directly above the road. As beautiful as this mountain is, it is also highly dangerous. Many of the avalanches that keep the road unplowable (and therefore open only to snow recreationists) are spawned on Silver Star.

*One of the views from the Silver Star route*

Just past the Silver Star Creek crossing at around 6 miles, all the Washington Pass peaks are visible on clear days. With Silver Star Mountain on the left and the Needles on the right, look for Tower Mountain, Cutthroat Peak, Whistler Mountain, and Liberty Bell Mountain (partially obscured by Silver Star) in between.

Because of the risk of avalanches caused by changing conditions, overnight camping is discouraged. For a quiet day outing, snowshoe up the road until lunch time, and then return home. Speedsters might work their way up the valley as far as Lone Fir Campground, but that makes a long day—it is more than 10 miles beyond the end of the plowed road.

## --31--

# Upper River Run

**Rating:** Easiest
**Round trip:** 7 miles
**Hiking time:** 4 hours
**Elevation gain:** 500 feet
**High point:** 2800 feet
**Best season:** December through early March
**Map:** Green Trails: Mazama No. 51
**Who to Contact:** Okanogan National Forest, Methow Valley Ranger District, Winthrop Office

Nothing beats an easy snowshoe stroll through the world-renowned winter wonderland of the Methow Valley. Rolling meadows of snow, nestled amid

the tall, willowy aspen trees, sturdy pines, and towering firs, offer a wonderful playground for snowshoers, and the River Run Trail system is the way to experience these wonders.

Although created with cross-country skiers in mind, the flat trails alongside the Methow River are just as enjoyable for snowshoers. They can hike along and soak in the beautiful scenery around the trail, and exult in the inspiring views of high ridges and towering peaks that surround the valley. From young kids to seasoned veterans, snowshoers of all abilities will enjoy the easy trails of River Run.

Because these trails are heavily used by skiers, snowshoers will be asked—sometimes told—to stay to the extreme edges of the trails, and when possible, to stay off the groomed track completely. Also,

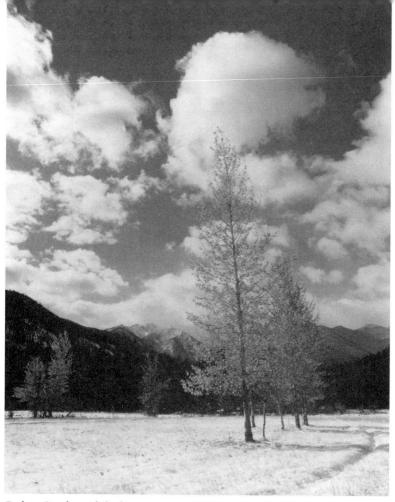

*By late October, while the aspens are still decked out in gold, there is often enough snow for snowshoeing along this route*

the trails cross private property occasionally, so visitors shouldn't wander far from the actual trail corridors.

To get there, from Winthrop drive west on State Route 20 (North Cascades Highway) to the Mazama turnoff and continue on SR 20 another mile before turning left (south) into the Early Winters/Arrowleaf property. Stay left, and follow the signs to Jacks Cabin a quarter mile down the road. (If you reach the Freestone Inn at the end of the 0.5-mile road, you have gone too far.) Purchase a trail pass at Jacks Cabin.

Hike west from the parking areas, passing Freestone Inn and, in 0.25 mile, several small cabins—the original Early Winters Cabins—alongside Early Winters Creek. Angle toward the highway, and cross the creek via the SR 20 bridge. Then cross the highway, and pick up the trail system on the north side of the road.

The trail turns right and leads away from the highway. A few hundred yards later, it veers left and follows the Methow River upstream. In the next 0.5 mile, several trail junctions are passed—one leads right, crosses the river, and ends at the North Cascades Basecamp property. Others merely cross meadows and create an intricate network of loops. The trails extend about 3.5 miles upstream from the highway crossing, for a trip of more than 7 miles. But shorter trips can be had by making use of the many connectors and cut-off trails.

A full loop is best done by sticking to the River Run Trail as it follows the river upstream. At the upper end of the route, stay left and cross the wide valley bottom to access Jacks Trail at the base of the western valley wall. Return to Jacks Cabin via this trail.

## --32--
# Cedar Falls

|  |  |
|---:|:---|
| **Rating:** | More difficult |
| **Round trip:** | 5.6 miles |
| **Hiking time:** | 5 hours |
| **Elevation gain:** | 800 feet |
| **High point:** | 3600 feet |
| **Best season:** | December through early March |
| **Map:** | Green Trails: Mazama No. 51 |
| **Who to Contact:** | Okanogan National Forest, Methow Valley Ranger District, Winthrop Office |

This trail represents one of the best chances for snowshoers to escape the ever-present hordes of skiers who clog the tracks and trails of the Methow Valley. While the occasional skier may struggle up the narrow trail, the route is mostly ignored simply because so many other trails are better suited to their long skis. Snowshoes, though, make easy work of this trail, climbing gently as it does through deep, dry-side forests to end at the site of a pretty little waterfall. This cascade is rather unspectacular in summer months, but cloaked in snow and ice, the falls becomes a wonderful work of water art.

Massive ponderosa pine, aspens, larch, cedar, and fir all fill this valley and provide habitat to an array of birds and animals. Chittering, begging

*The lower section of Cedar Creek*

camp-robber jays flit through the limbs, woodpeckers hammer on the trunks, and grouse and ptarmigan scurry around the roots of the big trees. Great horned owls are frequently seen hunting in this valley, which has plenty of prey animals for them to consume. Aside from the grouse and ptarmigan, the owls feast on the resident martens, weasels, mice, chipmunks, squirrels, and other small mammals.

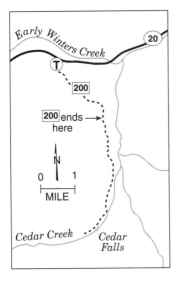

To get there, from Winthrop drive west on State Route 20 (North Cascades Highway) to the Early Winters Campground. Continue west 2.3 miles to find Forest Road 200 on the left. Park in the wide space (room for only one or two cars most of the time) at the base of this road, staying well clear of the traffic lanes of SR 20.

The hike begins with a gentle snowshoe walk up FR 200 to its end, about 1 mile up the valley. At that point, the true trail begins. It is a narrow hikers' path following the valley wall high above Cedar Creek. The trail is easy to follow even in heavy snow, although it is slow going at times as the route weaves up and down, in and out of tree wells. At 1.8 miles out, the trail angles down toward the creek and the last mile is right alongside the waterway. Views are limited, although periodic peeks open up of Sandy Butte to the east, and Driveway Butte can be seen to the north (best viewed on the return trip when facing north) from the lower sections of the trail.

At 2.8 miles, find a nice view of Cedar Falls, a small cascade on this little creek. The icy crust and snowy mantle that surround the falls give it a fairytale appearance that is worthy of a photo or two before returning home.

--𝄞𝄞--

# Paul Mountain

|  |  |
|---|---|
| **Rating:** | Easiest to more difficult |
| **Round trip:** | 7 miles |
| **Hiking time:** | 5 hours |
| **Elevation gain:** | 1500 feet |
| **High point:** | 3360 feet |
| **Best season:** | January through early March |
| **Map:** | Green Trails: Doe Mountain No. 52 |
| **Who to Contact:** | Okanogan National Forest, Methow Valley Ranger District, Winthrop Office |

This is a trek that can be tailored to any snowshoer: from an easy, flat walk perfect for families and first-time 'shoers, to a strenuous climb along a well-graded road for more adventurous sorts, or to a full-on snowshoe scramble to the top of a gnarly peak for snowshoe mountaineers. Generally, the best bet is to stick with the initial riverside walk, and maybe add a short snowshoe up the flank of the mountain to attain a better view of the glorious valley below. Leave the mountaineering to those fanatics who use snowshoes merely as tools to get to the top rather than as a specific form of recreation separate and complete in itself.

The gentle road walk provides excellent opportunities to see and experience the snowy ponderosa pine forests that line the beautiful Eightmile Creek. Along the way, and from the trail climbing the flank of Paul Mountain, there are stunning views of Buck Mountain (not the same Buck Mountain as Route 34) and Paul Mountain itself.

To get there, from Winthrop leave the north end of town on East Chewuch River Road. Nearly 7 miles out of town, turn left across the river and then go right onto the West Chewuch River Road (Forest Road 51) as it continues north. About 2.6 miles after crossing the river, turn left into the Sno-Park at the base of Eightmile Road.

Many snowshoeing options are available upon leaving this Sno-Park, but for this trail, head straight up the wide track of Eightmile Road (FR 5130). This route follows the pretty, tumbling waters of Eightmile Creek and provides countless opportunities to walk along its edge and listen to the gentle music of its water splashing over ice-crusted rocks. Generally in midwinter, several arching snow bridges span the small creek. As tempting as it may be to point your snowshoes across one of these, resist that urge, as the delicate bridges seldom are strong enough to bear the weight of a small animal, let alone a plodding snowshoer.

As the road approaches Flat Campground at 2 miles, it crosses the one

*Snow-covered trees along the trail to Paul Mountain*

truly safe bridge—one made of iron and wood—over the creek. Now on the north side of the creek, wander through the campground, enjoying the views of Paul Mountain (4210 feet) and the long crest of Eightmile Ridge that leads north away from the peak's summit.

To find a better view of Eightmile Valley, follow the road a few hundred yards farther up the valley to a small road leading off to the right. This route climbs steeply up the flank of Paul Mountain, and as it passes through increasingly thin forests, it offers many views along the length of Eightmile Valley and across it to Buck Mountain (4490 feet). The road continues for nearly 2 miles before it divides into a maze of spur roads, but from the first of these multiple road junctions at 3360 feet, the views are remarkable. With Paul Mountain towering overhead, the pretty ribbon of Eightmile Creek lies in the bottom of the deep valley spread out at your feet.

## --34--
# Buck Mountain

**Rating:** More difficult
**Round trip:** 8.5 miles
**Hiking time:** 6.5 hours
**Elevation gain:** 2500 feet
**High point:** 6100 feet
**Best season:** December through early March
**Map:** Green Trails: Loup Loup No. 85
**Who to Contact:** Okanogan National Forest, Methow Valley Ranger District, Twisp Office

The Okanogan National Forest seems to have more fire watchtowers still standing than any other national forest in the state. The Buck Mountain Lookout is one of them, and like many of the other towers in the Methow Valley region, Buck Mountain's lookout makes an excellent destination for winter recreationists. Not only are outstanding views to be had from the lookout-clad summit, but the local scenery on the way up the side of the peak is stunning in its own right.

Wildlife is also present along this quiet trail, and even when the animals are out of sight, their tracks give away their recent passing. Look for snowshoe hares, ptarmigans, and an array of birds flitting to and fro through the forest. This area is also home to bobcats, cougars, and coyotes and is well within the range of the tiny population of wolves living a precarious life in the North Cascades. (Although the odds of seeing one of these majestic pack animals are extremely low, just knowing they may hunt these hills is enough to give the region a special wild feel.)

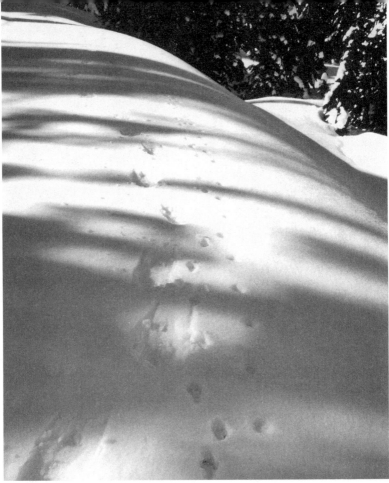

*Coyote tracks parallel those of snowshoers, Buck Mountain route*

If there is any question about the abundance of wildlife throughout this region, just consider the names of the hills and mountains that occupy the glorious views from Buck Mountain. (Yes, herds of deer—both mule deer and whitetails—browse the flanks of this peak, with many males, or bucks, in their ranks.) Bobcat Mountain sits beside Beaver Mountain to the northwest. Bear Mountain anchors the end of Coyote Ridge to the southwest, and the Salmon Creek valley is a dark cut in the hills to the northeast.

To get there, from Twisp drive east on State Route 20 to the summit of Loup Loup Pass and continue another 2.5 miles east to a junction with Buck Mountain Road (Forest Road 1100) on the left (north). Park in the plowed pullout at the base of Buck Mountain Road.

As you hike up Buck Mountain Road, you are likely to find plenty of cross-country ski tracks along the way. Try to avoid stepping on the primary ski tracks—those that look to have been used the most—whenever possible, and there is no reason snowshoers and skiers can't enjoy this route together.

The road climbs steadily, but not too steeply, for nearly 2 miles, passing several poorly marked side roads along the way. Stay on the main trail, which rolls due north until hitting a tight switchback at 2 miles followed by a long, looping curve back to the north. Once through this curve, which circles around the flank of a pretty, unnamed peak (4573 feet), the trail bears northwest.

At 3 miles, the top of a long ridge is reached. From here, the road weaves and wanders around the contours of the land as it bears northeast toward the top of Buck Mountain. You can forgo much of that roundabout navigation by heading more directly toward the tightly shuttered lookout cabin at the summit that is visible along the open ridge. Simply follow the path of least resistance, and shave as much as a mile off the road distance.

Depending on the winds, some dangerous corniced drifts may have built up along the top of the ridge. Generally, the east side of the ridge crest is the safest for snowshoeing, but the conditions will have to be evaluated during the hike.

The last few hundred feet involve a rather steep climb straight up to the lookout tower. This is worth the exertion because the narrow summit offers spectacular views in every direction. On clear days, gaze north into Canada, east into the Columbia Basin, west to the jagged crest of the North Cascades, and south over the Lake Chelan–Sawtooth Wilderness Area.

## -- 35 --
# Lookout Mountain

|  |  |
|---|---|
| **Rating:** | More difficult |
| **Round trip:** | 8.5 miles |
| **Hiking time:** | 5 hours |
| **Elevation gain:** | 2100 feet |
| **High point:** | 5500 feet |
| **Best season:** | December through early March |
| **Map:** | Green Trails: Twisp No. 84 |
| **Who to Contact:** | Okanogan National Forest, Methow Valley Ranger District, Twisp Office |

This is one of the classic snow routes in an area famous for nonmotorized winter recreation. The Methow Valley has long been recognized as a mecca

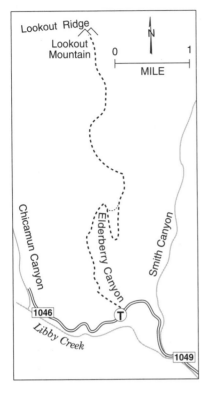

for cross-country fanatics, but snow-shoers will find the hills and valleys of this thinly forested mountain region just as much fun.

The Lookout Mountain route combines a modest warm-up hike up a narrow access road with a long cross-country climb along the open steppes of a windswept flank of Lookout Mountain. The route provides plenty of local scenery to admire and enjoy, but the real thrill is found on the upper slopes, where sweeping views encompass the majority of the Okanogan National Forest. Gaze out over the ragged crest of the Sawtooth Range to the south, admire the expansive Twisp River and Methow River valleys to the north and east, and stare in awe at the shimmering white peaks of the Cascade Crest to the west.

To get there, from Twisp drive south on State Route 153 to Carlton and continue another mile before turning right (west) onto Libby Creek Road (Forest Road 1049). Stay right at the first road junction at 2.5 miles, and at 3.6 miles turn left onto FR 1046. Drive 0.5 mile on this road, and park at the small unofficial snow-park area at the base of FR 200 on the left.

The first 1.5 miles follow FR 200 as it climbs the west side of Elderberry Canyon toward the summit of Lookout Mountain. The ascent along this section is gradual, gaining just over 1000 feet in that distance. As the road crosses the creek and starts to climb the opposite valley wall, the going gets tougher. For the easiest approach, stick to the road as it loops south 0.5 mile before switching back and climbing north to reach the ridge top.

Because the trees are thin from here on out, if you are feeling adventurous, leave the road to the skiers and put your snowshoe cleats to the test by angling up the valley wall at a steeper angle, crossing the road somewhere after it has started back from the long loop south. This will shave about a mile off the hiking distance, but it will put a burn in your thighs. Take a breather after you rejoin the road and enjoy the increasingly spectacular views. To the

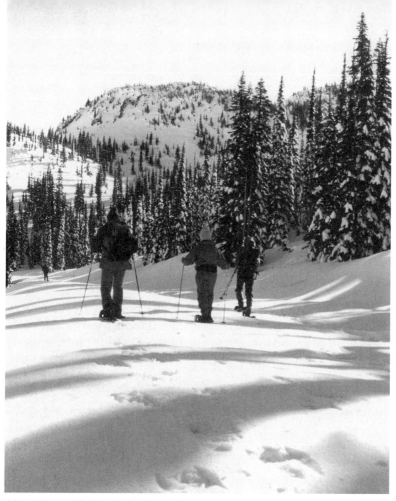

*Along the road below Lookout Mountain*

south, the Sawtooths are rising into view and to the north, straight up the ridge line, the small elevated wooden cabin at the summit of Lookout Mountain beckons.

Take a visual bearing off the lookout cabin, and lay in a course to intercept it. The upper ridge is open meadow and generally easy going. Nearly 1.5 miles separate the upper end of the road and the lookout structure, but the slope is only moderately steep and the snow is generally well packed by the breezes that continually caress this peak.

The lookout tower is boarded up for winter—no need to watch for fires when the forests are wrapped in a protective cocoon of snow—but you can enjoy a well-deserved snack on the leeward side of the building while soaking in the world-famous winter scenery of the sprawling Methow Valley.

## --36--

# Eagle Creek

**Rating:** Backcountry
**Round trip:** 5 to 16.6 miles
**Hiking time:** 4 hours to 2 days
**Elevation gain:** Up to 4900 feet
**High point:** 7300 feet
**Best season:** January through early March
**Map:** Green Trails: Buttermilk Butte No. 83
**Who to Contact:** Okanogan National Forest, Methow Valley Ranger District, Twisp Office

Although this route is recommended as a day hike, snowshoers with advanced skills and winter savvy may use this trail as the launching pad for adventures of several days in the wild, wonderful Lake Chelan–Sawtooth Wilderness Area. Eagle Creek Trail rolls around the flanks of Duckbill Mountain and beyond

*Snow pillows on the rocks of Eagle Creek*

to Eagle Pass in the shadow of Battle Mountain on the crest of the Sawtooth Range.

But most snowshoers won't get that far. Instead, snowshoe up the steadily climbing Eagle Creek valley for 3 or 4 miles for pretty views of Duckbill Mountain and out across the Twisp River valley to Canyon Creek Ridge. The trail pierces sundappled old-growth pine forests and climbs alongside a sparkling mountain stream. This route is virtually ignored when blanketed in snow, so snowshoers are almost assured of solitude in this winter paradise.

To get there, from Twisp drive 14 miles west on the Twisp River Road (Forest Road 44) to War Creek Campground. Continue 0.25 mile past the campground, and turn left onto a small road leading across a bridge spanning the Twisp River. After crossing the river, turn left onto FR 4420 and drive 1 mile to the base of a small spur road, FR 080, on the right. Park here. At times, the end of the plowed road will be at the bridge above War Creek. If that is the case, park in the wide plowed-out parking area at the end of the road and walk the mile to FR 080.

As you snowshoe up FR 080, pause at times to turn and look back at the wide Twisp River valley and the towering wall of Canyon Creek Ridge above it. The road angles west, and then switches back to the east to end at the Eagle Creek trailhead after just 1 mile. The trail then climbs alongside Eagle Creek, almost immediately weaving through a minicourse of switchbacks before entering a long, climbing run up the valley. The trail is generally easy to spot, even in heavy snow, as it boasts a wide corridor through the thin old forest. Watch for wildlife along the creek—birds and small mammals frequently scurry around the trail.

At 2.5 miles (3800 feet), the trail forks. This is an excellent place to pause for lunch, enjoy a leisurely exploration of the local flora, and then turn back.

If you want to put a few more miles under your snowshoes, you must make a decision. The left fork climbs a steep series of switchbacks to gain a high bench on the flank of Duckbill Mountain. It then traverses east to follow Oval Creek upstream into the Lake Chelan–Sawtooth Wilderness. The right fork is the preferred route. It loops through a single switchback, and then continues upstream along Eagle Creek.

After another 4 miles, near mile 6.5, the trail hooks right and climbs steeply toward the ridge at the head of the wall. At 8.3 miles, the trail crests the ridge at Eagle Pass (7300 feet). Getting to this point requires winter mountaineering skills and advanced avalanche-recognition skills.

--37--

# East Fork Foss River

|  |  |
|---|---|
| **Rating:** | More difficult |
| **Round trip:** | 13.6 miles |
| **Hiking time:** | 1 to 2 days |
| **Elevation gain:** | 1200 feet |
| **High point:** | 2400 feet |
| **Best season:** | Late December through early April |
| **Maps:** | Green Trails: Skykomish No. 175, Stevens Pass No. 176 |
| **Who to Contact:** | Mount Baker–Snoqualmie National Forest, Skykomish Ranger District |

*See map on page 120.*

Here's a route that lets snowshoers push themselves to the limit of their endurance, or if they'd rather, lets them enjoy a wonderful wilderness trek without much effort. The trail weaves through beautiful old-growth forest along the bottom of a wide river valley for much of its length before turning near-vertical to climb into a high alpine lakes basin. Those looking for a gentle stretch of the legs and a quiet snowy camp can call it a day at the bottom of the steep climb, while the "no pain, no gain" crowd can muscle their way up the slick slopes and right to the edge of the lakes before pitching camp for a well-deserved rest. Either way, enjoy wonderful scenery, stunning views, and a quiet solitude seldom experienced in the popular Alpine Lakes Wilderness.

To get there, from Everett drive east on U.S. Highway 2 toward Stevens

*Looking up the Foss River Valley*

Pass. After passing the Skykomish Ranger Station on the left, continue another 0.5 mile and turn right (south) onto Foss River Road (Forest Road 68). Follow this road nearly 2 miles to the end of the plowed road and a wide parking area at 1300 feet.

Snowshoe up the road as it gently climbs alongside the Foss River. The first mile is a multiple-use winter recreation area, so expect to see, or maybe just hear, snowmobiles along this section. But once past the Tonga Ridge Road (FR 6830) junction, the route is reserved for nonmotorized recreation, so plan on peace and quiet for the remainder of the journey.

At 1.8 miles from the parking lot, leave the wide roadway by climbing off the left side of the road onto the Foss River Trail. This narrow wilderness path follows the east bank of the East Fork Foss River for 5 miles. The trail is generally easy to follow, and is fairly flat and gentle, making easy going for snowshoers of all abilities. It was, in fact, once the route of a narrow-gauge railroad that steamed up and down the valley hauling ore out of mine claims and supplies up to the hardrock miners. But this trip is not all just boring trail walking. Along this stretch of trail there are countless opportunities for you to dip down into riverside meadows to explore the snowy landscape and the water's edge—just be careful not to get too close to the river's edge.

The river valley is wide and beautiful with enough openings in the old-growth forest to allow views up toward the jagged peaks of the Alpine Lakes Wilderness. Bald Eagle Peak towers over the western valley wall while glacier-studded Mount Daniel fills the sky to the southeast. Look straight up the valley to see the 7899-foot mountain as well as its neighbor, 7492-foot Mount Hinman.

Numerous fine campsites are all along this stretch of the trail, but the best are in the broad riverside meadows about 5 miles from your car, and again at 6.8 miles, where the trail suddenly veers west away from the river and climbs steeply into the high lakes basin of Necklace Valley. This corner near the river, with good views all around, and good selection of campsites in the surrounding forest, is the end of the road for all but the most fanatic snowshoers.

If you want to push your skills and endurance to the limits, and if the avalanche danger is low, struggle up the last 2.5 miles of trail as it climbs some 2200 feet to reach the lower lakes in the Necklace chain. The payoff is great, with the wide lakes basin, deep snow bowls, and awesome views of the major Alpine Lakes peaks. However, the expense is extreme physical exertion in an area highly prone to avalanche danger.

It's much more enjoyable to skip the last leg of the trail and simply bask in the glorious beauty of the winter wilderness environment of the East Fork Foss River. Save the high alpine lakes for summer hikes.

--*38*--

# Tonga Ridge

**Rating:** Easiest
**Round trip:** 7 miles
**Hiking time:** 5 hours
**Elevation gain:** 1400 feet
**High point:** 5100 feet
**Best season:** November through December
**Maps:** Green Trails: Skykomish No. 175, Stevens Pass No. 176
**Who to Contact:** Mount Baker–Snoqualmie National Forest, Skykomish Ranger District

This could be one of the best early-season snowshoe routes in the state. Ideally, visit this area when the snow is thin enough down low so that the road is passable to cars but the trail itself has enough snow to make snowshoes worthwhile. Mid- to late November is usually the time to find these conditions. Visit then and the trail will be uncrowded, the views unbelievable, and the memories unforgettable. By late December, however, the access road is blocked by snow and clogged with snowmobiles and weekend skiers. The route will be packed by the "multi-use" crowds until late spring when the road melts out, but the trail retains its blanket of snow. Come back then for one last hurrah on snowshoes before breaking out the hiking boots.

To get there, from Everett drive east on U.S. Highway 2 toward Stevens Pass. After passing the Skykomish Ranger Station on the left, continue another 0.5 mile and turn right (south) onto Foss River Road (Forest Road 68). Follow this road 3 miles to the junction with FR 6830, and turn left (east) onto FR 6830. Climb 3.3 miles up this road to the top of the ridge and a junction with a small spur road, FR 310. Turn right onto FR 310, and continue to the snow line or the end of the road (1.5 miles) at 4400 feet.

The Tonga Ridge Trail begins at the end of FR 310. From the trailhead, the narrow trail climbs modestly for a mile, gaining just 500 feet, as it heads to the crest of Tonga Ridge proper. The initial leg of the trail skirts an old clearcut before entering thick second-growth forest. That, in turn, gives way to old growth and periodic meadows along the ridge top. The trail rolls along just under the crest of the ridge for a total of 3 miles, passing under the high crown of Mount Sawyer before cresting at 4800 feet on Sawyer Pass.

If you're feeling adventurous, climb south from the pass and take a hard-to-follow trail through the trees to the crest of an unnamed knoll (5100 feet) before dropping down to Fisher Lake, some 2 miles distant from Sawyer

Pass. A better plan is to hunker down at the pass for a leisurely lunch while committing the outstanding vistas to memory. Terrace Mountain lurks to the south, providing a pretty foreground to the high, glacier-studded summits of Mounts Daniel and Hinman beyond. To the north, Mount Sawyer lines the afternoon sky. To the east are the high peaks of the Cascade Crest: Surprise Mountain, Spark Plug Mountain, and Mac Peak among them. To the west is the deep cut of the Foss River valley.

*Heavily laden trees along the Tonga Ridge route*

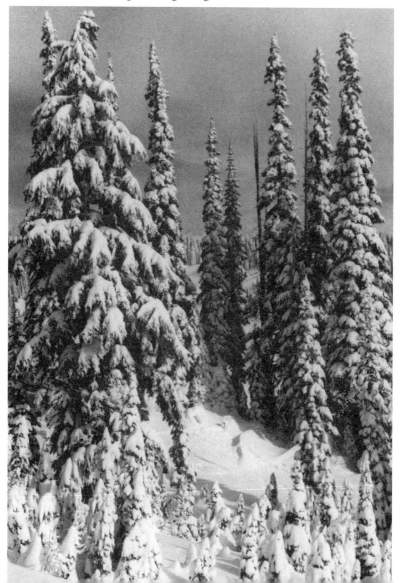

## --39--

# Surprise Lake

**Rating:** Backcountry
**Round trip:** 8 miles
**Hiking time:** 6 hours
**Elevation gain:** 2300 feet
**High point:** 4500 feet
**Best season:** December through early April
**Map:** Green Trails: Stevens Pass No. 176
**Who to Contact:** Mount Baker–Snoqualmie National Forest, Skykomish Ranger District

This trail climbs a narrow side valley above the Skykomish River, offering pretty views, sparkling waterfalls, and deep forest environments to explore and experience. The trail is popular with snowshoers, but don't expect to encounter many skiers here. The trail is far too narrow and the forest is way too close for most skiers' comfort.

*Descending a slope near Surprise Lake*

All but the first 0.5 mile of trail is within the Alpine Lakes Wilderness, so the forest is ancient, undisturbed old growth. That provides healthy habitat for an array of wildlife, and even in winter a lot of scurrying and flittering occurs along the trail. Snowshoers can look for, and frequently see, animals such as martens, hares, and deer. They can also find tracks of cougars, bobcats, coyotes, and foxes, though these animals seldom allow themselves to be seen by humans. Birds in the area include the always-present whiskey jacks, ptarmigans, owls, ravens, falcons, and woodpeckers. Delicate waterfalls and deep blue pools are found along the plunging creek, and views of the rocky summits of Spark Plug and Thunder Mountains are spectacular along the upper end of the trail.

To get there, from Everett drive east on U.S. Highway 2 to the town of Skykomish and continue east another 10 miles. Turn right (south) into the small community of Scenic just before the railroad underpass on the highway. Cross the river, and turn right again onto a small spur road signed as the Surprise Creek/Surprise Lake trailhead.

The snowshoe hike begins with a short walk up an old, narrow dirt road. Cross Surprise Creek about 0.5 mile up, pass under the powerlines, and start up the Surprise Creek valley proper. Just above the powerlines, the road gives way to a narrow hiking trail, at 2200 feet, and begins to climb steadily. For 0.5 mile, the trail stays well above the creek, but it then tapers down the valley wall and, at 1 mile, comes abreast of the creek and stays there most of the way to the lake. Several small side creeks are crossed, and near the 1.8-mile mark, the trail crosses to the west side of Surprise Creek.

Several small, unnamed waterfalls and miniature sets of rapids accent the little stream. These features are beautiful any time of year, but when the stream banks are cloaked in snow and the river rocks rimmed with ice, the tumbling waters are like sparkling jewels, glinting in the cold, winter sunshine.

At 3 miles, the trail leaves the creekside to climb east through a series of steep, tight switchbacks before banking south a bit and rolling the final 0.25 mile on fairly gentle slopes to the lakeshore. From the banks of the big lake, enjoy views of 6311-foot Spark Plug Mountain to the west, Thunder Mountain (6556 feet) to the south, and the deep Skykomish River valley due north.

--*40*--

# Lake Susan Jane

| | |
|---:|:---|
| **Rating:** | More difficult |
| **Round trip:** | 7 miles |
| **Hiking time:** | 3.5 hours |
| **Elevation gain:** | 1200 feet |
| **High point:** | 5200 feet |
| **Best season:** | December through early April |
| **Map:** | Green Trails: Stevens Pass No. 176 |
| **Who to Contact:** | Mount Baker–Snoqualmie National Forest, Skykomish Ranger District |

Few sections of the Pacific Crest Trail (PCT) can be enjoyed in midwinter, but this is one of them. The trail leads from a crowded ski area to a tiny wilderness lake amid a snow-blanketed forest. Snowshoers can amuse themselves watching the out-of-control antics of downhill skiers and snowboarders on the first mile of the hike and then put those crowds behind them and

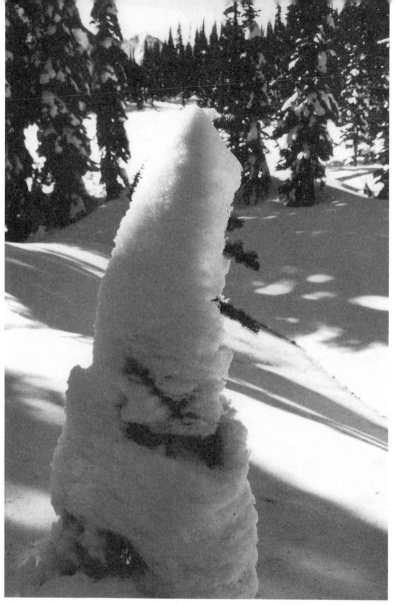

*Tree in disguise near the shores of Lake Susan Jane*

enjoy a quiet day amid wildlife of a different sort—whiskey jacks, snowshoe hares, snowy white ptarmigans (large, ground-roosting birds), martens, and even an occasional fox may be seen darting through the drifts.

To get there, from Everett drive east on U.S. Highway 2 to the summit of Stevens Pass. Park in the ski area parking lots on the south side of the highway.

Before strapping on the snowshoes, walk up the slope past the ski lodge and angle off to the left to get clear of the downhill ski runs. The PCT actually slices diagonally across the ski area, but snowshoeing on groomed ski runs is frowned upon. So stay on the outside edge of the ski runs on the left, and climb up along the border of the ski area. As the ski runs taper south to merge at the top of the Tye Chairlift, veer southwest, still skirting the downhill runs, to traverse along a wide bench at the base of a steep hillside. Continue to climb, slanting off to the right, until the top of the ridge is reached in about 1.5 miles (5200 feet).

Turning south, drop off the back side of the ridge to skirt around the headwall of Mill Creek valley, and pass under the high-tension powerlines that carry electricity from the upper Columbia River dams across Stevens Pass to the Puget Sound area.

The PCT drops steeply downslope, looping through a few switchbacks. Most winter recreationists find it easier to just angle down and across the slope. Continue almost due south, staying above the 4500-foot level on the eastern flank of the ridge that is the Cascade Crest. An old road is passed at about 2.5 miles, and Lake Susan Jane—a small pond set in a quiet forest glade—is reached at 3.5 miles.

## --*41*--

# Skyline Lake

|  |  |
|---|---|
| **Rating:** | More difficult |
| **Round trip:** | 3 miles |
| **Hiking time:** | 2 hours |
| **Elevation gain:** | 1100 feet |
| **High point:** | 5100 feet |
| **Best season:** | December through early April |
| **Maps:** | Green Trails: Benchmark Mountain No. 144, Stevens Pass No. 176 |
| **Who to Contact:** | Mount Baker–Snoqualmie National Forest, Skykomish Ranger District |

A short but strenuous climb to a high alpine lake, buried deep in snow, is what awaits snowshoers here. The length of the trail and the steepness with which it climbs are secondary considerations, however, for snowshoers will find an inordinate amount of natural beauty and winter wilderness on this

*Lookout tower and weather station near Skyline Lake*

trail. The idyllic little lake basin is situated in such a way that snowshoers who pause here for lunch may enjoy unmatched views of the whole of the Alpine Lakes Wilderness Area—from Mount Daniel to Mount Stuart—as well as the Glacier Peak Wilderness Area to the north, the Lake Chelan–Sawtooth Wilderness Area to the east, and the beautiful Skykomish Valley to the west.

To get there, from Everett drive east on U.S. Highway 2 to the summit of Stevens Pass. Park in the ski area parking lots on the north side of the highway.

From the parking area, climb north along a groomed road leading past a number of small skier cabins on the edge of the forest above the highway. The groomed snow-cat track angles north away from the highway and ends abruptly near a power shack about 0.25 mile up the slope. Dig your snowshoe cleats into the hillside, and continue straight up the hill. Stay near the trees on the west side of the open slope to minimize avalanche danger and collisions with telemark skiers whooshing down the slope. After nearly a mile of climbing, at the 5000-foot level, the slope tapers off a bit and the climbing becomes easier. Pause here to catch your breath and soak in the views.

Turn and look south. At what seems just an arm's length away, the Stevens Pass Ski Area sprawls out across the slopes on the opposite side of the highway. Above and beyond those groomed runs (long, white scars on the dark green forest) stand the summits of the Alpine Lakes peaks. Mount Stuart, like a massive granite wall, looms in the southeast. Mounts Daniel and Hinman, the glaciated peaks in the center of the wilderness, rise like twin towers to the southwest. Nearer in, Thunder Mountain rises on the Cascade Crest just south of the ski area, and Bulls Tooth sits on the southern horizon.

After a well-deserved rest, continue climbing the now moderate slope, and in just 0.5 mile, trudge through a young stand of fir to come upon the shores of Skyline Lake. At 5100 feet, this lake is generally high enough that the ice cap on it freezes solid enough to support skiers and snowshoers; indeed, the broad flat surface of the lake is almost always crisscrossed with ski and snowshoe tracks. Unless you have a desperate need to cross a frozen lake, however, it's always a good idea to skirt the lake's shore rather than risk the ice. The combination of generally mild winters and the volcanic nature of the Cascade Range makes all lake ice suspect. Even if temperatures are cold enough long enough to freeze a lake solid, the geothermal activity below the mountains creates a lot of warm and hot springs, some of which can spout out of the ground in the middle of a lake, keeping it warmer than you might expect. In effect, these unseen warm springs sometimes melt the surface ice from underneath.

A long, relaxed lunch along the shores of the lake allows ample time to marvel at views to the south as well as the now-revealed vistas to the north, which include views of Glacier Peak and Lichtenberg Mountain. To extend the outing, amble west along the crest of Skyline Ridge for up to 2 more miles before returning to your car.

## --42--
# Lake Valhalla

**Rating:** More difficult
**Round trip:** 7.5 miles
**Hiking time:** 5.5 hours
**Elevation gain:** 1700 feet
**High point:** 4800 feet
**Best season:** December through early March
**Map:** Green Trails: Benchmark Mountain No. 144
**Who to Contact:** Wenatchee National Forest, Lake Wenatchee Ranger District

According to Norse mythology, Valhalla is the beautiful home of heroes slain in battle. Fortunately for snowshoers, this Valhalla is no myth, and visiting it doesn't require mortal combat. Lake Valhalla is a wondrous basin nestled alongside the Pacific Crest Trail (PCT) just north of Stevens Pass. Tucked between Mount McCausland and Lichtenberg Mountain, the lake appears remote and isolated. The snowshoe hike to the lake belies that wildness, though, because the trail is generally easy enough for novices and family groups.

Although summer hikers can access Lake Valhalla by way of the PCT, snowshoers will find it easier, and safer, to make use of the narrow road leading up Smith Brook valley to the east, and then to traverse cross-country through the head of that valley to the lake basin. This path provides good footing, safety from avalanche danger, and stunning views along its route.

To get there, drive east on U.S. Highway 2 to the summit of Stevens Pass and continue another 6 miles east to the Mill Creek exit. Make a U-turn at Mill Creek to get into the westbound lanes of the divided highway, and drive west 1.2 miles to a narrow parking strip on the right (north) side of the highway. This is the nearest parking area to the Smith Brook trailhead, which is another 0.1 mile to the west.

With snowshoes in hand, follow the shoulder of the highway west to the start of Forest Road 6700 (Smith Brook Road). The plows will have left a high, vertical wall of snow between the road surface and the top of the untracked snow, so a climb is generally required. In heavy snow years, this embankment has been known to be as much as 18 feet high, but generally it is less than 10 feet. An ice ax can be handy here, not only for added traction in climbing but to chop out steps. If you don't want to chop your own, bear in mind that by midmorning Saturday on most winter weekends someone will have dug a rough staircase into the bank.

The trail follows the narrow Smith Brook Road through a thin stand of forest along a near-level bench for the first 0.25 mile before beginning a gentle climb up the creek valley. The lower section of the valley has been logged, so

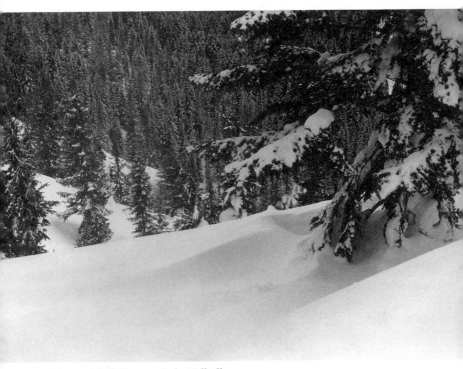

*Forested hillside near Lake Valhalla*

the second-growth forest is dotted with clearcut sections for the first 1.5 miles of the hike. Look for birds and small animals where the forests and meadows meet: generally, camp-robber jays (a.k.a. whiskey jacks) flit through the area, and snowshoe hares leave tracks by the edges of the meadows.

At nearly 2 miles, the road switches back twice to gain elevation above the creek bed. Here, in the midst of a sloping clearcut meadow, some nice views open up west toward Mount McCausland and north to Union and Jove Peaks. The route then follows the creek as it banks toward the west.

Just over 2.5 miles up, at 4000 feet, the road again loops through a switchback turn. This is the end of the road, but not the trail. Leave the road at the apex of that switchback, and traverse the open hillside above Smith Brook. Climb slightly while snowshoeing across the valley wall to get near the 4600-foot level in the next mile. There, at 3.5 miles from the trailhead, catch the snow-obscured PCT, cross the head of the Smith Brook valley, and hike another 0.25 mile southwest to the Lake Valhalla basin at 4800 feet. Enjoy a rest at the lake while soaking in the views of Lichtenberg Mountain, Nason Ridge, Union and Jove Peaks, Mount McCausland, Valhalla Mountain, and Skyline Ridge.

--43--

# Lanham Lake

| | |
|---|---|
| **Rating:** | More difficult |
| **Round trip:** | 3.2 miles |
| **Hiking time:** | 3 hours |
| **Elevation gain:** | 1100 feet |
| **High point:** | 4100 feet |
| **Best season:** | December through early March |
| **Map:** | Green Trails: Benchmark Mountain No. 144 |
| **Who to Contact:** | Wenatchee National Forest, Lake Wenatchee Ranger District |

This narrow forest trail climbs gently alongside a gurgling ice-rimmed creek and leads to a picturesque alpine lake. The trail is often attempted by cross-country skiers, but the narrow path and thick forest often send them packing before they complete the first mile, so a high degree of quiet solitude can be found at this lake despite the shortness of the access trail. The lake is ringed with snow-laden trees, but some nice views of the jagged top of Jim Hill

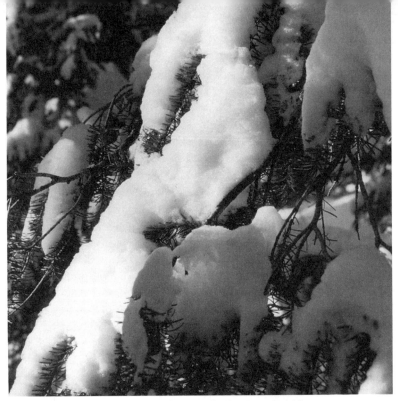

*One of the snowy scenes that make snowshoeing so enjoyable*

Mountain appear to the south. The lake is also an ideal destination for novice winter campers—not too far to snowshoe but far enough to get into a true wilderness setting. The thick old growth around the lake provides plenty of shelter for a snug winter camp.

To get there, drive east on U.S. Highway 2 to the summit of Stevens Pass and continue another 6 miles east to the Mill Creek exit. Turn right onto Mill Creek Road, and drive a few hundred feet to park in the Mill Creek Sno-Park (the lower lot). The lot nearest the buildings is provided for the commercial Nordic ski facilities run by the Stevens Pass Ski Area. To avoid conflicts, avoid snowshoeing on the groomed trails wherever possible.

The Lanham Lake Trail starts about 10 yards up Mill Creek Road—one of the ski area's groomed trails, so snowshoe along the uphill edge of this groomed track to avoid incurring the wrath of skiers on your way to the trailhead. Bear left into the trees at the well-marked start of the Lanham Lake Trail.

This narrow hikers' trail follows the west bank of Lanham Creek as it climbs the gentle valley to its headwaters in the lake. About 0.25 mile up, the trail crosses a clearing, passes under high-tension powerlines—these carry the juice that keeps Puget Sounders out of the dark—and crosses a groomed ski trail (part of the commercial operation).

Try to ignore the buzzing electrical lines and the unnaturally flat track left by the groomer. The trail leaves both behind quickly as it continues the steady climb up the creek valley. About a mile up the trail, the valley narrows considerably. The trail is now close to the creek, and footing is sometimes slick where the trail enters a brief, steep pitch for a couple hundred yards.

The last 0.5 mile is only moderately steep as the valley widens again and finally opens into a deep bowl cradling the lake. If you are the adventurous type, trek up the slope on the far (south) side of the lake to explore the flanks of Jim Hill Mountain, but if avalanche danger is moderate or higher, skip this added adventure and stick to the lake basin for any extra exploration.

--*44*--

# Wenatchee Ridge

**Rating:** Easiest to more difficult
**Round trip:** Up to 11 miles
**Hiking time:** 7 hours
**Elevation gain:** 2000 feet
**High point:** 4000 feet
**Best season:** January through late February
**Map:** Green Trails: Wenatchee Lake No. 145
**Who to Contact:** Wenatchee National Forest, Lake Wenatchee Ranger District

This trail combines the serene beauty of the Little Wenatchee River valley with the thrilling vistas found on the high benches of Wenatchee Ridge. Stick to the lower half of the route and enjoy a quiet day in a picturesque mountain valley, or trek the entire route, climbing to panoramic views of peaks and ridges of the eastern Cascades.

Kids will love the flat, snowy track along the Little Wenatchee River, and families can make a day of it by hiking along the valley bottom, reveling in the musical sounds of the river splashing over the icy rocks of its bed. Nice views up to the jagged crest of Wenatchee Ridge to the north and the high, snowy crowns of Mounts Mastiff and Howard to the south round out this part of the trail. Adventurers will love the moderate climb up the snout of Wenatchee Ridge, with strikingly beautiful views across the valley toward those two great peaks, Mastiff and Howard, that anchor the northern end of Nason Ridge.

To get there, from Leavenworth drive north on U.S. Highway 2 to Coles Corner and turn right (north) onto State Route 207. Continue north on SR 207 for 11 miles, passing Lake Wenatchee, and turn left (west) onto the Little Wenatchee River Road (Forest Road 65). Drive 1.5 miles to a Sno-Park area at the end of the plowed road.

Hike FR 65 as it heads upstream alongside Little Wenatchee River. Actually, the road is several hundred feet from the river, with some broad meadows and thin groves of alder and pine between, but a mile up the valley, the road and river come together to provide some waterside entertainment. Look for the quick movements of water ouzels—small birds dipping in and out of the frigid waters—and small flotillas of ducks in the pools of the stream.

At 2 miles, a side road (FR 6502) angles off to the right. This is the route up the ridge. Snowshoe up it as it traverses for 0.5 mile before climbing more steeply through a wide series of switchbacks. FR 6502 passes three side roads in its first mile—stay left at the first main intersection and right at the next two. At mile 3, the track begins a long curving traverse east around the snout of the ridge. There are some nice views through openings in the forest cover. To the south, over the Little Wenatchee Valley, Nason Ridge is in view—anchored on the west by Mount Mastiff and on the east by Round Mountain.

At mile 4, the route turns sharply to the left to climb around a small knob at 3300 feet. The road continues to climb gradually for the last 1.5 miles, rolling around to the north side of the ridge before ending at 4000 feet before the jagged crest of the ridge.

*Ice formation near the crest of Wenatchee Ridge*

## --45--

# Chiwaukum Creek

**Rating:** More difficult
**Round trip:** 10.4 miles
**Hiking time:** 6 hours to 2 days
**Elevation gain:** 1200 feet
**High point:** 3200 feet
**Best season:** December through early March
**Map:** Green Trails: Chiwaukum Mountains No. 177
**Who to Contact:** Wenatchee National Forest, Leavenworth Ranger District

This narrow wilderness trail follows the Chiwaukum Creek upstream to a junction with several other trails, providing opportunities for unbounded rambling in the winter wonderlands of the Alpine Lakes Wilderness. Most snowshoers, though, will find plenty of beautiful country, awesome views,

*Snow pillows on the rocks in a creek in the Chiwaukum Valley*

and outstanding snowshoeing along the first 5 miles of the trail. The trail pierces pine and fir forests, nicely blanketed in pristine white snow. Along the way, snowshoers can gawk in wonder at the towering ramparts of Big Jim and Snowgrass Mountains. They can enjoy the musical stylings of Chiwaukum Creek as it bounds over ice-crusted boulders and snow-laden logs. And, unfortunately, they can skip the whole thing if the avalanche danger is moderate or higher. The last mile of the road to the summer trailhead and the first mile of trail are at the base of a steep, slide-prone slope and should only be crossed when the risk of avalanche is low or nonexistent. But if the conditions are right, this trail is not to be missed.

To get there, from Leavenworth drive north on U.S. Highway 2 about 9 miles to Tumwater Campground. Continue north another mile and turn left onto Chiwaukum Creek Road (Forest Road 7908). Drive 2 miles to the end of the road at 2200 feet, or to the snow line if it is lower than that. The summer trailhead is at the road end.

Chiwaukum Creek cuts through a narrow valley along its lower reaches. It is nearly flat, gaining just 1200 feet in more than 5 miles, and it pierces some of the most beautiful old forests of pine and fir in the region. The ponderosa pine is particularly pretty in this setting, with its bright-orange bark scales offsetting the brilliant white of the snow and the sparkling blue of the creek.

The trail rolls upstream, curving gently to the west and opening up views of McCue Ridge towering above the upper Chiwaukum Creek valley and Big Jim Mountain to the south. Numerous wide areas in the sheltering forests offer excellent sites in which to pitch a camp, and the possibilities of making an extended snowshoeing adventure out of this trip are endless.

At 5.2 miles the trail splits. This is where most of you will turn back, but if you are a hearty winter fanatic, consider pushing on into the deeper regions of the Alpine Lakes Wilderness. Do this only if you are adequately prepared for extended winter exposure.

At the trail fork, the path on the right climbs steeply to the Chiwaukum Lake and Larch Lake basins. This trail crosses several avalanche slopes and is best left for summer explorations. The left trail, though, follows the South Fork Chiwaukum River for 3 miles, passing several other trails along the way. Good campsites are found at Timothy Meadows, about 2 miles upstream from the original trail split.

## --*46*--

# Eightmile Creek

**Rating:** Backcountry
**Round trip:** 12.4 miles
**Hiking time:** 1 to 2 days
**Elevation gain:** 2600 feet
**High point:** 4600 feet
**Best season:** December through early March
**Map:** Green Trails: Chiwaukum Mountains No. 177
**Who to Contact:** Wenatchee National Forest, Leavenworth Ranger District

One of the most heavily visited trails in summer, the Eightmile Trail is virtually ignored by winter recreationists. Cross-country skiers find the narrow trail and occasional steep pitches difficult to navigate while wearing their long boards, but today's snowshoes are tailor-made for tromping in and around tightly spaced trees and up steep slopes.

In addition to peaceful solitude, this trail offers unmatched wilderness beauty. High alpine lakes appear in table-flat meadows covered by blankets of billowing white fluff. Crystalline creeks rush through icy channels alongside the trail. Above it all towers the monarch of the central Cascades—Mount Stuart. Joining that great bulk on the horizon are Cannon, Eightmile, and Cashmere Mountains. This trail can be more tiring than one might think, but don't fret if forced to turn back before reaching the upper end of the trail. There is plenty to see and enjoy on the lower half of this route to make even an abbreviated snowshoe trek here worthwhile.

Bear in mind that this trail is at the bottom of a narrow valley in steep mountain country, so avalanche hazards are extreme. Knowledge of how to recognize and avoid avalanche dangers is essential for visitors on this trail.

To get there, from Leavenworth drive north on U.S. Highway 2 and, at the northern edge of town, turn left (west) onto Icicle Creek Road. Continue west 8.5 miles to Bridge Creek Campground. Turn left onto Forest Road 7601, and park near the bridge over Icicle Creek. In heavy snow years, it may be necessary to park farther down the valley and snowshoe a few miles up Icicle Creek Road to Bridge Creek Campground (2000 feet). In light snow years, it is sometimes possible to drive another mile or so up FR 7601 before being stopped at the snow line. Mileage figures for the hike are measured from Bridge Creek Campground.

The snowshoeing begins on the wide, moderately pitched FR 7601. This road contours along the hillside above Mountaineer Creek, gaining just 1300 feet in the 3 miles to the junction with Eightmile Creek. The lower valley is wide and scenic, providing plenty of pretty views south to Cannon Mountain and east to Icicle Ridge. At 3 miles, the road crosses Eightmile Creek. Instead of crossing the creek with the road, turn right and start up the narrow Eightmile Creek Trail, which weaves through the tight forest of pine and fir on the lower flanks of Cashmere Mountain.

The trail climbs gently for nearly a mile until, at 4 miles out, the route steepens as the valley narrows. At times, the trail is obscured completely, and routefinding skills are tested. But getting lost isn't much of a threat because the trail parallels the creek, so routefinding is merely an exercise in finding the most efficient path up the steep slopes. Fortunately, the steepest pitch is only a few hundred feet long. Then the trail returns to its moderate pitch. In fact, there is a mere 1100-foot gain from the point where the trail leaves the road to Little Eightmile Lake, encountered at 5.7 miles. Some potential campsites are found around this little pond, but much better sites can be found 0.5

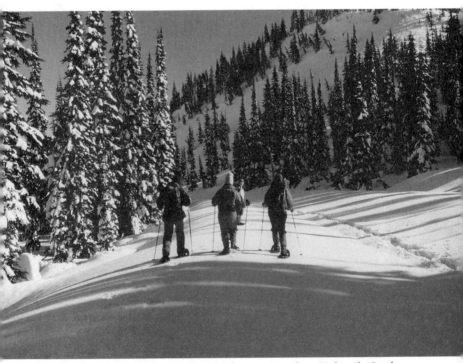

*On the road leading toward the backcountry trail up Eightmile Creek*

mile farther up the valley—and another 200 feet higher in elevation—at Eightmile Lake.

This sprawling plain of ice and snow is in the shadow of Eightmile Mountain, which looms to the north, and you will find that a camp here is blessed with magnificent sunrises. Watching the morning sky brighten and seeing the icy face of Eightmile Mountain glow with dawn's orange light is an experience of a lifetime.

## --47--

# Talapus Lake

**Rating:** Most difficult
**Round trip:** 8.5 miles
**Hiking time:** 7 hours
**Elevation gain:** 1600 feet
**High point:** 3280 feet
**Best season:** January through early March
**Map:** Green Trails: Bandera No. 206
**Who to Contact:** Mount Baker–Snoqualmie National Forest, Snoqualmie Ranger District, North Bend Office

Overcrowded in summer months, this trail is too often overlooked in the winter. Sure, the route requires a modest hike up a snowy road before getting to the trailhead, but that's the perfect way for snowshoers to warm up and swing into stride. The trail ascends through open fir and hemlock forests, dips low and rolls alongside a pretty mountain stream a time or two, and finally deposits dedicated snowshoers on the shores of a wide, pretty alpine lake nestled below a steep, avalanche-ravaged ridge. The views from the lake basin include looks up to Bandera Mountain and Pratt Mountain, and east to Granite Mountain.

The trail is easy to find, although it can be a bit difficult to follow if the snow is crusty and slick. Be sure to have good cleats on both heel and toe to ensure a solid "bite" on the crusty snow that is often the curse of this trail.

To get there, from North Bend drive east on Interstate 90 for 15 miles to exit 45. After exiting the interstate, turn left, cross under the freeway, and follow Forest Road 9031 west 1 mile to its junction with FR 9030 on the right. Park here, or if the road isn't plowed, park at the end of the plowed area, well clear of the freeway exits, and snowshoe the mile to FR 9030.

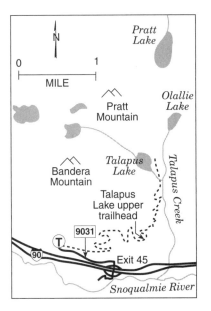

Start up FR 9030, signed as the access to Talapus Lake trailhead, as it rolls up through a series of small switchbacks. The road offers good views upslope toward the summit of Bandera Mountain thanks to several open clearcut areas that flank the road. The 2.5 miles of the road hike goes fast. At the end of the road, in the wide parking area of the Talapus Lake trailhead, enjoy stunning views of Granite Mountain before starting up the narrow trail.

Usually you will have the trail to yourself from this point on. Skiers often kick their way up the road as far as the trailhead, but few of those folks care to struggle with their long skis on the winding, forest trail. With snowshoes, you will have no problems with the twisting, turning trail as it rolls around trees and rocks. At 3.5 miles,

*Taking a break along the trail to Talapus Lake*

after a mile of snowshoeing on the narrow trail, the path dips into a valley to follow close alongside Talapus Creek the last 0.75 mile to the lake.

The lake basin is the most likely place to find snowslides, so be aware of avalanche potential as you approach the lake. If the avalanche hazard was reported as moderate or higher for this part of the Cascades, it's best to skip the trail component of this outing. The roadway makes a nice, gentle outing on snowshoes without the danger of being swept away.

## --48--
# Granite Mountain

|  |  |
|---|---|
| **Rating:** | Backcountry |
| **Round trip:** | 5 miles |
| **Hiking time:** | 8 hours |
| **Elevation gain:** | 3750 feet |
| **High point:** | 5629 feet |
| **Best season:** | December through early March |
| **Map:** | Green Trails: Snoqualmie Pass, No. 207 |
| **Who to Contact:** | Mount Baker–Snoqualmie National Forest, Snoqualmie Ranger District, North Bend Office |
| **Note:** | Avalanches routinely sweep down the flanks of Granite Mountain. Before attempting this route, make sure you thoroughly assess the snow conditions and the avalanche risk. Only travel this route when avalanche risks are low. |

Regardless of the air temperature, be prepared to sweat. Summer hikers know the Granite Mountain Trail as a real thigh burner. But as strenuous as the well-trod summer path maybe, it's nothing compared to the snow route up the big mountain. Snowshoers don't have the benefit of the long, looping switchbacks and hillside traverses. Instead, they must climb steeply and fairly directly to the top, gaining more than 3700 feet in about 2.5 miles—or nearly 1500 feet per mile! Take your time, and watch the snow conditions as you climb.

To get there, from North Bend drive east on Interstate 90 for 17 miles to exit 47—signed Denny Creek. After exiting the interstate, turn left, cross under the freeway, and turn left again on the north side of the highway. Drive as far west as possible, or if the road is not plowed, park well clear of the highway interchange.

*Raven on Granite Mountain*

The route begins at the summer trailhead for the Granite Mountain Trail, but you won't stick to the trail for long. The winter route climbs nearly due north, staying on the low ridgeline that climbs in a gentle westward arc toward the summit. Avoid drifting east into the obvious—and hazardous—avalanche chute there. The summer hiking trail pierces the heart of that chute, but in winter, snow flushes that valley regularly. Steer clear of it.

The safe route climbs steeply from the get-go, passing first through a tight tangle of Douglas fir and cedar trees, then breaking out into open snowfields at about 3500 feet. If you have climbed straight north, you should be nearly due south of the summit at this point. Keep mobbing upward, staying near the spine of the ridge. You might encounter bare rock on this windswept ridgeline, but keep your shoes on for traction since the snow is not gone, just blown somewhere else.

As you push up toward the summit, views open and you can enjoy spectacular panoramas to the south and east. Humpback Mountain towers due south, and Mount Catherine sits to the southeast. If you're tired and worried about getting back down before dark, skip the summit and turn around anytime after you break out of the trees.

--*49*--
# Source Lake

Rating: More difficult
Round trip: 3.5 miles
Hiking time: 5 hours
Elevation gain: 1000 feet
High point: 4100 feet
Best season: January through early March
Map: Green Trails: Snoqualmie Pass No. 207
Who to Contact: Mount Baker–Snoqualmie National Forest,
Snoqualmie Ranger District, North Bend Office

It all starts here. Source Lake is the headwaters of the main branch of the South Fork of the Snoqualmie River system. The waters of this lake run down the Snoqualmie River, flowing alongside Interstate 90 to North Bend, then carving north into the fertile Snoqualmie Valley before merging with the Skykomish River to form the fish-rich Snohomish River. But that's downstream. We are looking for the headwaters here.

When planning a trip along this route, be aware that when snow is unstable, avalanche dangers are scary. But when avalanche danger is listed as moderate or lower, the trail to Source Lake makes a wonderful outing for snowshoers.

Snowshoers can bask in glorious views of Denny Mountain, The Tooth, Bryant Peak, Chair Peak, and Snoqualmie Mountain. Those with sharp eyes can sometimes spot radical extreme skiers sneaking away from the Alpental Ski Area to launch themselves down the near-vertical snow-laden slopes of these peaks. Those who would rather watch a more natural variety of wildlife can scan the skies to spot red-tailed hawks, golden eagles, ravens, and falcons. Martens, hares, weasels, and squirrels burrow through and scamper over the snow around the trail.

To get there, from Seattle drive east on Interstate 90 to exit 52 (Snoqualmie Pass, West Summit) and turn north, crossing under the freeway. Continue north to the end of the road at the Alpental Ski Area parking lot.

When snow levels are low, you can begin the snowshoe trek by either finding the Snow Lake trailhead on the east side of the lower parking lot and following it as it climbs up the slope before looping northwest on a level traverse for 0.5 mile to Source Lake; or go the easier route and, from the upper end of the parking area, snowshoe cross-country up the slope at

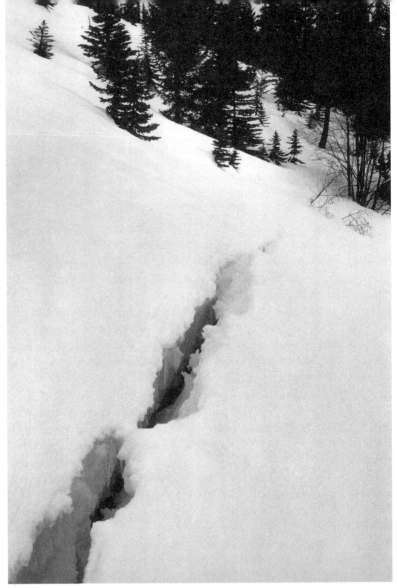

*A slab of snow calving off at the base of a steep avalanche slope above Source Lake*

the base of Snoqualmie Mountain to catch the trail as it passes the ski area. By midwinter when the snows are deep and the brush all well buried, ignore the summer trail and instead head northwest from the ski area, staying on the west side of the river basin. Don't walk in the bottom of the valley—there is a danger of punching through snow and taking a dip in the creek. Rather, stay up above the river course, but stay parallel to it.

The route climbs at a gentle pitch up the Snoqualmie River valley, passing through alder thickets, old stands of forest, and open meadows, for a bit more than 1 mile—gaining more than 700 feet along the way—before a final steep pitch of several hundred yards to the lake.

The lake is a small, circular tarn at the base of a steep wall below Chair Peak. This is the headwaters of the South Fork Snoqualmie River, although in winter, with its thick ice cap, it looks more like a flat bench than a deep lake. Enjoy a rest and picnic here while soaking in the views of the surrounding panorama.

Denny Peak lies to the south, flanked by The Tooth; Bryant Peak and Chair Peak are to the west. To the north, a high ridge links Chair Peak to Snoqualmie Peak on the northeast, which is in turn flanked by Lundin Peak, Red Mountain, and finally Guye Peak to the southeast.

## --*50*--

# Snow Lake

|  |  |
|---|---|
| **Rating:** | More difficult |
| **Round trip:** | Up to 10 miles |
| **Hiking time:** | 7 hours or 2 days |
| **Elevation gain:** | 2000 feet |
| **High point:** | 5100 feet |
| **Best season:** | January through early March |
| **Map:** | Green Trails: Snoqualmie Pass No. 207 |
| **Who to Contact:** | Mount Baker–Snoqualmie National Forest, Snoqualmie Ranger District, North Bend Office |
|  | *See map above.* |

Snow Lake may be the most popular wilderness trail in the Pacific Northwest. From June through September, it gets thousands—maybe tens of thousands—of hiker visits. But come winter, only a few hardy folks make the long slog though deep snow to the glorious lake basin. Part of the reason for this is that

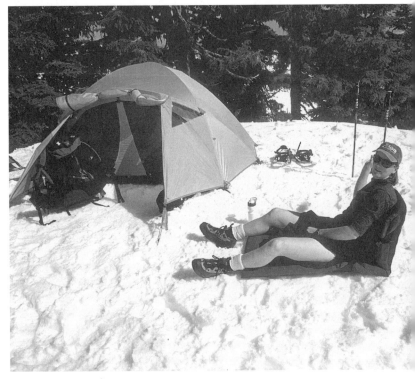

*Camp at Snow Lake*

the route crosses some pretty substantial avalanche chutes, creating a danger for unwary snow travelers. But those who take the time to check avalanche snow conditions and closely monitor avalanche dangers can find a safe time to trek this route.

The route begins by heading to Source Lake (Route 49), but pushes on past that easy-to-reach day-hiking destination and climbs steeply to crest the saddle separating Snow Lake from the Snoqualmie River drainage. This makes for a rigorous outing, but one well worth the effort—especially for those seeking a winter camping destination.

To get there, from Seattle drive east on Interstate 90 to exit 52 (Snoqualmie Pass, West Summit) and turn north, crossing under the freeway. Continue north to the end of the road at the Alpental Ski Area parking lot.

From Alpental, follow the route to Source Lake (Route 49), staying on the west side of the river basin. From Source Lake, swing north and start climbing the increasingly steep slope below Chair Peak, angling north and east up the slope. At about 3 miles, you'll find the slope tapers off and you enter a broad, tree-dotted meadow atop a broad saddle between Chair Peak and Snoqualmie Mountain. Stop and catch your breath here as you peer out at the surrounding glory. Denny Peak lies to the south, flanked by The Tooth, Bryant Peak, and Chair Peak to the west. To the north, a high ridge links Chair Peak to Snoqualmie Mountain on the northeast, which is in turn flanked by Lundin Peak, Red Mountain, and finally Guye Peak to the southeast.

Due north, just a few hundred feet below you, lies the long, flat oval of Snow Lake. You can descend to the lakeshore to find camp, or find a comfortable place to pitch your tent on the ridgeline, where the views are far better. Just find a nice flat in the lee of a stand of trees and you'll be warm and comfy. To continue your outing, and to gain a panoramic view of the basin, head east from the lake and climb to the low ridge above the lake, exploring to your heart's content.

## --51--
# Commonwealth Basin

| | |
|---|---|
| **Rating:** | Backcountry |
| **Round trip:** | Up to 10 miles |
| **Hiking time:** | 7 hours |
| **Elevation gain:** | 2300 feet |
| **High point:** | 5300 feet |
| **Best season:** | January through early March |
| **Map:** | Green Trails: Snoqualmie Pass No. 207 |
| **Who to Contact:** | Mount Baker–Snoqualmie National Forest, Snoqualmie Ranger District, North Bend Office |

The section of the Pacific Crest Trail (PCT) north of Snoqualmie Pass is overrun with hikers every summer weekend, but put a few feet of snow on the trail, and the crowds ignore it. That's great news for snowshoers because the trail is easy to get to and enjoyable for snowshoeing. The route to Commonwealth Basin follows the PCT for more than 2 miles through shadowy old-growth forest—with an occasional break in the trees for views of the surrounding peaks—before setting off on a smaller path into the wide, rocky basin at the base of Red Mountain.

Commonwealth Basin affords excellent views of the iron-rich flanks of Red Mountain, although snowshoers will be at a loss to explore the source for the mountain's name since it is covered in a deep quilt of white snow all

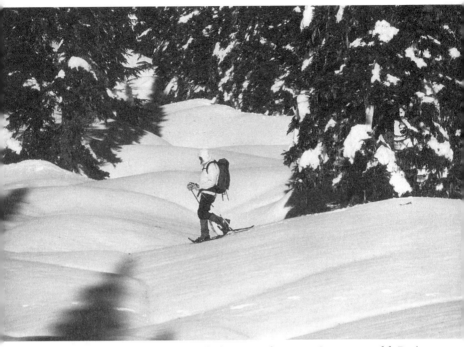

*Snowshoer trudging over drifted snow in the upper Commonwealth Basin*

winter. There are also excellent views up to Kendall Peak and Snoqualmie Mountain from the basin.

To get there, from Seattle drive east on Interstate 90 to exit 52 (Snoqualmie Pass, West Summit) and turn north, crossing under the freeway. Continue north to the first wide, plowed pullout along the road, usually no more than 0.25 mile beyond the freeway. Park in the first available space, making sure your vehicle is well clear of the roadway. If parking is not available on the lower road, park on the south side of the freeway and walk through the underpass to reach the trailhead.

Just north of the freeway underpass, a small snow-covered road climbs off to the right. Snowshoe up this road into a wide summer parking area at the PCT trailhead. The trail leads off from the east end of the parking lot, rolling up through thick forest on a long traverse to the east before looping through a switchback corner near 0.7 mile and climbing northwest. After looping through a couple more short switchbacks, the trail rolls north to a junction at 2.5 miles (4000 feet).

An alternate route, when snow is very deep, is to snowshoe up the narrow valley directly above the PCT parking area. Stay left and climb through the trees, keeping the small creek basin on your left until reaching the broad mouth of Commonwealth Basin.

The route to this point is easy to follow because the trail corridor is wide and obvious in the heavy forest. The trail stays under the forest canopy nearly all of the first 2.5 miles, although it does cross the base of a large avalanche slope and then recross the slope higher up after climbing through a switchback. Cross this slope with care, and if the avalanche danger is higher than moderate, avoid the area. The point where the trail crosses the slope is on the run-out section of the chute rather than the trigger area, so it is unlikely that you will trigger a slide here, but caution is still required.

At the trail junction, stay left—the PCT climbs steadily to the right—and follow the Commonwealth Creek valley up into the basin. The trail is a long, straight ascent up the valley, climbing gradually as it enters the basin. The forest thins, and finally falls away at 4 miles, leaving you on open slopes at the base of Red Mountain. Potential for avalanches exists here beyond timber line, so care and common sense must be used in heavy doses. If the snow is stable and safe, it's possible to scramble up to the 5300-foot level (about 5 miles from the trailhead) at a low saddle on the ridge between Red Mountain and Lundin Peak. The last 0.5 mile of climbing is steep and should be attempted only by those with experience in snowshoe mountaineering.

## --52--
## Kendall Peak Lakes

Rating: Most difficult
Round trip: 9 miles
Hiking time: 7 hours
Elevation gain: 1700 feet
High point: 4400 feet
Best season: January through early March
Map: Green Trails: Snoqualmie Pass No. 207
Who to Contact: Mount Baker–Snoqualmie National Forest, Snoqualmie Ranger District, North Bend Office
*See map on page 151.*

The roar of the highway is unmistakable when starting up this track, but soon the beauty of the winter wilderness surrounding the trail makes everything else fade into the background. The dark green firs and hemlocks lining the ridge, the open, quilted meadows of snow, and the wide avenue of the trail make this a perfect destination for snowshoers.

The trail leads to a pair of small alpine ponds nestled in a deep cirque on the flank of towering Kendall Peak (5675 feet). The mountain dominates the skyline from the lakes basin, as well as along the last mile of the trail leading

*Mother and child on lower section of Kendall Peak Lakes route*

into the basin. But Kendall isn't the only peak on the horizon. To the east is Alta Mountain and the long line of Rampart Ridge. To the south is Mount Catherine with its lower flanks lined with the wide white slashes of alpine ski runs. Below the lakes, the broad meadows along the bottom of the Gold Creek valley glimmer a brilliant white in the afternoon sun.

Although the trail ascends nearly 2000 feet, the climbing is gradual and the trail is easy to follow. Because of that, first-time 'shoers and young kids will enjoy this outing as much as experienced snowshoe enthusiasts. Of course, all of those features coupled with the trail's close proximity to the Seattle metropolitan area means a lot of snowshoers and skiers on any winter weekend. Strap on the snowshoes midweek, though, and the trail will be virtually deserted.

To get there, from Seattle drive east on Interstate 90 over Snoqualmie Pass to exit 54, 2 miles east of the pass's summit. Exit I-90, turn left, and cross under the freeway to reach the Gold Creek Sno-Park just a few hundred feet north of the highway interchange.

Snowshoe up the Gold Creek valley, staying close to the left (west) side of the valley, and in a few hundred yards, find an old logging road climbing left into the trees and up the valley wall. This road is steep for 0.25 mile, and then the ascent moderates considerably. The road enters an old clearcut just past the 0.5-mile mark and twists and turns its way up the slope. You can either stay with the moderate pitch of the road or take a steeper, more direct, northerly approach straight up the slope, cutting off the switchback corners. Pause often to rest. Use the excuse of stopping to admire the increasingly pretty views south over the Gold Creek basin, Hyak Ski Area, and Mount Catherine if you are the competitive sort who doesn't like to admit to fatigue!

At 1.7 miles, the route hooks through a sharp hairpin turn to the right. A wide spur road heads off to the left, leading to a nice overlook of the lower Coal Creek basin and the ski areas at Snoqualmie Pass. Stay right if you are bound for the lakes. The road traverses east toward the snout of a narrow ridge and, at that leading edge of the ridge, turns north and climbs steeply through forest and meadow. The track stays on the west side of the ridge crest, banking right at 2.6 miles, and at 3.5 miles hooking sharply south in a switchback turn.

Stay north, snowshoeing off the road at the apex of the hairpin corner, to find a narrow path just below the ridge crest leading to Kendall Lakes. The trail nears Coal Creek at 4.2 miles and follows it the remainder of the way to the lakes' basin, rolling over two small knolls before reaching the lower of the twin Kendall Lakes. Avoid the upper lake because the tight, avalanche-prone walls of the cirque are not a safe way to approach it.

## --53--
# Lower Gold Creek Basin

|  |  |
|---:|:---|
| **Rating:** | Easiest to more difficult |
| **Round trip:** | 4 miles |
| **Hiking time:** | 4 hours |
| **Elevation gain:** | 400 feet |
| **High point:** | 3000 feet |
| **Best season:** | December through February |
| **Map:** | Green Trails: Snoqualmie Pass No. 207 |
| **Who to Contact:** | Mount Baker–Snoqualmie National Forest, Snoqualmie Ranger District |

*See map on page 151.*

Hiking through a wide, level valley in the shadow of looming Kendall Peak to the north and Rampart Ridge to the east would be an ideal outing, if only so many people didn't know about it. Fortunately, a few miles up the trail, the crowds thin—or at least spread out—and snowshoers can get on with the business of learning to travel in a beautiful wilderness valley. That's right, just a few miles after leaving the buzzing Interstate 90 corridor, the Alpine Lakes Wilderness unfolds. By mid-December, the snow is usually deep enough for the outing to be enjoyable, making this a great destination for families who gave each other snowshoes for Christmas.

To get there, from Seattle drive east on I-90 over Snoqualmie Pass to exit 54, 2 miles east of the pass's summit. Exit I-90, turn left, cross under the freeway, and just a few hundred feet north of the highway interchange, turn right onto a narrow paved road and drive east parallel to the freeway for 1 mile. Cars generally line both sides of this road, as the shoulder is the primary parking area for the long Gold Creek Sno-Park. Park at the end of the plowed road, near the small bridge over the stream connecting Mardee Lake to Keechelus Lake.

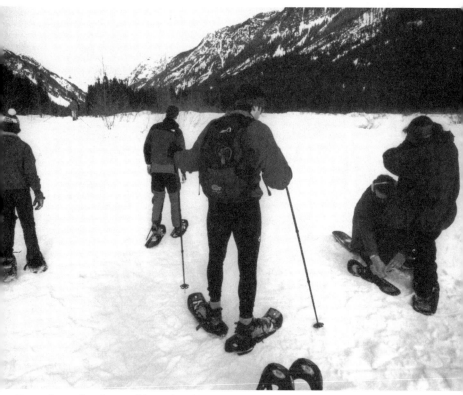

*Preparing to head up Gold Creek Valley*

Start the hike by heading north along a narrow access road (Forest Road 144) on the eastern side of Mardee Lake. The road stays tight to the eastern wall of the valley, but if the snow is deep enough to bury all the ground cover, drop off the road in a few hundred yards—just past Mardee Lake—and snowshoe up the open meadow and through the thin stands of forest. As you hike up the valley, the view of Kendall Peak gets better and better, while on your right, Rampart Ridge rolls majestically along. As the valley tapers in, the meadows give way to wide stands of trees and small forest clearings. The walls close in tighter and tighter on the valley floor, and the views become more dramatic. At about 2.5 miles in, stop and enjoy the scenery and the feeling of power that this winter wilderness emits.

At the northern end of Rampart Ridge is the bulky summit of Alta Mountain; directly opposite is the vertical face of Kendall Peak. The steep walls of these mountains seem to rise from the ground at your feet. Continue to press on up the valley, but only if you know how to evaluate avalanche dangers. Even on the valley floor, hikers are susceptible to avalanches. The mammoth slides can come barreling off the valley walls with enough momentum that they sweep well out onto the basin's floor.

Stroll to your heart's content along the valley floor, then weave your way through the trees back to the starting point for a gentle day on the snow.

## --*54*--

# Alaska Lake

|  |  |
|---:|:---|
| **Rating:** | Easiest to more difficult |
| **Round trip:** | 12 miles |
| **Hiking time:** | 8 hours or 2 days |
| **Elevation gain:** | 1600 feet |
| **High point:** | 4200 feet |
| **Best season:** | January through March |
| **Map:** | Green Trails: Snoqualmie Pass No. 207 |
| **Who to Contact:** | Mount Baker–Snoqualmie National Forest, Snoqualmie Ranger District, North Bend Office *See map on page 151.* |

Trek for miles up the long, gently sloping valley under the towering wall of Rampart Ridge before the route turns steep and you slog upward to increasingly picturesque views to reach a deep, steep lake cirque. The valley approach,

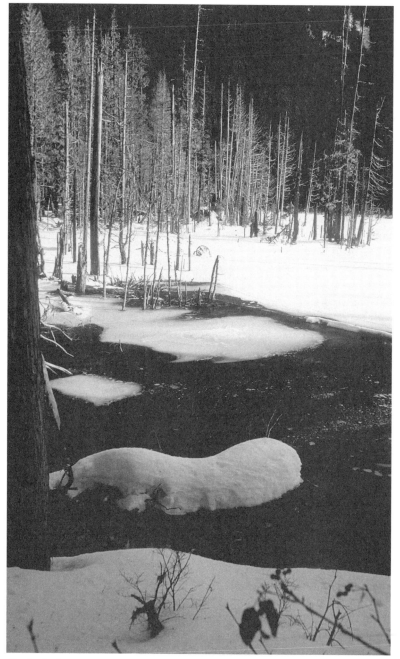

*Alaska Lake*

though fairly flat itself, is an avalanche danger zone, with several avalanche-chute runouts reaching the valley bottom. Don't trek up this valley unless the avalanche risk is low. But when the snow is stable, this can be a stunning place to visit, even though the first few miles are within hearing of Interstate 90 to the south. In addition to the vertical wall of Rampart Ridge to the east, there is the high summit of Alaska Mountain at the head of the valley, and the rocky spires of Kendall Peak to the west.

To get there, from Seattle drive east on I-90 over Snoqualmie Pass to exit 54, 2 miles east of the pass's summit. Exit I-90, turn left, cross under the freeway, and just a few hundred feet north of the highway interchange, turn right onto a narrow paved road and drive east parallel to the freeway for 1 mile. Cars generally line both sides of this road, as the shoulder is the primary parking area for the long Gold Creek Sno-Park. Park at the end of the plowed road, near the small bridge over the stream connecting Mardee Lake to Keechelus Lake.

Head up the Gold Creek valley as described in Route 53, Lower Gold Creek Basin. Moving up the valley, you'll find the walls slowly drawing closer together. To the left (west) is the rocky bulk of Kendall Peak, while to your right (east) is the high, skyscraping wall of Rampart Ridge. The towering cliffs, topped with a ragged line of spires and pinnacles, create an impressive skyline even from the valley floor directly below.

At about 2.5 miles, the valley floor is narrow and many steep gullies and couloirs drop from the peaks above. These deep channels serve as natural avalanche chutes with snowslides regularly scouring them and depositing the fast-running slides on the valley floor. If the snow is stable during your visit (you did check with the Northwest Weather and Avalanche Center before your outing, right?), push on up the valley for another 2.5 miles, crossing in front of the mouth of Silver Creek valley on the north side of Kendall Peak, before reaching a small draw leading off to the left. This is the outlet stream from Alaska Lake. Leave Gold Creek, and begin your ascent of the valley wall here, heading north-northwest. Stay to the left (south) of the creek basin itself, hiking up the low ridge above the creek. The lake is just 1 mile up the slope, but the elevation gain in that mile is more than 1000 feet, so take your time.

Alaska Lake fills a small basin directly below Alaska Mountain and Ridge Lake, which both lie alongside the Pacific Crest Trail. Steep walls surround the lake, except at the outlet end, so plan your camp there to avoid potential avalanche chutes. Although the lake will most likely be frozen over, stay off the ice because it is usually thin and subject to cracking.

--*55*--

# Mount Margaret

**Rating:** Easiest to more difficult
**Round trip:** 9 miles
**Hiking time:** 6 hours
**Elevation gain:** 2800 feet
**High point:** 5200 feet
**Best season:** Late December through late February
**Map:** Green Trails: Snoqualmie Pass No. 207
**Who to Contact:** Wenatchee National Forest, Cle Elum Ranger District
*See map on page 151.*

Views of the entire eastern half of the Snoqualmie Pass area, including the sprawling blue waters of Keechelus Lake and the snow-covered summits of Mount Catherine and Tinkham Peak to the south, can be had from the upper reaches of this route. The lower section, though, is unremarkable. The flat roadway, parallel to noisy Interstate 90, is a great place for novice snowshoers to get a feel for hiking with the broad "foot boards," and it does serve as a good warm-up for the long climb ahead. The real treasures of the Mount Margaret trek are found beyond the second mile.

Because this area is close to the metropolitan centers, a lot of skiers and snowshoers share the trail. That, combined with the closeness of the busy freeway, means the chances of seeing wildlife are pretty slim. Still, where people play in the woods, camp-robber jays look for handouts. This valley is also patrolled by many red-tailed hawks and ravens, so watch the skies for raptors and corvids, and look for the tiny tracks of their prey (mice, hares, and grouse) in the meadows.

To get there, from Seattle drive east on I-90 over Snoqualmie Pass to exit 54, 2 miles east of the pass's summit. Exit I-90, turn left, cross under the freeway, and just a few hundred feet north of the highway interchange, turn right onto a narrow paved road and drive east parallel to the freeway for 1 mile. Cars generally line both sides of this road as the shoulder is the primary parking area for the long Gold Creek Sno-Park. Park at the end of the plowed road, near the small bridge over the stream connecting Mardee Lake to Keechelus Lake.

The first 1.5 miles of the snowshoe hike follow the road southeast from the parking area, parallel to I-90. This leg of the journey is frequently used by

*View over the valley from below Mount Margaret*

cross-country skiers who are just learning their craft, and it makes a nice place to familiarize yourself with your snowshoes. The road curves around the base of Rampart Ridge, with just a few modest views west toward Mount Catherine and Roaring Ridge above the waters of Keechelus Lake.

After crossing Wolfe Creek, the road climbs gradually, switches back to recross the creek, and just a few hundred yards beyond the second crossing, switches back once more to start a long, traversing climb through intermittent forest and clearcuts to mile 2.5. Two more switchbacks are encountered in the next 0.5 mile, and at 3.2 miles, the road splits. The left fork continues to climb while the right stays at a level traverse before dropping toward the I-90 valley. Staying left, climb for another 0.5 mile to 3600 feet and a gate marking the Mount Margaret trailhead.

The trail is wide for a hiking path—it's actually an old jeep road—so it is very easy to follow even when deep in snow. The path zigzags steeply up the side of a ridge, through broad clearcut meadows. Save some travel time by angling east, still climbing steeply, to the eastern edge of a large meadow. Pause here to soak in the views of the Snoqualmie Pass area, Keechelus Lake, and the sprawling clearcut-pocked mountains of the South Cascades. On clear days, Mount Rainier and sometimes even Mount Adams are visible to the south.

Continue uphill toward the ridge crest (now heading north), following the road through a small forested area, another meadow, and finally a solid, respectable stand of trees. The last 0.5 mile is along a true hiking trail in deep forest. It climbs, weaving around trees, along the crest of the ridge to a high promontory below the craggy summit of Mount Margaret. Below, on the eastern side of the ridge, is tiny Margaret Lake. Reaching its shores, though, requires a steep descent along an avalanche-prone slope, so stay on the ridge and enjoy the wonderful views.

## --56--
# Keechelus Ridge

**Rating:** More difficult
**Round trip:** 6.4 miles
**Hiking time:** 5 hours
**Elevation gain:** 2100 feet
**High point:** 4900 feet
**Best season:** Late January through late February
**Map:** Green Trails: Snoqualmie Pass No. 207
**Who to Contact:** Wenatchee National Forest, Cle Elum Ranger District

Snowshoers who like to climb will love this route. Although the trail is broad and easy to follow all the way to the ridge crest, ample opportunities exist for snowshoers who want to show off their climbing abilities by heading straight up the open slopes.

But this trail isn't all work. Plenty of rewards await the dedicated athletes who point their snowshoes toward the top of this ridge. Best of all, even those who cut their trips short of the top will find the journey pays off tremendously. Views from the route are incredible, and the higher snowshoers go, the better the panoramic scenery. The jumbled peaks of the South Cascades spread away to the southern horizon with Mount Rainier dominating the skyline.

To get there, from Seattle drive east on Interstate 90 over Snoqualmie Pass to exit 62, signed Kachess Lake, about 10 miles east of the summit. After exiting the interstate, turn left, cross over the freeway, and turn left onto the freeway on-ramp and drive westbound I-90 for 1.5 miles to the Price Creek Westbound Sno-Park. (Although another Sno-Park is located on the other side of the freeway, there is no way to cross the interstate to reach it.)

A small trail leads northwest from the Sno-Park for a 0.25 mile to Forest Road 4832. Turn left and hike west a couple hundred feet to leave the multi-use crowds behind. (Snowmobilers, skiers, skijorers—skiers pulled by one or more dogs—and even dogsledders use this trail.) Climb to the right onto a small side road, FR 124. This road climbs steeply up the flank of Keechelus Ridge alongside Price Creek for 0.5 mile before angling west away from the creek in a long, looping route that isn't too steep but does cover several miles. You can stick with the road, but a faster, more enjoyable route is to head cross-country up the slope, slicing across old clearcuts and thin stands of forest.

The best cross-country "trail" is found about 1.3 miles out from the Sno-Park. As the road rolls farther west away from Price Creek, snowshoe up the slope away from the track, staying right while the road goes left. Parallel Price Creek uphill, but stay on the bench above the stream rather than descending into the brambles alongside it. The slope rolls upward over several small benches and false summits, crossing clearcuts old and new. In light snow years, take care to avoid hooking a snowshoe on some of the brush protruding in the older, grown-over cuts.

The climb covers about a mile of distance before crossing another heavily used road, FR 4934, just below the ridge crest (4300 feet). Emerge onto that road at about the same place as FR 124, which finally loops back from its long journey around the ridge flank.

Rather than joining FR 4934—a popular snowmobile route that creates a long loop when coupled with several other roads in the area—merely snowshoe across it, and head toward the ridge crest. This last 0.5 mile of climbing is also cross-country travel, although you can follow the road (FR 124) here too, if you are nervous about routefinding on the open ridge. The top is easily identifiable on the approach by tall radio relay towers. Once there, put the towers behind you (thus keeping them out of sight) and enjoy the panoramic vistas of the eastern Cascades.

*Icicles on evergreen bough*

--*57*--

# Amabilis Mountain

**Rating:** Most difficult
**Round trip:** 8 miles
**Hiking time:** 6 hours
**Elevation gain:** 2100 feet
**High point:** 4554 feet
**Best season:** Late January through late February
**Map:** Green Trails: Snoqualmie Pass No. 207
**Who to Contact:** Wenatchee National Forest, Cle Elum Ranger District

Sometimes it's nice to cut a switchback or two; to go where skiers and snowmobilers can't; to work up a sweat on a cold day while enjoying spectacular local scenery and distant views. This trail offers all that. A road loops, bobs, and weaves its way to the top of the mountain, but snowshoers don't need roads. There is enough open country on the side of the mountain that snowshoers can just point their shoes uphill and go, jumping onto the road when necessary to avoid particularly steep pitches or brambly clearcuts.

All that open country makes prime hunting habitat for raptors—red-tailed hawks and falcons—and ravens. Owls prowl the forest fringes, and bald eagles soar through between fishing trips up the Yakima River. Those birds are here for a reason, and that reason is rabbits, or more accurately, hares— snowshoe hares, which bound through the meadows and burrow in the snow to eat the grasses underneath. Even if the white rabbits aren't seen, their tracks frequently are.

This route is steep and has a high danger of avalanche at times, so avoid the mountain when forecasters report moderate or higher avalanche danger.

To get there, from Seattle drive east on Interstate 90 over Snoqualmie Pass to exit 63, signed Cabin Creek. Turn right after exiting the interstate, and enter the Cabin Creek Sno-Park on the right.

Before strapping on the snowshoes, walk north across the freeway overpass and find the start of Forest Road 4826 on the left. Snowshoe north on this wide, flat road. Note that the road is usually groomed, with tracks frequently set for skiers (twin, parallel grooves carved into the snow by a grooming machine), so steer your snowshoes well clear of the tracks. A quarter mile up the road, turn off onto FR 4822 and start to climb toward the summit of Amabilis. This trail switches back and forth a few times before slanting off to the south on a long traverse of the middle section of the mountain.

*Looking up the valley, Amabilis Mountain route*

Cross a small creek, and at about 2 miles the road forks. A hard hairpin turn to the left leads you on a long looping route to the mountaintop. Snowshoeing straight off on the right-hand road leads to an even longer loop to the same point at the summit (which, incidentally, is almost directly up-slope from this intersection).

Either road will get you to the top, but if you are looking to avoid the roads, start off along the left fork, and in 0.5 mile leave the road by climbing on a more direct route up the slope while still slanting slightly to the left. The views are now spectacular. Looking south and west, the Yakima River and Keechelus Lake valley spread out at your feet, and beyond the rolling hills (with their many square scars of open clearcuts) the South Cascades sprawl to the horizon.

A half mile farther on, near the 3-mile mark, cross the road, which has flipped through a switchback turn and is now climbing south, and head

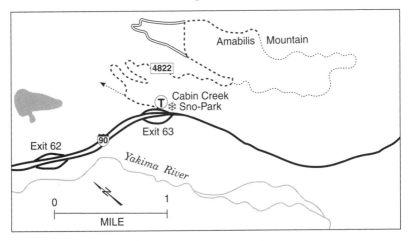

straight upslope to the ridge crest. Turn right and follow the crest another mile to the 4554-foot summit. A thin stand of trees lines the summit crest, providing a degree of protection from the wind while you enjoy a scenic lunch before heading down the steep slopes.

## --58--

# Twin Lakes

**Rating:** Easiest
**Round trip:** 4 miles
**Hiking time:** 5 hours
**Elevation gain:** 400 feet
**High point:** 3100 feet
**Best season:** December through late February
**Map:** Green Trails: Snoqualmie Pass No. 207
**Who to Contact:** Wenatchee National Forest, Cle Elum Ranger District
*See map on page 170.*

This is a pleasant forest walk, offering a fairly easy outing for the family. The route holds to a broad, easy-to-follow road for the first 1.5 miles before dropping into the woods to ramble along a narrow hiking path. At the end of the route, you'll find a small lake set deep in the woods. Despite its proximity to the popular ski areas of Snoqualmie Pass and the busy roadway of Interstate 90, this is a wonderful place to find wildlife in the winter.

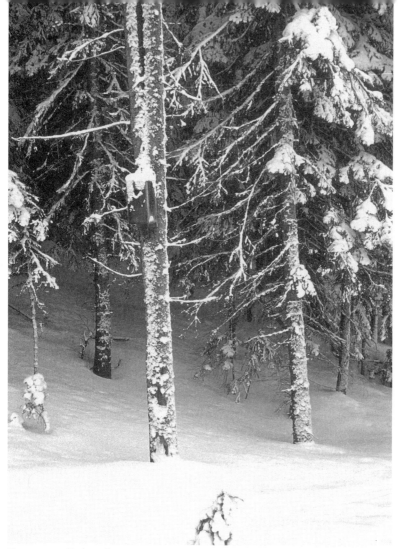

*Forest near Twin Lakes*

Deer frequent this valley, as they find forage in the deep forests, but it is far more likely you'll see tracks and trails of snowshoe hares, martens, weasels and—hot on the trail of those three—bobcats and cougars. You'll find grouse perched in the trees, and gray jays flitting through the branches. The only thing missing is expansive views, but sometimes its nice to focus on beauty close at hand, and this route offers that aplenty.

To get there, from Seattle drive east on I-90 over Snoqualmie Pass to exit 54, signed Hyak. Turn left and drive about 1.5 miles south on Forest Road 2219 to the Keechelus Sno-Park.

From the Sno-Park, cross the Iron Horse Trail (a.k.a. John Wayne Trail) and head up FR 9070. At various times during the winter, both the Iron Horse and FR 9070 are groomed by the Cross Country Ski Center of The Pass Ski Resort. Be sure to stick to the outside edges of the trail if it is groomed, and if not groomed, avoid any well-laid ski tracks whenever possible.

FR 9070 climbs the Cold Creek valley, heading west around the southern flank of Mount Catherine. The going is easy as the road climbs just 400 feet in nearly 1.5 miles. Watch the edges of the road, and peer under the eaves of the forest along the road for signs of wildlife.

At 1.5 miles and 3000 feet, the road rounds a sharp hairpin turn. Leave the road, dropping off the left side of the road just before the apex of the turn, and continue trekking west (the road begins to climb north-northwest to Route 59, Windy Pass/Mount Catherine). There is a narrow hiking trail here, but with a blanket of snow the trail is nearly impossible to find. No need to worry, though. Just pick a route that carries you west at a fairly level pace—a slight ascent is what you're actually going for, but not much. At just 0.5 mile past the point where you left the road, you'll find a small lake nestled in the deep second-growth forest. (The "twin" of this Twin Lake is further up the valley, and is too small and insubstantial to bother with.) Stay off the lake ice—the forest and the relatively low elevation prevent thick ice from forming.

## --59--

# Windy Pass/Mount Catherine

Rating: Most difficult
Round trip: 8 miles
Hiking time: 8 hours
Elevation gain: 2300 feet
High point: 5052 feet
Best season: December through late February
Map: Green Trails: Snoqualmie Pass No. 207
Who to Contact: Wenatchee National Forest, Cle Elum Ranger District

As you approach Snoqualmie Pass while driving east on Interstate 90, you notice a large forested mountain straight ahead. As you near its base, the road swings north in a large loop through the pass, then back south along Keechelus Lake before turning east once more. That big, forested mountain that pushed the highway on that northern jag is Mount Catherine, and snowshoers can

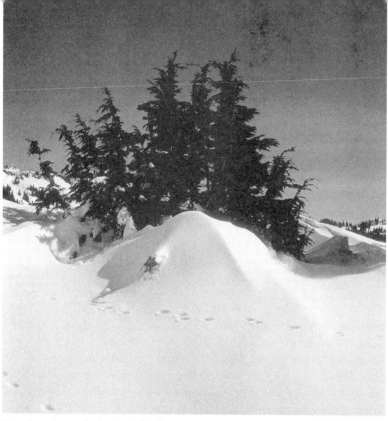

*Foxes' tracks on Catherine's flank*

explore its flanks and summit by trekking up the eastern side. Along the way, you'll enjoy ample opportunities to experience wildlife, and some glorious views of the Snoqualmie Pass peaks.

To get there, from Seattle drive east on I-90 over Snoqualmie Pass to exit 54, signed Hyak. Turn left and drive about 1.5 miles south on Forest Road 2219 to the Keechelus Sno-Park.

Begin your trek by crossing the Iron Horse Trail (a.k.a. John Wayne Trail) and heading up FR 9070 (as on Route 58, Twin Lakes). Remember that the lower sections of the road may be groomed. Be sure to stick to the outside edges of the road if it is groomed, and if not groomed, avoid any well-laid ski tracks whenever possible.

At 1.5 miles, the road rounds a sharp, switchbacking turn to the right (Route 58 to Twin Lakes continues straight ahead). Continue up the road and soon it swings back to the west, now climbing a bit more steeply, gaining 800 feet in the next 1.5 miles. The route cuts across the southern flank of Mount Catherine to reach Windy Pass (3800 feet) at 3 miles. Windy Pass provides wonderful views west into the South Fork Snoqualmie River valley (home to I-90) and across to Granite Mountain. To the south, Silver Peak looms tall, while to the northeast Mount Catherine awaits.

From Windy Pass, you'll likely see a well-groomed track leading to the top of Mount Catherine. This is part of the pay-to-play trail network of the commercial ski area. Stay off those groomed trails. Instead, from Windy Pass turn east and pick a route up the low ridgeline leading toward the top of the mountain in about a mile.

## --60--

# Keechelus Lake/John Wayne Trail

| | |
|---|---|
| **Rating:** | Easiest |
| **Round trip:** | 4 miles |
| **Hiking time:** | 3 hours |
| **Elevation gain:** | 200 feet |
| **High point:** | 2700 feet |
| **Best season:** | December through late February |
| **Map:** | Green Trails: Snoqualmie Pass No. 207 |
| **Who to Contact:** | Wenatchee National Forest, Cle Elum Ranger District |
| | *See map above.* |

Well pardner, if you're looking for a gentle, but rustic outing, John Wayne can help you out. The old railroad right-of-way that runs across the state is known

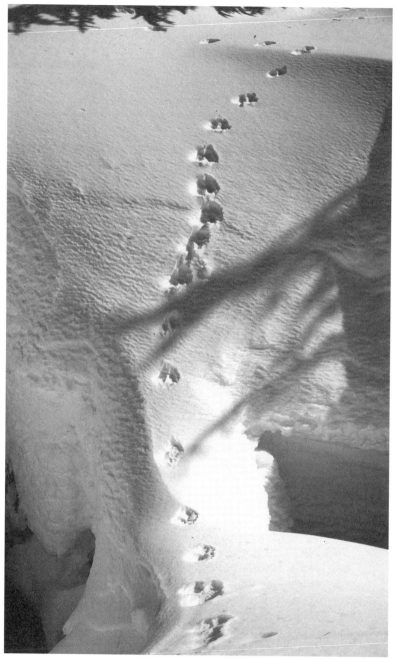

*Hare tracks near Keechelus*

as the John Wayne State Park, while the actual physical trail (the old railbed) is the Iron Horse Trail. But whether you call it the John Wayne Trail, the Iron Horse Trail, or the Keechelus Lake Trail, you'll find this a great route to enjoy with the family. The flat, well-graded trail is perfect for kids of all ages.

To get there, from Seattle drive east on Interstate 90 over Snoqualmie Pass to exit 54, signed Hyak. Turn left and drive about 1.5 miles south on Forest Road 2219 to the Keechelus Sno-Park.

Climbing slightly west from the trailhead to get on the trail, turn left (south) and stroll south along the trail as it hugs the slope above the waters of Keechelus Lake. The trail (like the old train route before it) pushes east to Idaho, but there's no need to think so far out. The trail is often groomed, and when it is, snowshoers should stick to the outside edges of the path—and don't tread on established ski tracks if it can be avoided.

From the trail, you can look across the lake at the rushing traffic on I-90, and above that ribbon of frenetic activity, you'll see the jagged crown of Rampart Ridge and the high summit of Mount Margaret at the northern end of Keechelus Ridge.

At about 2 miles from the trailhead, you'll find the trail diving into some old wood and concrete structures. These are snow sheds—basically, roofs held over the railroad tracks to divert avalanche snows over the train route. This is a great place to turn around—move much farther east and you risk running out of snow as the trail continues to drop in elevation.

## --61--
# Hex Mountain

**Rating:** More difficult
**Round trip:** 7 miles
**Hiking time:** 6 hours
**Elevation gain:** 2600 feet
**High point:** 5034 feet
**Best season:** Late December through March
**Map:** Green Trails: Kachess Lake No. 208
**Who to Contact:** Wenatchee National Forest, Cle Elum Ranger District

This trail represents the epitome of snowshoeing in the Cascades: a long, steady, often-steep climb through lush old forests ending at a high ridge with panoramic views of unmatched beauty. After soaking in the scenic splendor at the summit, snowshoers then reverse direction and follow their tracks back down the slope.

What sets this trail apart from others is that the slopes are well forested and sheltered, so avalanche hazards are minimal and snowshoeing, though steep at times, is relatively easy. Starting from Salmon la Sac Road (State Route 903), the snowshoe hike begins with a climb on an old, winding logging road through mixed forest and small clearcuts. Some nice views are found on the way up the trail, but the best are left until snowshoers top the ridge and turn around to see the breathtaking vistas to the west. Cle Elum Lake sprawls directly underfoot, and just beyond that is Mount Baldy, Thomas Mountain, West Peak, and Thorp Mountain along the crest of Kachess Ridge.

To get there, from Seattle drive east on Interstate 90 over Snoqualmie Pass to exit 80, signed Roslyn. Turn north onto the Bullfrog Cutoff Road, and drive to its end at a junction with SR 903. Turn left and continue north 9 miles, passing through the towns of Roslyn and Ronald, to reach the junction of Forest Road 116 on the right. If a turnout is plowed out here, park in it; otherwise, go back down SR 903 about 300 yards to a plowed area on the west side of the highway near where it crosses Newport Creek.

If you park at Newport Creek, walk up the highway to FR 116 before strapping on your snowshoes and starting the climb. The road leads northeast, always climbing, past several spur roads and side trails. Most of these are easily discernible as secondary roads, but at times the forks and junctions can be confusing. Unfortunately, trying to map all the junctions and byways is difficult, so you will have to use your best judgment and occasionally backtrack if you make a wrong turn. (Fortunately, the side roads are generally short, so you'll quickly realize your errors. For example, if the road dips or heads too far off the northeast bearing that is required, it's the wrong road.)

After the first mile of the road, the options decrease and the main road is the only one to follow until, at 1.2 miles, the road traverses above a small

*Foggy day on the Hex Mountain trail*

creek valley and, at 1.7 miles, ends at the summer trailhead parking area. Here is where the fun really begins. Snowshoeing up the narrow forest trail as it climbs the ridge crest toward Hex Mountain is a wonderful experience. With snowshoes you can easily climb, weave around trees, and generally enjoy the day as you soak in the beauty of the forest environment. This area is home to red foxes and an assortment of birds and small animals. Of course, whiskey jacks pester every human who enters the forest, thus living up to their alias, camp-robber jays, and great horned owls silently patrol the woods in search of mice, voles, martens, and hares.

The trail climbs for more than 1.5 miles, with only occasional glimpses of the world beyond the trees. At 3.3 miles from the start of the hike, the trail tops out on the south end of Sasse Ridge, just below the summit of Hex Mountain (Route 62 continues along Sasse Ridge). Turn right onto the Sasse Ridge Trail, and hike 0.25 mile to the summit for striking views of the eastern Cascades.

## --62--
# Sasse Ridge

**Rating:** Backcountry
**Round trip:** 15 miles
**Hiking time:** 2 days
**Elevation gain:** 2700 feet
**High point:** 5400 feet
**Best season:** Late December through March
**Map:** Green Trails: Kachess Lake No. 208
**Who to Contact:** Wenatchee National Forest, Cle Elum Ranger District
*See map on page 173.*

After a modest climb to the ridge crest, this route lets snowshoers stay high and enjoy an endless bounty of beautiful views and remarkable scenery. The trail rolls south to north and opens up on views of the Alpine Lakes Wilderness peaks, Cle Elum Lake, and the entire eastern Cascade Mountains.

Few folks visit the north end of this trail in winter, so those snowshoers who do venture out along the route will find it empty of human company. Still, they won't be alone. A host of wintering animals thrive here, including a few who perform chameleon acts by changing into snowy white coats each winter. Snowshoe hares, ptarmigans, and weasels are seen as flashes of white

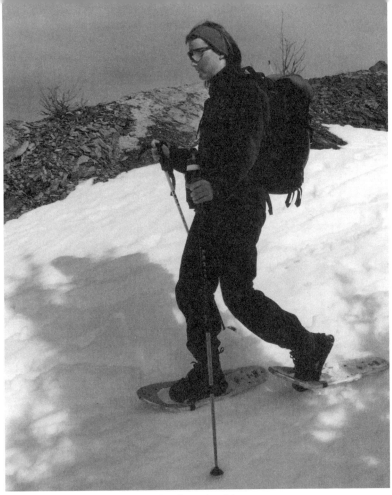

*Heading toward Sasse Mountain along the ridge crest*

against the white snow only when they move. But even their winter camou-
flage can't save them from the predators who prowl this area. Coyotes, bobcats, cougars, red-tailed hawks, golden eagles, falcons, and great horned owls
all compete for the few small animals that scamper about the snowy forests
and meadows of Sasse Ridge.

To get there, from Seattle drive east on Interstate 90 over Snoqualmie
Pass to exit 80, signed Roslyn. Turn north onto the Bullfrog Cutoff Road, and
drive to its end at a junction with State Route 903. Turn left and continue
north 9 miles, passing through the towns of Roslyn and Ronald, to reach the
junction of Forest Road 116 on the right. If a turnout is plowed out here, park
in it; otherwise, go back down SR 903 about 300 yards to a plowed area on the
west side of the highway near where it crosses Newport Creek.

Start up FR 116 as described in Route 61, Hex Mountain. At the top of the trail, at 3.3 miles, instead of turning right for a short scramble to the summit of Hex, turn left onto the Sasse Ridge Trail and start the long, scenic snowshoe north. The trail follows the crest of the ridge for more than 7 miles, but you can find plenty of fine, protected campsites all along the route, so tailor the length of the snowshoe trek to your own preferences.

From the 4900-foot junction with the Hex Mountain Trail, the Sasse Ridge Trail heads north, dropping gradually through thin forests in the first mile before climbing once more until, at 5.3 miles, the trail rolls under the crown of a high, unnamed peak (5159 feet). The trail then banks right, drops slightly into a high saddle, and climbs again to 5400 feet at 5.8 miles. Wind exposure and potential avalanche dangers are possible on this stretch of the trail. If conditions are unstable, head back and make camp in the first sheltered site, either near the saddle or on the south side of the unnamed peak.

The trail curves north again at 5.9 miles and at 7.5 miles passes just under the summit of Sasse Mountain. The scramble to the summit is easy because the peak is open and round. Enjoy unmatched views from the top of Sasse, and either find a suitable campsite in the thin forests on the mountain's protected southern flank or head back down the trail to find a sheltered camp.

North of Sasse Mountain, the trail crosses a steep, open ridge section that is a dangerous avalanche area. The windswept ridge is seldom stable or secure, so only highly experienced winter mountaineers should even consider going farther, and they should do so only when avalanche dangers are low.

## --63--
# Thorp Mountain

**Rating:** Backcountry
**Round trip:** 15 miles
**Hiking time:** 2 days
**Elevation gain:** 2800 feet
**High point:** 5100 feet
**Best season:** Late December through March
**Map:** Green Trails: Kachess Lake No. 208
**Who to Contact:** Wenatchee National Forest, Cle Elum Ranger District

Thorp Mountain is one of the preeminent summer hiking trails in the area, but winter recreationists often overlook the beautiful peak because it requires a long snowshoe slog along a road before jumping on the narrow trail to the summit. Still, snowshoers who don't mind making camp in the snowy forest will find Thorp Mountain Trail to be extraordinarily beautiful and serene.

The route climbs steeply at times, along both the road and the trail, but generally the snowshoeing is easy. Because the trail is in the bottom of the creek valley most of the way, there are few panoramic views; but looking upvalley, Thorp Mountain captivates snowshoers working their way toward it, and the creek valley itself provides plenty of pretty scenery.

To get there, from Seattle drive east on Interstate 90 over Snoqualmie Pass to exit 80, signed Roslyn. Turn north onto the Bullfrog Cutoff Road, and drive to its end at a junction with State Route 903. Turn left and continue north a little more than 14 miles, passing through the towns of Roslyn and Ronald, to reach the junction with French Cabin Creek Road on the left, just past the Cle Elum River Campground. Park near the start of French Cabin Creek Road in wide plowed turnouts.

Start snowshoeing up French Cabin Creek Road as it crosses the Cle Elum River and ambles 0.25 mile to the base of the valley wall. Then climb steeply up the ridge on the north side of French Cabin Creek. The road stays above the creek basin for 1.5 miles, switching back time and again. Take advantage of the open terrain, and cut straight up the slope rather than rambling around the looping turns. Near 2 miles, the summit of Red Mountain is seen to the north. This mountain will remain in view much of the next mile, and at 3.4 miles, the road crosses Thorp Creek and comes to a junction with the Thorp Creek Road.

Turn right onto Thorp Creek Road (3200 feet), and 1.5 miles up this road—5 miles from the start of the route—turn right to cross the creek and

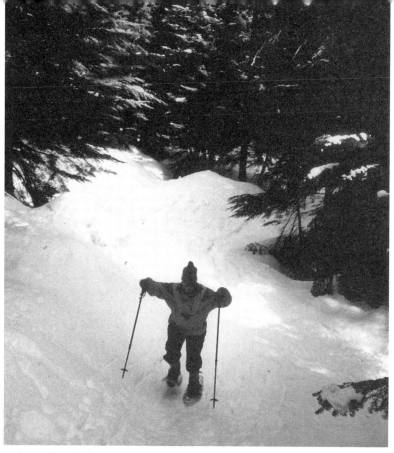

*Using poles to help ascend the Thorp Mountain trail*

pick up the start of the narrow Thorp Mountain Trail. Consider pitching camp near here, so you can make an early-morning start of the steep climb toward the summit of Thorp Mountain. If the avalanche danger is moderate or higher, this is the end of the trail, period. From this point on, there are some severe avalanche slopes.

The trail follows the north side of Thorp Creek upvalley for another mile, crossing through old pine forest, dense alder thickets, and the base of a major avalanche chute. At 6 miles, the trail is up against the head of the creek valley and the serious climbing begins. In the next 1.5 miles, the trail gains 1600 feet to reach the 5100-foot bench on the ridge below the summit of Thorp Mountain. The scramble to the true summit at 5854 feet requires winter mountaineering skills. Better to stop at the ridge crest (if that is even attained) and enjoy the vistas offered there. Red Mountain, No Name Ridge, and West Peak tower all around, while the Cle Elum Lake basin is nestled below to the east and Kachess Lake lies below to the west.

## --*64*--

# Salmon la Sac Creek

**Rating:** Most difficult
**Round trip:** 6.4 miles
**Hiking time:** 5 hours
**Elevation gain:** 1300 feet
**High point:** 4700 feet
**Best season:** Late December through March
**Map:** Green Trails: Kachess Lake No. 208
**Who to Contact:** Wenatchee National Forest, Cle Elum Ranger District

A number of good trails lead out of the Salmon la Sac area, but this is one of the few that is almost completely ignored by snowmobilers and skiers, leaving it for snowshoers to explore in quiet solitude. The trail rolls east, climbing gradually through pretty ponderosa pine and larch forest. The forest shelters the trail for most of its length, but there are enough openings in the canopy to provide some nice views of the Cle Elum River basin and the mountains beyond. Between those panoramic peeks, the sparkling little creek and snow-swaddled forest offer all the scenic diversion any snowshoer could want.

To get there, from Seattle drive east on Interstate 90 over Snoqualmie Pass to exit 80, signed Roslyn. Turn north onto the Bullfrog Cutoff Road, and drive to its end at a junction with State Route 903. Turn left, and continue north a little more than 17 miles, passing through the towns of Roslyn and Ronald, to the end of the plowed road at the Salmon la Sac Picnic Area and Sno-Park.

The trail leaves the Salmon la Sac area from behind the Cayuse Horse

*Pausing to enjoy the view*

Camp facilities. Follow the signs for Trail 1307. The path weaves through the trees, climbing gradually for the first 0.5 mile before finally traversing south to the Salmon la Sac Creek basin. The creek is a tiny rivulet that sparkles and splashes along its ice-laden banks, providing a pretty picture for winter recreationists.

The trail becomes steep, and for the next mile it climbs ruthlessly through a long series of switchbacks, staying high above the creek. At 1.6 miles, the trail levels somewhat and begins a long, climbing traverse into the creek basin, crossing the creek at 2.7 miles (4300 feet) and following it another 0.5

mile to a trail junction at 4700 feet. This is a good turnaround point. If you have plenty of energy and daylight left, follow the right fork for another mile to a bench below the summit of Jolly Mountain.

This trail climbs steeply toward its end, but a few avalanche chutes should keep you away any time the avalanche danger is moderate or higher. The left fork at the junction is steep and slide prone much of the time, so avoid it at all times.

## --65--

# Cooper River

**Rating:** More difficult
**Round trip:** 8 miles
**Hiking time:** 6 hours
**Elevation gain:** 400 feet
**High point:** 2900 feet
**Best season:** Late December through March
**Map:** Green Trails: Kachess Lake No. 208
**Who to Contact:** Wenatchee National Forest, Cle Elum Ranger District

Thank goodness the Salmon la Sac area has plenty of roads because they keep the snowmobilers off quiet trails like this one that parallels Cooper River upstream to Cooper Lake. This route is occasionally used by cross-country skiers, but more often than not, snowshoers will find they have the wide, pretty trail all to themselves.

*Stones and snow along the Cooper River*

The trail is relatively flat, and finding the route is not difficult, even in heavy snow years, because the trail corridor is wide and nearly straight. Snowshoers can enjoy their surroundings here as they stroll up the path, gazing in wonder at the beautiful snow-shrouded landscape. The forest is a mixed bag of old pine and fir, so it is generally open and light. Sun streaks in through the thin canopy to keep the valley bright and sunny. Deer are frequently seen in this valley, even in winter, and many small birds and animals can be seen along the trail as well. Kids and adults alike will enjoy studying and trying to identify the many animal tracks left in the snow beside the trail and along the riverbanks.

To get there, from Seattle drive east on Interstate 90 over Snoqualmie Pass to exit 80, signed Roslyn. Turn north onto the Bullfrog Cutoff Road, and drive to its end at a junction with State Route 903. Turn left and continue north a little more than 17 miles, passing through the towns of Roslyn and Ronald, to the end of the plowed road at the Salmon la Sac Picnic Area and Sno-Park.

Snowshoe up the road past the ranger station, and cross the river toward the Salmon la Sac Campground. The trail is well signed and easy to find. Stay right, and snowshoe up a small service road. The trailhead is located on this road, about 200 feet past the gated entrance to the campground. The trail stays alongside, but not too near, Cooper River for its entire length. If you have difficulty finding the trail—especially in the first 0.5 mile—just head northwest, keeping the river off to your left, but no more than 50 or 60 yards away.

The first 0.5 mile is in fairly open, airy forest, so the snow piles deep and obscures landmarks and trail tread. Beyond this section, the route is easy to find. The wide corridor skirts the bottom edge of the Polallie Ridge wall where it meets the Cooper River valley bottom. The views, while not amazing, are quite picturesque. In addition to the scenic river views, you can catch occasional glimpses up the valley of Polallie Ridge on the right and Chikamin Ridge straight ahead.

The valley narrows considerably after the first 0.5 mile, and at 1 mile, the trail is squeezed tight into a narrow gorge. The river quickens, and the trail climbs until, at 2 miles, it levels out and the valley opens up again. The walls stay close, but not nearly as confining as the section just passed. The last 1.5 miles of trail ramble gently and serenely to a junction with Forest Road 4616 along the banks of Cooper Lake. To see the lake, and enjoy a lunch spot with pretty views of the lake and the high ridges around it, turn right onto the road and hike up a few hundred yards to catch the Lake Shore Trail on the left. Drop down along this trail, and skirt the lake to any one of a dozen good viewpoints and picnic areas. Owhi Campground is just a 0.5 mile up the lakeshore if a larger lunch spot is needed.

## --66--
# Indian Creek

| | |
|---|---|
| **Rating:** | Easiest to more difficult |
| **Round trip:** | Up to 14 miles |
| **Hiking time:** | 2 to 10 hours |
| **Elevation gain:** | 1300 feet |
| **High point:** | 3600 feet |
| **Best season:** | Late December through March |
| **Map:** | Green Trails: Mount Stuart No. 209 |
| **Who to Contact:** | Wenatchee National Forest, Cle Elum Ranger District |

Many individual mountains in Washington are extremely beautiful, but no range of peaks is more spectacular than the long, jagged line of the Stuart

Range. Along this route, snowshoers will amble up the wide Teanaway Valley and gaze in awe at the impressive summits. The pretty Wenatchee Mountains, a lower, less spectacular range, provide a picturesque foreground for the more massive Stuarts behind.

Because of the wonderful views, not to mention the beautiful forest and river environments of the Teanaway Valley itself, this area gets a lot of winter visitors. Snowshoers will find the road well traveled by skiers and snowmobilers, as well as other snowshoers. The route described here lets snowshoers enjoy the views, while tolerating the crowds, before climbing a side valley that is much quieter and less visited. Indian Creek Road climbs the deep basin of the creek, but the road ends before the valley does. That, and the fact that the Stuart Range isn't visible from the valley, keeps most snowmobilers out of the basin, and skiers prefer the more scenic valleys farther up the Teanaway. Snowshoers might consider these other routes, too, but since skiers can travel faster on the flat Teanaway Road, they beat the 'shoers to the viewpoints. So Indian Creek valley is the snowshoers' best bet for a Teanaway trek.

To get there, from Seattle drive east on Interstate 90 over Snoqualmie Pass to exit 85 and turn north onto State Route 970. Drive 5 miles before turning left (northwest) onto Teanaway Road (Forest Road 9737). About 7 miles up the valley, when the road (and river) splits, stay right on the North Fork Teanaway Road and continue 2 miles to the end of the plowed road at the wide Lick Creek Sno-Park.

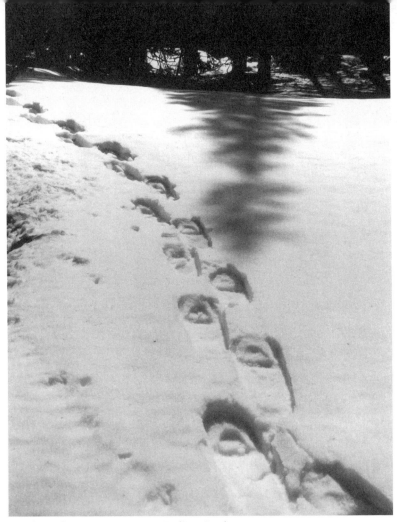

*Tracks in thin snow, Teanaway/Indian Creek route*

Start up the North Fork Teanaway Road as it curves northeast alongside the pretty Teanaway River. Stop to enjoy the meadows along the river bottom by stepping off the road now and again and ambling out across the open snow for close-up looks at the river. Or head off into the stands of trees that separate the many meadows, keeping a close eye out for small birds and animals that thrive in these protected woods.

The valley slowly hooks north, gradually revealing more and more of the snowcapped rocks of the high Stuart Range. The road crosses the river at about 1.5 miles, and at about the 2-mile mark, the road and the valley it climbs in are pointed due north. This is where Mount Stuart bursts onto the horizon. The western end of the staggeringly beautiful Stuart Range is anchored by this mountain—a high, near-vertical wall of rock and ice. In front of the great range lies the lesser but also beautiful Wenatchee Mountains. The peaks along this front are less dramatic—no vertical walls of granite here—but they are high enough, and craggy enough, to provide an outstanding foreground to the towering Stuarts in the background. Together, the two ranges create a perfect picture, so make sure to bring along a camera and plenty of film.

At 3 miles, just after crossing Indian Creek, find the Indian Creek Road angling off to the right. A gate across the bottom of the road—and the fact that the road dead-ends in a few miles—keeps snowmobilers out. Hike up the little-used road, crossing meadows, clearcuts, and deep forests for up to 4 more miles before turning back. A half mile up the valley, all views of the Stuarts are cut off, but Indian Creek is a pretty little stream, and the snowbound valley is a fun playground. Enjoy this route for its own sake rather than for rewards at its end, because on this route the rewards are found as you go.

## --67--
# Swauk Forest Discovery Trail

**Rating:** Easiest
**Round trip:** 2 to 5 miles
**Hiking time:** 2 to 5 hours
**Elevation gain:** 450 feet
**High point:** 4552 feet
**Best season:** December through late March
**Map:** Green Trails: Liberty No. 210
**Who to Contact:** Wenatchee National Forest, Cle Elum Ranger District
*See map on page 190.*

Snowmobilers, and skiers, and snowshoers, oh my!

No, Dorothy, you aren't in Kansas, you are in the wonderful world of winter recreation. The Blewett Pass area may be one of the finest snow recreation spots in the state, with trails set aside for motorized and nonmotorized recreation. The Sno-Parks are often used by all, but the snowshoers and skiers can find quiet solitude away from the motors even in this popular winter playground. What's more, you can find richly rewarding routes to explore whether you have just a few hours to roam, or a few days.

*Forest along Swauk Forest Discovery Trail*

The Swauk Forest Discovery Trail—popular in summer as a wonderful place to learn a little about our woodland ecosystems—provides a great easy day outing for snowshoers. The actual summer trail meanders for about 2 miles through the woods and meadows near the Blewett Pass summit, but snowshoers can take advantage of the heavy cushion of snow to cut corners and shorten the route or push beyond the trail's limits and extend their travels out into the adjacent Tronsen Meadow. Whether you slog a mile through the snow, or 5 miles, you'll find great winter wonderlands opening at your feet. A huge colony of snowshoe hares reside here, and where there are hares, there are also foxes, coyotes, and bobcats. Keep your eyes open for the cautious critters—if you don't see the beasts themselves, you're sure to spot their tracks.

To get there, from Seattle, drive east on Interstate 90 to Cle Elum. Take the second (eastern-most) exit, and continue northeast on State Route 970 about 12 miles to a junction with U.S. Highway 97. Continue north on US 97 (following signs to Wenatchee). At the crest of Blewett Pass, about 27 miles from I-90, turn right (south) into the Blewett Pass Sno-Park.

Strap on your snowshoes and start up the well-traveled snow track on the south side of the parking lot (this frequently groomed road is used by snowmobilers, skiers, and snowshoers). A short way up the road, veer right along a break in the trees and leave the groomed track behind. You'll climb gently now, heading almost due west away through the forest, picking a path of least resistance. If you stay on a nearly level contour along the slope—or better yet, maintain a slightly ascending route—in less than 0.5 mile from the groomed track you'll find yourself veering south once more as the hillside banks that way. Keep climbing, and you'll top a small knoll at 4552 feet. Modest views are found from this little hillock, including peeks south to the rocky monolith of Diamond Head.

Bear left now, heading east and in 0.5 mile or so you'll encounter the groomed road once more. Turn left on the road and descend (northbound). If you want to keep your outing short (2 miles), just trek on back to the trailhead along the road. If you want to push on a little farther, leave the road within a few hundred yards. Simply look for an opening on the right that looks promising and step off into the untracked snow. Heading east now, you'll find yourself slanting through stands of trees interspersed with broad meadows. Skiers and snowshoers frequent these meadows—the upper reaches of the Tronsen Meadow area—but snowmobiles are prohibited from leaving the main road routes.

Moving north, downhill, you'll penetrate deeper into the interconnected series of meadows, while traversing east will extend your trip and keep you up in the trees a little longer. While exploring the forested sections of the route, stay quiet and move slowly and you might see wildlife. At the very least, you'll likely see the endless tracks of snowshoe hares left as they scurry in search of forage in these snowy timberlands.

When tired or out of time, cut northwest and you'll close your loop. If you head too much to the north, you'll come out on US 97—no problem, just head back up the hill a little ways, then turn and parallel the highway back to the trailhead.

## --*68*--
# Diamond Head

| | |
|---:|:---|
| **Rating:** | More difficult |
| **Round trip:** | 5 miles |
| **Hiking time:** | 7 hours |
| **Elevation gain:** | 1800 feet |
| **High point:** | 5915 feet |
| **Best season:** | December through late March |
| **Map:** | Green Trails: Liberty No. 210 |
| **Who to Contact:** | Wenatchee National Forest, Cle Elum Ranger District |

No sand, no surf, no bikinis. Indeed, this Diamond Head is far from Waikiki. Nestled deep in Washington's winter wonderland, this rock is a mighty

monolith amidst the Wenatchee Mountains. The only thing it has in common with its Hawaiian namesake is a general abundance of sun. Diamond
Head, set on the eastern flank of the Cascades, offers a great chance to tromp
through the deep snows under a clear blue sky and sparkling sunshine. Look
for an array of wildlife—from snowshoe hares underfoot to soaring raptors
overhead—while enjoying this somewhat strenuous trek.

To get there, from Seattle, drive east on Interstate 90 to Cle Elum. Take
the second (eastern-most) exit, and continue northeast on State Route 970
about 12 miles to a junction with U.S. Highway 97. Continue north on US 97
(following signs to Wenatchee). At the crest of Blewett Pass, about 27 miles
from I-90, turn right (south) into the Blewett Pass Sno-Park.

From the Sno-Park, head south on the frequently groomed road (Forest
Road 9716) leading up into the trees. About 0.25 mile out, a small, poorly
marked skier/snowshoer trail leaves the road on the left (west)—snowmobilers
can and do use the road as an access route to farther-out snowmobiling trails.

The snowshoer trail parallels the road, staying well above it most of the
way, for about 1 mile, to the 4400-foot level. Then, with Diamond Head looming before you, veer left and angle southeast, climbing around the northern
flank of Diamond Head. A poorly blazed ski trail coming up out of the Tronsen
Meadow area is found near 4800 feet as you cross over onto the east side of
the mountain. Follow this trail, or if you can't find the blazes, just keep

*Diamond Head and Swauk Meadow*

moving south now, staying well above the creek that runs in a broad valley on the east side of Diamond Head.

As you climb to a low saddle—5500 feet—at the end of the creek valley, turn west and follow the ridgeline directly to the summit of Diamond Head. Awesome views await you there. Peering west over the Wenatchee Mountains and the long dark shadow of the Teanaway country, you'll see Mount Stuart looming on the horizon. To the south is Table Mountain and to the east is the long line of Tronsen Ridge. Retrace your steps when you are ready to return.

## --69--
## Haney Meadow Loop

Rating:  More difficult
Round trip:  7 to 12 miles
Hiking time:  8 hours to two days
Elevation gain:  1600 feet
High point:  5700 feet
Best season:  December through late March
Map:  Green Trails: Liberty No. 210
Who to Contact:  Wenatchee National Forest, Cle Elum Ranger District
*See map on page 190.*

When you want solitude and serenity without a lot of uphill effort, the Haney Meadow Loop is a great option. The route doesn't soar up onto high, wind-swept viewpoints, but it does roll through a plethora of open meadows, dark forests, and a few low ridges that sport modest views. What's more, you'll find a great diversity of plants and animals to examine and enjoy along the way, and you'll likely have all or part of the route to yourself. From a trailhead shared by snowmobilers, skiers, dogsledders, and snowshoers, you can venture out and in a couple hours be off by yourself exploring untracked snow.

To get there, from Seattle, drive east on Interstate 90 to Cle Elum. Take the second (eastern-most) exit, and continue northeast on State Route 970 about 12 miles to a junction with U.S. Highway 97. Continue north on US 97 (following signs to Wenatchee). At the crest of Blewett Pass, about 27 miles from I-90, turn right (south) into the Blewett Pass Sno-Park.

Begin as if you were heading to Diamond Head (Route 68). Walk up Forest Road 9716 as it leads south into the trees. About 0.25 mile out, climb left off the road to find a poorly marked, but generally well-traveled trail

*Group in Swauk Meadow*

paralleling the road for the next mile. At the 4400-feet level, veer left and angle southeast, climbing across the northern flank of Diamond Head to catch another poorly marked (look for white or orange reflective blazes nailed onto trees) skier trail at 4800 feet. If you miss the trail, just keep angling upward as you slide around to the east flank of Diamond, being sure to stay well up on the wall above the creek that runs in a broad valley on the east side of peak.

At about 2 miles, you'll emerge on the crest of a low saddle (5500 feet) between Diamond Head and an unnamed peak to the east. Here, turn east and skirt the unnamed hillock on its southern flank. As you move east, you'll slowly gain elevation, climbing a whopping 200 feet in the next mile before descending just as slowly back to 5500 feet at the edge of Haney Meadow. FR 9712 passes the meadow and snowmobilers occasionally venture out along this road (but not too often, since it's a dead end for them).

You can find wonderful campsites around the broad meadow. Rolling drifts create a pillowy texture on the expansive field of snow, and watching the golden rays of twilight dance on the shimmering white hills is a great way to end a day.

Whether you camp or not, when you leave the meadow you'll turn northwest and descend along the walls of a small creek valley. You can choose your own path, east or west. A summer hiking trail drops along the eastern wall, but the western side is less steep. In just over a mile, you'll find FR 7240 on the upper edge of Tronsen Meadow. Stick to a course that moves northwest along the edge of the hillside meadows before turning and angling west, parallel to US 97, to close the loop at the Sno-Park.

## --70--
# Wenatchee Crest

**Rating:** Easiest
**Round trip:** 6 miles
**Hiking time:** 5 hours
**Elevation gain:** 400 feet
**High point:** 4500 feet
**Best season:** December through late March
**Map:** Green Trails: Liberty No. 210
**Who to Contact:** Wenatchee National Forest, Cle Elum Ranger District
*See map on page 190.*

If you don't mind company, but prefer to have an easy-to-follow, modestly graded route to explore, this is it. It's perfect for families or for first-timers who just want to get a feel for their new snowshoes. The trail sticks to an old dirt road—groomed on a semiregular basis—that follows the crest of the Wenatchee Mountains from Blewett Pass Sno-Park to a point directly above the Pipe Creek Sno-Park.

To get there, from Seattle, drive east on Interstate 90 to Cle Elum. Take the second (eastern-most) exit, and continue northeast on State Route 970 about 12 miles to a junction with U.S. Highway 97. Continue north on US 97 (following signs to Wenatchee). At the crest of Blewett Pass, about 27 miles from I-90, turn left (north) into the North Blewett Pass Sno-Park. If this small parking area is full, cross the highway to the main Blewett Pass Sno-Park.

From the trailhead, find the start of Forest Road 800 on the north end of the parking lot and start walking. The trail sticks to this road for the next 3 miles to the road end. The road rolls up and down modestly, providing plenty of opportunity for novices to practice different snowshoeing techniques and build their skills. About 0.5 mile out, the road splits. Stay left (west) to follow

*Big ponderosa pine on Wenatchee Crest route*

the ridgeline. The right-hand road drops steeply into Scotty Creek basin. This is another area you can explore, but remember that every foot you drop down has to be regained in the long slog back up.

FR 800 hugs the crest of the ridge separating Scotty Creek basin from the Swauk Creek basin (home to US 97). You'll encounter occasional clearings with stellar views north and south. Looking north, you'll see Tronsen Ridge stretch before you, while to the south Diamond Head and Table Mountain rise above Blewett Pass.

The road ends at an open clearing about 3 miles from the trailhead. Enjoy the views here while having a picnic lunch, then return the way you came to close out the day.

-- *71* --

# Sun Top

|  |  |
|---|---|
| **Rating:** | More difficult |
| **Round trip:** | 10 miles |
| **Hiking time:** | 7.5 hours |
| **Elevation gain:** | 3000 feet |
| **High point:** | 5280 feet |
| **Best season:** | Early January through late February |
| **Map:** | Green Trails: Greenwater No. 238 |
| **Who to Contact:** | Mount Baker–Snoqualmie National Forest, Snoqualmie Ranger District, Enumclaw Office |

The route to the top of Sun Top is often groomed for cross-country skiers, but snowshoers will still enjoy this trek. After all, the views are just as spectacular, and the winter landscape just as pretty, even when the trail has been leveled for skiers. Just stick to the edges of the road to avoid tromping on skiers' tracks, and take advantage of any opportunity to climb off the road and cross open meadows for maximum snowshoeing fun.

Attaining the summit of Sun Top requires considerable energy, but the workout is well rewarded with unmatched views of the country northwest of Mount Rainier. The White River valley stretches below the mountain, and Mount Rainier towers above. The lower section of the route is sometimes visited by the White River elk herd, so keep an eye out for the big beasts. This is also prime cougar country (due, in large part, to the presence of the elk). Seeing one of the big cats is a pleasure. Cougars pose little threat to adult humans, although kids shouldn't be allowed to run ahead. The odds of seeing a mountain lion are extremely low, but a couple lucky snowshoers

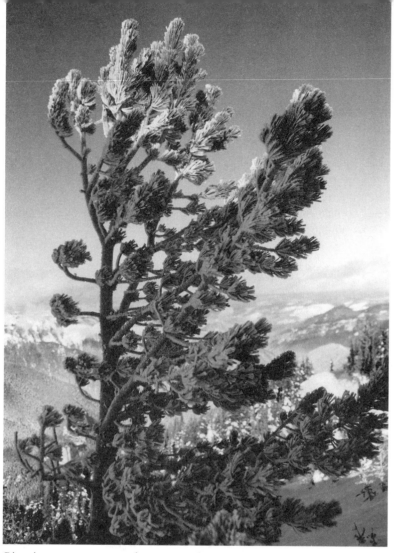

*Rime ice coats a tree near the summit of Sun Top*

have excitedly reported seeing the tawny cats streaking away from the road when the elk are nearby.

To get there, from Enumclaw drive east on State Route 410 for 24 miles and turn right (south) onto Forest Road 73 (Huckleberry Creek Road). Drive south 1.5 miles to the Sun Top Sno-Park.

The route to the summit follows FR 7315. Snowshoe up the only road leaving the Sno-Park, pass the gate, and in a couple hundred feet, turn left up FR 7315. The road climbs steadily to the summit, and because of the frequent clearcuts encountered along the hike there are ample opportunities to stop, rest, and savor the scenery spread out before you. As the trail climbs the ridgeline, look down into the wide White River valley and the narrower, darker Huckleberry Creek basin. The best place to find elk is along the lower clearcuts, although from the higher clearcuts it's possible to look down into the open meadows along the rivers. Using a good pair of binoculars, scan the river meadows for the large herds that live in the White River drainage.

A few spur roads are found along the way, and these make nice diversions from the well-traveled main road. Snowshoe out along them for a new view, and then angle up through the trees and meadows to rejoin the main trail. By climbing straight through the larger clearcuts rather than following the looping road, you can save nearly a mile and enjoy some untracked snow.

Following the road all the way, it is 5 miles to a high bench below the summit of Sun Top. The summit approach requires crossing some serious avalanche slopes, so attempt the top only when conditions are stable and avalanche dangers are reported as low. For the best views south to Rainier, angle southwest around the bench about 400 yards to an open view of Mount Rainier and all the lesser peaks between.

## --72--

# Bullion Basin

|  |  |
|---|---|
| **Rating:** | Backcountry |
| **Round trip:** | 4.5 miles |
| **Hiking time:** | 4 hours |
| **Elevation gain:** | 1500 feet |
| **High point:** | 5800 feet |
| **Best season:** | Early December through early March |
| **Map:** | Green Trails: Bumping Lake No. 271 |
| **Who to Contact:** | Mount Baker–Snoqualmie National Forest, Snoqualmie Ranger District, Enumclaw Office |

Snowshoers flock to this trail on winter weekends, but there is something unusual about a lot of the snowshoers here. Many of them have long planks strapped to their backs as they ascend the steep trail. These are cross-over 'shoers. They use their shoes to get them to the top of steep, deep slopes and then trade their snowshoes for snowboards and swoosh down the smooth slopes. Even nonboarding snowshoers will appreciate the artistry these backcountry snowboarders exhibit on their downhill runs.

*The view from Crystal Mountain Ski Area, Bullion Basin route*

But Bullion Basin has a lot more to offer than just the chance to watch some backcountry thrill seekers shred powder. This trail has high, subalpine meadows blanketed in deep snow, wonderful views of the surrounding craggy peaks, and an array of destination options to assure solitude for those who want it. The trail climbs steeply, and there are some serious avalanche slopes around the area, so snowshoers here need to be ready for a workout and must know how to recognize and avoid avalanche dangers. But when the conditions are stable, this is a wonderful winter world to explore and experience.

To get there, from Enumclaw drive east on State Route 410 to the end of the plowed highway and turn left onto Crystal Mountain Road (Forest Road 7190). Continue up this winding road to the Crystal Mountain Ski Area. Park in the upper parking lot if space is available. The ski area asks that backcountry travelers sign in with the ski patrol so they can account for any cars left in the lot after the lifts close down.

The route follows Trail 1156 east toward Blue Bell Pass. The trailhead is found to the east (left, as you face the ski slopes) side of the ski area parking lot behind the condominiums and buildings on the hillside. From the upper end of the parking lot, angle left up the steep slope, skirting the beginners' ski slope at the base of the valley wall. Snowshoeing along the tree line, find an old roadway and more skier cabins. A small ski lift on the right ends near the road—stay well to the left of it to the first switchback on the narrow road. The trail sign should be visible at this switchback in all but the heaviest snow years.

Trail 1156 climbs left along a traverse across the slope to 5000 feet, and then switches back a few times before settling in for a long climb up the small Bullion Creek draw. If the trail is drifted over and difficult to find, simply pick a route along the north side of the creek and, in just over 1.5 miles, traverse right to cross the creek (near 5600 feet). Hike through a thin stand of forest, climbing straight up the slope above to reach the open meadows of Bullion Basin at 5800 feet.

Plenty of variations are available on the approach route, but generally, evaluate the slopes and find a path as near to the actual route of the summer hiking trail as possible while steering clear of the steep slide-prone slopes. Lots of open country is found along the way, so views are spectacular all the way up. From Bullion Basin enjoy views of the ski area as well as of the snowboarders playing nearby. If you are the adventurous sort, choose to scramble another mile (gaining some 600 feet) up steep slopes to the ridge crest at Blue Bell Pass. However, Bullion Basin is so pretty and scenic, there is really no need to go any higher in your explorations. Scramble around the basin to find a nice, quiet picnic spot, enjoy a leisurely meal, and then head back down.

## --73--

# White River

|  |  |
|---|---|
| **Rating:** | Easiest |
| **Round trip:** | 2 to 4 miles |
| **Hiking time:** | 3 hours |
| **Elevation gain:** | 400 feet |
| **High point:** | 3200 feet |
| **Best season:** | Early December through February |
| **Map:** | Green Trails: Bumping Lake No. 271 |
| **Who to Contact:** | Mount Baker–Snoqualmie National Forest, Snoqualmie Ranger District, Enumclaw Office |

Bring the kids, even if the kids are too young to snowshoe themselves. On this easy route, you can pull them in a sled or carry them on your shoulders.

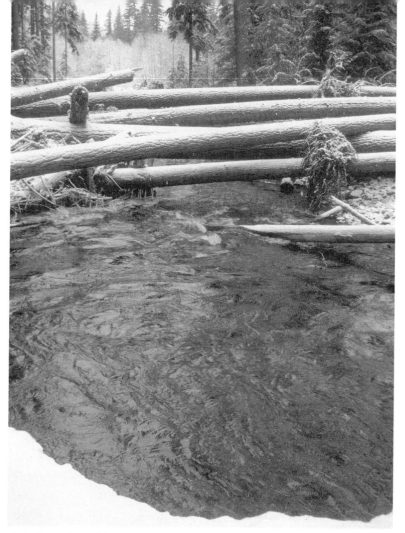

*Side channel of White River*

This is a route perfect for novices who want to practice walking on snow-shoes for the first time, or for anyone seeking a gentle, relaxing day in the snow without a lot of exertion or fuss.

To get there, from Enumclaw drive east on State Route 410 to the end of the plowed highway and turn left onto Crystal Mountain Road (Forest Road 7190). Immediately (about 20 yards) after turning onto Crystal Mountain Road, turn right into the Sno-Park. If the Sno-Park has not been plowed, turn around and return to the highway. Park well off the highway on the edge of the chain-up area adjacent to the highway.

From the Sno-Park, angle south through the trees and hop on the snow-covered expanse of State Route 410. You can follow the highway south into Mount Rainier National Park as far as you'd like, but you can also drop off the road and stomp through the snow along the rocky shores of the White River for a mile or so. Be sure you and your kids stay well clear of the river itself and be careful around side channels and creeks, since running water can hollow out holes under the snow—you don't want to crash through and land in an icy bath.

I recommend strolling south at least a mile to enjoy views across the river to a high wall of cliffs on the far bank. In summer, this is just another damp wall of rock, but come winter, it's a mosaic of rock and ice as the water oozing out of the rock freezes in long beards of ice. At about a mile, the river forces hikers back onto the road, making this a nice place to turn around—if you have slogged up the river bed, you can relax and return on the road. Or vice versa. If you want to continue, follow the road south another mile or so before turning back. Beyond that point, the scenery doesn't change much, but the road gets steeper.

## --74--
## Mowich Lake

**Rating:** Easiest
**Round trip:** 10 miles
**Hiking time:** 6 hours or 2 days
**Elevation gain:** 1400 feet
**High point:** 5000 feet
**Best season:** Early December through late March
**Map:** Green Trails: Mount Rainier West No. 269
**Who to Contact:** Mount Rainier National Park

Mowich Lake is the destination of choice for most folks who want to play on the northwest side of Mount Rainier National Park. The road is closed at the park boundary shortly after the first heavy snowfall, and the 5.5-mile trip to

*Mount Rainier from Mowich Lake Road*

the lakeshore is a favorite of skiers and snowshoers who want to enjoy the beauty of the park, without working too hard at their sports. The road is steep in places, but overall it is moderately sloped and wide enough for snowshoers and skiers to enjoy together.

Snowshoers will find themselves climbing through lush, old cedar forests—some truly massive trees are found in this area—and thinner stands of fir and hemlock before arriving at the lake with its views of Tolmie Peak, Paul Peak, and Mount Rainier. The lake has an array of excellent campsites, each well sheltered but with great views all around. The gentle road hike in makes this a good destination for novice winter campers as well as seasoned cold-weather fanatics.

To get there, from Enumclaw drive 5 miles west on State Route 410 to the small town of Buckley and, on the west end of town, turn left (south) onto SR 165. Continue for 10 miles through the communities of Carbonado and Wilkeson before crossing the one-lane bridge over the deep Fairfax Gorge on the Carbon River. Just beyond the bridge, turn right onto Mowich Lake Road (FR 79), a narrow road that climbs through a clearcut slope. Drive 11 miles to the national park boundary or to the snow line. Park along the road, leaving the roadway clear so that other vehicles can pass and turn around safely.

From the gate at the park boundary (3000 feet), hike up the road as it skirts around the flank of Martin Peak and climbs gradually up the Meadow Creek valley, passing the Paul Peak Trail (Route 75) at 1 mile. The thick tree cover is broken by an occasional small clearing, but dense, ancient forests dominate the first 2 miles of the route. At this point, the road rolls through the Mowich Meadows—small fields of snow nestled among the trees. The road curves right past the meadows and climbs steeply for a few hundred yards, rolling south through a sweeping curve. At 3 miles, rather than following the road down through a roundabout course, find a small trail on the left and climb steeply for 0.25 mile to rejoin the road at 4400 feet, thus trimming more than a half mile off the distance to the lake.

Instead of rejoining the wandering road at the junction, cross the road and start up another trail as it climbs steeply to the south, cutting across the neck of a long northerly loop in the road. A half mile up this trail, at 3.8 miles, cross the road once more and stay on the small forest trail as it continues to angle up the slope on a southern bearing. This 0.5-mile trail cuts nearly a mile off the road distance. Road hikers will sweep west with the road as it rounds a sharp switchback and returns.

Back on the road at mile 4.3, turn left and hike 0.5 mile to the east to find Mowich Lake. Once at the lakeshore, turn right and follow the road along the shoreline to a flat area at the end of the road. Tolmie Peak is visible to the north from here. To see Mount Rainier, hike 0.25 mile south to a viewpoint on the ridge above the lake. A small, level area for campers is nearby, with plenty of places for picnickers to plop down and enjoy lunch while gazing at the stony north face of the mighty mountain.

## --75--

## Paul Peak

**Rating:** Most difficult
**Round trip:** 5.6 miles
**Hiking time:** 6.5 hours
**Elevation gain:** 1800 feet
**High point:** 4800 feet
**Best season:** Early December through late March
**Map:** Green Trails: Mount Rainier West No. 269
**Who to Contact:** Mount Rainier National Park
*See map above.*

Although this trail is within Mount Rainier National Park, no views of the big mountain are visible along this route. In fact, there are no sweeping panoramic views at all. Plenty of beautiful local scenery surrounds this trail, though,

*Tracks of a snowshoe hare lead to a burrow under a cedar tree*

including a sparkling forest stream and lush old-growth forests that have stood here for eons. Quiet solitude is also a feature of this often-overlooked winter trail.

To get there, from Enumclaw drive 5 miles west on State Route 410 to the small town of Buckley and, on the west end of town, turn left (south) onto SR 165. Continue 10 miles through the communities of Carbonado and Wilkeson before crossing the one-lane bridge over the deep Fairfax Gorge on the Carbon River. Just beyond the bridge, turn right onto Mowich Lake Road (Forest Road 79), a narrow road that climbs through a clearcut slope. Drive 11 miles to the national park boundary or to the snow line. Park along the road, leaving the roadway clear so that other vehicles can pass and turn around safely.

Start hiking up the Mowich Lake Road as it gradually climbs through deep old-growth forest. In a mile, turn right onto the well-signed Paul Peak Trail and drop a couple hundred feet in the next 0.5 mile until the trail crosses the beautiful Meadow Creek at 3450 feet. The bridge over the creek is narrow and can be hazardous when snow covered. If footing is too insecure, it might be necessary to slip out of your snowshoes and, using trekking poles for balance, stomp a narrow track across the center of the bridge wearing just your boots.

The trail stays fairly level from the creek crossing, following the hillside south another 0.5 mile before curving east along the flank of Paul Peak. At 2.8 miles (3500 feet), the trail suddenly turns south again and drops into a long set of switchbacks. Rather than following the trail down, turn around here and return the way you came for a modest, quiet outing. For a more energetic trip, turn left and angle up the slope above the trail. Traversing northwest, climb the slope above the trail, and near the 4000-foot level, turn northeast and angle up a small ridgeline toward the forested summit of Paul Peak.

There are no views along the climb, but the forest is a wonderful example of mixed old growth, with cedar, Douglas fir, and hemlock and a few bigleaf maples tossed in for good measure. Camp-robber jays, ptarmigans, grouse, hares, red foxes, coyotes, and cougars patrol the area. Best of all, few other snowshoers or other recreationists intrude on a quiet communion with nature in this popular national park.

## --76--
# Copper Creek Hut

|  |  |
|---|---|
| **Rating:** | More difficult |
| **Round trip:** | 8.8 miles |
| **Hiking time:** | 5 hours or 2 days |
| **Elevation gain:** | 1000 feet |
| **High point:** | 4200 feet |
| **Best season:** | December through early April |
| **Map:** | USGS: Mount Wow |
| **Who to Contact:** | Mount Tahoma Trails Association |

The Mount Tahoma Trails Association system comprises a series of huts and yurts set in the well-roaded foothills just outside Mount Rainier National Park. In the summer months, these hills are a marred world of clearcuts and densely packed tree farms. But come winter, the heavy blankets of snow turn the clearcuts into expansive meadows, and the roads into meandering trails.

The north district of the trail system provides one of the easiest to reach and most scenic huts in the network. The Copper Creek Hut lacks the expansive views of some of the others, but it is an ideal destination for families and novice snowshoers looking for a comfortable winter camping experience. The hut sleeps twelve and offers a gas-fired kitchen and a large common room for lazing away the long dark evenings. Reservations are required.

To get there, drive east from Tacoma on State Route 7 to Elbe and turn left onto SR 706—the Road to Paradise—and continue east toward Ashford. Just past milepost 6, turn left (north) onto Forest Road 92. Drive up to 6 miles,

*Big snowdrift near Copper Creek Hut*

passing a white Mount Rainier Lions building in the first 0.5 mile, to the lower or upper Sno-Park—depending on the snow level—at the road's end. This route is described from the upper Sno-Park.

From the trailhead, the road climbs steeply for the first 50 feet, but then tapers off for a long, moderate ascent through the rich second-growth forests of the area. The trail slices through meadows, and forests and at 3.9 miles, turns right at a well-signed junction. Follow the signs for the Rainier Vista Trail. The next 0.5 mile slants upward, with the final 0.1 mile ascending ruthlessly to the hut. From the hut, you can look down on the Nisqually River valley and east to Mount Rainier.

--77--

# Busywild Overlook

**Rating:** Easiest
**Round trip:** 6.5 miles
**Hiking time:** 4 hours
**Elevation gain:** 900 feet
**High point:** 3500 feet
**Best season:** December through early March
**Map:** USGS: Mount Wow
**Who to Contact:** Mount Tahoma Trails Association
*See map above.*

This is a perfect route when the snows have been falling heavy and low down on the hills. In those situations, you'll be using the lower Sno-Park, giving

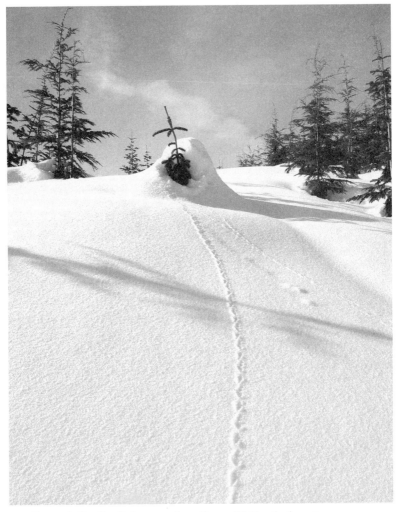

*Small snowball rolls off tiny tree along Busywild Overlook route*

you an extra mile of snow to enjoy. And enjoy it you will. This route provides an easy alternative for snowshoers who'd rather avoid the popular path to the Copper Creek Hut (Route 76). The trail climbs steadily but gradually, piercing rich second-growth forests full of wildlife and winter wonders. At the trail's end, you'll find views down into the green-gray valley of Busywild Creek. Beyond the creek stretch the long gray hills of the Rainier Timber Company's tree farms, and to the east lie the old-growth stands of the Glacier View Wilderness abutting Mount Rainier National Park.

To get there, drive east from Tacoma on State Route 7 to Elbe and turn left onto SR 706—the Road to Paradise—and continue east toward Ashford. Just past milepost 6, turn left (north) onto Forest Road 92. Drive up to 6 miles, passing a white Mount Rainier Lions building in the first 0.5 mile, to the lower or upper Sno-Park—depending on the snow level—at the road's end. This route is described from the lower Sno-Park.

Head north along the road. After 0.5 mile or so, the road curves sharply to the south and climbs a bit more steeply over the next mile. As you trek up the road, scan the undisturbed snow under the eaves of the forest adjacent to your path. Chances are good you'll be able to pick up the tracks of snowshoe hares, and maybe even the wily critters that hunt them—bobcats, red (and gray) foxes, and coyotes.

At about 3300 feet, the road grade levels out somewhat, still climbing but far more gently. A bit over 2.5 miles from the lower Sno-Park, the road forks. Straight ahead on the main path is the route to Copper Creek Hut. Turn left onto the faint trail climbing north. This road, the Overlook Trail, rolls nearly due north for about 0.75 mile to a broad open area above Busywild Creek. This is your turnaround point. But before heading back, stop and enjoy the views down into Busywild and north to Puyallup Ridge and beyond.

## --78--
# Snow Bowl Hut

**Rating:** More difficult
**Round trip:** 8.4 miles
**Hiking time:** 7 hours or 2 days
**Elevation gain:** 2000 feet
**High point:** 4400 feet
**Best season:** December through early April
**Map:** Green Trails: Randle No. 301
**Who to Contact:** Mount Tahoma Trails Association
*See map on page 214.*

The south district of the Mount Tahoma Trails Association (MTTA) network offers spectacular snow recreation, even though you're seldom above 4500 feet. Though the route is relatively low, you'll generally find good snow, and great views of impressive mountains and craggy peaks are to be had. From

*View of Snow Bowl Hut's "snow bowl"*

the ridge above Snow Bowl, you can stare north to Mount Rainier, while closer at hand, the dark wall of High Rock stands like a black monolith to the east. Griffin Mountain looms to the southeast.

Snow Bowl Hut sleeps eight, and sports a wide, view-rich deck complete with barbecue pit. Make the effort to pack a few extra provisions if you're planning to stay to take advantage of the hut's amenities. Reservations are required.

To get there, drive east from Tacoma on State Route 7 to Elbe and turn left onto SR 706—the Road to Paradise—and continue east to Ashford. At the edge of town, watch for the brown South District Access Road sign, and take the next right onto 1 Road. At the T intersection (2.8 miles from the highway), turn left at the brown sign pointing toward 1 Road. At mile 4, veer left at the fork. The first, lower Sno-Park is located at mile 6.4. If the snow line is higher, continue to the second, upper Sno-Park, staying left at 6.7 miles (following the signs to the Outer Loop Trail). The second Sno-Park is at mile 7.5.

From the lower Sno-Park, trek up the road to the second. From there, you'll continue on the road, climbing at a brisk pace. The road is wide and frequently groomed by MTTA volunteers, but it isn't easy. The road climbs a touch over 2000 feet in 3 miles. Take your time, and enjoy frequent breaks. Even if you aren't tired, stop for a break now and then if only to enjoy the increasingly nice views east toward High Rock.

At about 2.5 miles, the road forks. To the right is the High Hut ridge (and Route 79). Stay left and start climbing south. The road now pushes on to a more moderate final mile. You're now largely above tree level. Or rather, you are now in broad ridgetop meadows broken by periodic stands of forest. As a result, the winds are more active here and the road is often swept with deep drifts. Take your time crossing this final mile, since this is where the hard work of the lower 2.5 miles really pays off. As you near the hut, you'll find clear views north to Mount Rainier and south across the expanse of the Gifford Pinchot National Forest.

If there are skiers in your party, or sharing the hut with you, you can enjoy watching them carve up the pristine snow in the perfect slope of the snow bowl behind the hut. The skiers can shred 600 vertical feet of Cascade snow here, but snowshoers can get in on the act, too— just remember to bring a lightweight sled, and note that if you slide down, you'll have to hike back up.

## --79--

# High Hut

| | |
|---|---|
| **Rating:** | More difficult |
| **Round trip:** | 7.8 miles |
| **Hiking time:** | 7 hours or 2 days |
| **Elevation gain:** | 2400 feet |
| **High point:** | 4800 feet |
| **Best season:** | December through early April |
| **Map:** | Green Trails: Randle No. 301 |
| **Who to Contact:** | Mount Tahoma Trails Association |

High Hut is the jewel in the crown of the Mount Tahoma Trails Association. This ridgetop lodge offers an incredible winter getaway for snowshoers and skiers. With gas-powered lights and cooking stove, and a wonderful wood-fired heating stove, this hut is comfortable and cozy. But in addition to the getaway's amenities, High Hut is situated on the windswept ridge with un-matched views of Mount Rainier, High Rock, Griffin Mountain, and all of the Gifford Pinchot National Forest, offering a glorious retreat from the hectic business of modern life. Whether you are out just for the day, or are over-nighting, the hut is worth the considerable effort required to make the visit.

To get there, drive east from Tacoma on State Route 7 to Elbe and turn

*High Hut and Mount Rainier*

left onto SR 706—the Road to Paradise—and continue east to Ashford. At the edge of town, watch for the brown South District Access Road sign, and take the next right onto 1 Road. At the T intersection (2.8 miles from the highway), turn left at the brown sign pointing toward 1 Road. At mile 4, veer left at the fork. The first, lower Sno-Park is located at mile 6.4. If the snowline is higher, continue to the second, upper Sno-Park, staying left at 6.7 miles (following the signs to the Outer Loop Trail). The second Sno-Park is at mile 7.5.

From the lower Sno-Park, continue up the road, sharing the first 2.5 miles with the route to Snow Bowl (Route 78). But as the road climbs out of the broad valley and attains the ridge saddle (4000 feet) at 2.5 miles, bear right instead of left. This leads you northeast on a long slant to the ridge crest. The last 0.9 mile climbs 800 feet, leaving you winded and tired when you finally push over the last of the wind-scoured ridge to stomp onto the hut's broad deck.

If you have the energy after reaching the hut, you can explore the ridgeline as it drops northeast away from the hut, or head back to the west and tromp around the wind drifts and small tree stands along the ridge behind the hut.

## --80--
## Kautz Creek

**Rating:** More difficult
**Round trip:** Up to 11 miles
**Hiking time:** 7 hours
**Elevation gain:** 2800 feet
**High point:** 5300 feet
**Best season:** January through early March
**Maps:** Green Trails: Mount Rainier West No. 269, Randle No. 301
**Who to Contact:** Mount Rainier National Park
*See map on page 218.*

Kautz Creek offers not only an excellent snowshoe excursion but also a chance to experience the geologic history of Mount Rainier. The trail climbs along the route followed by mudflows, lahars, and floods that date back tens of thousands of years. Lest one think that is all ancient history, bear in mind that the last massive mudflow in this valley occurred in 1947 when some 50 million cubic yards of mud, water, and debris flashed through the valley, burying the Road to Paradise and killing most of the trees in the lower valley bottom. A forest of silver snags is what remains today. But the picture isn't all that bleak. Although the valley is routinely the scene of geologic destruction, the area is awash in beauty between those catastrophic events. This route follows the tumultuous creek, then climbs through ancient forests, and finally rolls through wide, open meadows with spectacular views.

To get there, drive east from Tacoma on State Route 7 and bear left onto SR 706 at the town of Elbe. Continue east through the Nisqually Entrance of Mount Rainier National Park, and proceed 3 miles farther to the parking area on the right just beyond the Kautz Creek Bridge. The trail begins on the north side of the road.

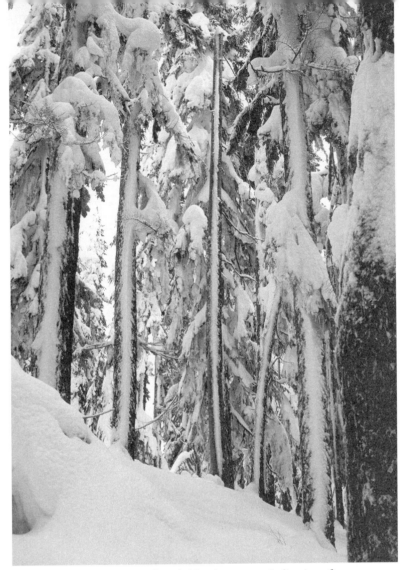

*Wet, sticky snow on the windward side of trees—an indication of avalanche danger*

The trail is wide and easy to follow. The early section may be thinly covered in snow some years, so you might have to begin the outing with your snowshoes attached to your pack instead of your feet. However, the trail climbs steadily, and the snow is generally deep enough to require snowshoes well before the footbridge is reached at the 1-mile mark. Check with a ranger before heading out in early spring to make sure this bridge is intact: spring floods sometimes wash it away. Exercise caution when crossing the bridge.

The snow accumulated on it tends to pile up at an angle, so the first person across should take his or her time and kick out good, solid footpads for those following. It may be necessary to remove your snowshoes to increase your stability when crossing.

Once over the creek, the trail begins to climb the valley wall, angling up through the forest between Tumtum Peak and Satulick Mountain. You can catch occasional peeks at these summits as you climb. The climb begins as a gradual straight-on pitch, and then turns into steep switchbacks. Around the 4000-foot level, the trail swings into a long hillside traverse around the head of a small creek valley (a tributary to Pyramid Creek), followed by another series of switchbacks.

At 4 miles from your car, the route enters the first long, broad meadow. Views south to the Kautz Valley and north to the glacier-covered flank of Mount Rainier are found here. This makes an excellent place to have lunch and turn around. If you prefer an extended adventure, carefully climb through the meadow and a tricky traverse through another clearing in the next mile before finding a long 0.5-mile traverse around the flank of Mount Ararat to reach the beginning of Indian Henry's Hunting Ground.

## --*81*--
# Eagle and Chutla Peaks Trail

Rating: Most difficult
Round trip: 7 miles
Hiking time: 6 hours
Elevation gain: 2900 feet
High point: 5600 feet
Best season: January through early March
Maps: Green Trails: Mount Rainier West No. 269, Randle No. 301
Who to Contact: Mount Rainier National Park

Climbing through mossy old-growth forest, this trail ascends the western flank of the Tatoosh Range. The trail is quiet and often overlooked by snow-shoers—it is often overlooked by summer hikers as well—but it offers an excellent opportunity to get out and enjoy the wonders of a winter woodland environment; not to mention a chance to interact with an array of wildlife, including the ever-present camp-robber jays (a.k.a. gray jays or whiskey jacks), red foxes, bobcats, and blacktail deer. A flash of white movement seen in the snowy forest could be a ptarmigan, a weasel, or a snowshoe hare, all of which trade in their brown summer coverings for white winter coats.

To get there, drive east from Tacoma on State Route 7 and bear left onto SR 706 at the town of Elbe. Continue east through the Nisqually Entrance of Mount Rainier National Park, and proceed to the Longmire Ranger Station and Lodge. Park in the plowed area behind the lodge.

The route begins with a hike up the service road behind the ranger station, passing the employee housing area and crossing the Nisqually River via a narrow one-lane bridge. Continue up the road 100 yards to the trailhead on the left. In low-snow years, you may not need your snowshoes for the first 0.5 mile or so; but even when the snow is relatively shallow, snowshoes and their sure-grip cleats and crampons can be helpful on the trail.

The route climbs through a couple of moderate switchbacks, each followed by long traverses across the hillside, before entering a series of increasingly short switchbacks in the shady forest. The trail is always climbing, but never too steeply. At 2 miles, the trail crosses a tiny creek—the stream it has followed up the hillside for the previous mile.

The forest around the trail is thick, and the trail rolls through an endless series of tree wells and snow mounds. These features form when a large opening in the forest canopy allows more snow to reach the ground, piling it deeper than that accumulated under the trees. The walking isn't overly difficult, but the constant up-and-down motion does make the going slow. But this is a trail to be savored and enjoyed, not rushed through. The broad canopy and forest of ancient trees is worth experiencing. Stop and listen to the birds. Smell the wet cedars. Feel the sun as it streams through openings in the canopy, and taste the water as it drips off the fir limbs and onto your face.

Near the 3.25-mile mark, the trail enters a sidehill meadow. This clearing provides good views of Eagle and Chutla Peaks ahead. If snow conditions allow it, continue up through this meadow to reach Eagle Saddle—between Eagle and Chutla Peaks—for vistas that sweep over Mount Rainier, Tumtum Peak, and Eagle and Chutla Peaks, as well as the rest of the Tatoosh Range. On very clear days, the top of Mount Adams may be seen peeking up on the southeastern horizon.

## --82--

# Rampart Ridge

| | |
|---|---|
| **Rating:** | More difficult |
| **Round trip:** | 4.5 miles |
| **Hiking time:** | 5 hours |
| **Elevation gain:** | 1200 feet |
| **High point:** | 4050 feet |
| **Best season:** | January through early March |
| **Map:** | Green Trails: Mount Rainier West No. 269 |
| **Who to Contact:** | Mount Rainier National Park |

*See map on page 218.*

This is a forest trek through ancient cedars and firs, with panoramic views of the wide Nisqually Valley and nearby peaks. There are also occasional glimpses of the snowy face of Mount Rainier, but the real beauty of this route is the wonderful local scenery. The deep old-growth forest is home to an assortment of birds and animals, including ravens, red foxes, and snowshoe hares. Because it is on the lower flanks of the mountain, this trail gets its snow later than the routes near Paradise. But once the big winter storms of January and February hit, Rampart Ridge is an excellent option, especially on those days when the Road to Paradise stays gated at Longmire well into late morning.

*The view to the southeast from Rampart Ridge*

The route is a loop trip that is best when hiked clockwise from Longmire Lodge, as there are gentler slopes to climb this way.

To get there, drive east from Tacoma on State Route 7 and bear left onto SR 706 at the town of Elbe. Continue east through the Nisqually Entrance of Mount Rainier National Park, and proceed to Longmire Ranger Station and Lodge. Park in the plowed area behind the lodge, and find the start of the trail in the meadows across the road.

The snowshoe hike begins on the well-marked Trail of the Shadows nature walk. Go left on this small loop trail, and in just a few hundred yards, bear left again, leaving the meadow and starting up a wide, well-signed trail (Rampart Ridge Trail) into the trees. Even under deep snow, the trail is easy to follow through the woods. Continue upward, weaving between the mammoth old trees as the trail goes from one wide switchback to another.

In 2 miles, you'll reach the crest of the ridge and open views to the west of Nisqually Valley and the cone-shaped Tumtum Peak. A short bit beyond, you'll pass the high point of the route, and look down over the cliffs that give the ridge its name—The Ramparts. From here it's a relatively flat mile of forest hiking, with occasional meadows and views of Rainier, before reaching a trail junction with the Wonderland Trail.

If you want a bit more adventure, and a few more clear looks at the mountain, go straight to continue along the upper reaches of Rampart Ridge. The trail leads another 2.5 miles to Van Trump Park, gaining another 1500 feet along the way. This extension would increase your round-trip mileage to nearly 10 miles.

To close the loop, go right at the junction with the Wonderland Trail and descend through a long series of switchbacks, slicing through thick forest along the way. The final 0.5 mile of the trail is pretty much a gentle straight shot back to the road, just above Longmire. Hike the last 100 yards west along the shoulder of the Road to Paradise to reach the Longmire Lodge area.

## --*83*--
# Wonderland Trail

|  |  |
|---|---|
| **Rating:** | Easiest |
| **Round trip:** | Up to 7.6 miles |
| **Hiking time:** | 5 hours |
| **Elevation gain:** | 1300 feet |
| **High point:** | 4100 feet |
| **Best season:** | December through early April |
| **Map:** | Green Trails: Mount Rainier West No. 269 |
| **Who to Contact:** | Mount Rainier National Park |

*See map on page 218.*

Snowshoe through some of the oldest, most beautiful ancient forest left in Washington's Cascades while enjoying views of the rolling, crashing waters of the milky Nisqually River. Families will appreciate the nearly flat, easy trek through the trees along the first half of the route, while those with an appetite for more adventure will enjoy the last half of the hike as it skirts the base of a steep slope, climbs steadily along the rushing river, and passes a pair of pretty waterfalls on its way to Paradise River Camp.

To get there, drive east from Tacoma on State Route 7 and bear left onto SR 706 at the town of Elbe. Continue east through the Nisqually Entrance of Mount Rainier National Park, and proceed to Longmire Ranger Station and Lodge. Park in the plowed area behind the lodge.

From the ranger station, hike east along the Wonderland Trail. (Find the trailhead to the left of the ranger station.) The trail is nestled alongside the Road to Paradise for the first 0.5 mile, and then is pinched tight between the road and the Nisqually River for a few hundred feet before the road angles left away from the river and trail. The forest around the trail is Douglas fir and cedar. An assortment of wildlife thrives in this rich forest environment, and the most visible member of the forest community is the fearless gray jay, a.k.a. camp-robber jay, a.k.a. whiskey jack. These birds act as if they are all starving as they flit from limb to limb in the trees around the trail whenever hikers are near. The brazen beggars will even go so far as to land on a raised arm, a shoulder, or a head if there is a chance of a quick bit of bread or granola.

*A clump of moss, insulated by a covering of snow, endures a cold winter*

The chittering, flittering chaps are harmless, and if you can resist their piteous begging, they will leave you alone. But be warned, feed one and all will want a bite.

At 0.75 mile, the trail skirts the line between forest and riparian environments, with the Nisqually River just a stone's throw away to the right. The trail stays fairly level alongside the river to the 2-mile mark, where it passes the picnic area of Cougar Rock Campground. This is the last time the trail approaches the road—the trail crosses the wide Nisqually on a stout bridge and climbs up the Paradise River valley while the road sticks to the Nisqually River valley.

Paradise River is a smaller, more scenic stream, and the trail sticks close to its banks, skirting the base of the steep slope of a narrow gorge for 0.5 mile. There is a danger of snow slides here, so avoid this trail section in times of high or moderate avalanche conditions. The gorge slowly opens up and, at 3.3 miles, passes Carter Falls and, at 3.6 miles, Madcap Falls. Both cascades are pretty plunges of the Paradise and are worthy of a photo and leisurely contemplation. Just above Madcap Falls is Paradise River Camp (a small backcountry campsite). Turn around here for a modest day's outing.

# --84--
# Reflection and Louise Lakes

**Rating:** More difficult
**Round trip:** 7 miles
**Hiking time:** 4 hours or 2 days
**Elevation gain:** 560 feet
**High point:** 5100 feet
**Best season:** December through early May
**Maps:** Green Trails: Mount Rainier East No. 270, Paradise No. 270S
**Who to Contact:** Mount Rainier National Park
*See map on page 226.*

This trail stays right along the edge of timber line, making it one of the most spectacular routes for snowshoers (and cross-country skiers) in Mount Rainier National Park. The trail provides a wonderful experience in a winter forest, the chance to visit a frozen alpine lake, and subalpine meadows in which to play and soak up the scenery.

To get there, drive east from Tacoma on State Route 7 and bear left onto SR 706 at the town of Elbe. Continue east through the Nisqually Entrance of the park, and proceed to the Narada Falls View Area parking lot, which is kept plowed each winter.

From the upper end of the parking area, go right along a plowed driveway, passing a warming hut and restrooms, as well as a long maintenance shed, to find the trail. If the snow is stable and not too deep, climb the steep, open slope directly ahead to reach the main trail. If conditions are icy, or the climb looks too steep, follow the orange blazes to the left through the trees as the trail parallels the bottom of the hill. Soon you'll begin angling uphill and will quickly top out on a wide, level trail—it is actually the Paradise–Stevens Canyon Road.

Turn right, and snowshoe along this road as it loops out around the flank of Inspiration Point. The road quickly bears to the left and enters a long corridor in the forest. The way has little elevation gain, but it can't be called level because the snow rolls through tree wells and snowdrifts.

This trail through the trees brings you right to the edge of Reflection Lakes at 1.5 miles—although don't count on seeing your reflection because the lakes stay frozen over until June. That doesn't mean, however, that the ice is safe. This is an active volcano, and all that geothermal power keeps warm

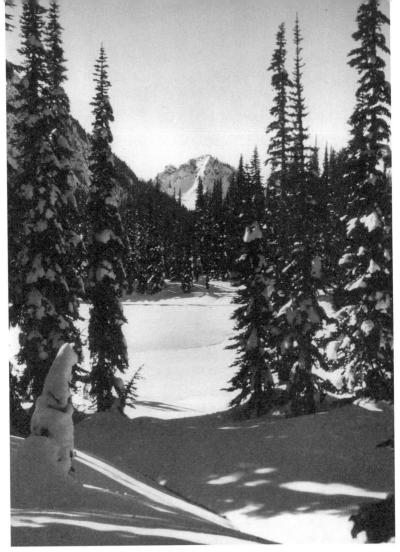

*The view east over Reflection Lakes*

springs bubbling around and in most of the lakes in the area. That, in turn, keeps the ice on the lake surface thin and dangerous. But do take some time and expend a little energy exploring this lake basin and enjoying the stunning views of Mount Rainier, as well as the jagged line of peaks in the Tatoosh Range to the south.

From Reflection Lakes, push on east along the road as it curves through a big southern bend and then drops nearly 300 feet in 1 mile to loop down to the shore of Louise Lake. If the snow is stable, drop off the road just as it enters that big bend and angle down the slope directly to the lakeshore.

A camp on the eastern edge of the lake offers great views of a climbing route up Mount Rainier—someone always seems to be making an attempt at the summit. You'll also find that a camp on the east slope above the lake gives you a fantastic surprise in the morning—a stunning sunrise as the towering peak of Mount Rainier starts to glow first and then the sunlight moves slowly downslope until the entire 14,411-foot peak is brightly lit.

## --85--
# Pinnacle Saddle

|  |  |
|---|---|
| **Rating:** | Most difficult |
| **Round trip:** | 6 miles |
| **Hiking time:** | 5 hours |
| **Elevation gain:** | 1400 feet |
| **High point:** | 6100 feet |
| **Best season:** | December through early May |
| **Maps:** | Green Trails: Mount Rainier East No. 270, Paradise No. 270S |
| **Who to Contact:** | Mount Rainier National Park |

Imagine a view that encompasses the three great volcanoes of southern Washington, with Oregon's Mount Hood and Mount Jefferson tossed in for good measure, and the jagged line of the Goat Rocks peaks capping off the panoramic splendor. That's exactly what's found at the end of this scenic, if somewhat strenuous, trek up the flank of the Tatoosh Range to a wide saddle between Pinnacle Peak and Denman Peak.

To get there, drive east from Tacoma on State Route 7 and bear left onto SR 706 at the town of Elbe. Continue east through the Nisqually Entrance of Mount Rainier National Park and proceed to the Narada Falls View Area parking lot, which is kept plowed each winter.

Proceed up the trail to Reflection Lakes (Route 84) at 1.5 miles, and from the southern shore of the larger lake, start a slow, steady climb up the steep meadows to the south. The route heads up a wide, open bowl near the lake's eastern end, providing the most gradual ascent and the least danger of avalanche. Near the top of the snowy meadow, the trail bears right near the tree line and traverses out around a small ridge crest. The snowshoe route lies roughly along the path of the Pinnacle Peak Trail from this point on.

At the end of the small ridge, bear left with the trail and climb along the crest of the ridge as it angles due south toward Pinnacle Peak. The ridge is thinning forest, so the snowshoeing is easy. Pick the path of least resistance through the pretty snow-laden trees, and keep climbing the moderately sloped ridge crest. Just 1 mile past Reflection Lakes, the route steepens significantly. To avoid the steep climb, angle left into an open snowfield. Although still pitched at an angle, this bowl is less steep than the route straight up Pinnacle Peak. Follow the open snowfield up to a high saddle with Pinnacle Peak on the right and The Castle to the left.

Fanatic peak baggers may be tempted to scramble to the summit of one or the other of these summits. But before succumbing to that temptation, bear in mind that well-honed winter climbing skills, and the necessary hardware, are required to make either summit (and the narrow summits are typically crowned with dangerous cornices). The views from this saddle are comparable to what's found at the top of either peak anyway.

Speaking of views, as soon as you reach the saddle, turn around and soak in the awesome sight of Mount Rainier looming to the north. The saddle looks out across the valley to easily seen Paradise and, higher on the mountain, Camp Muir. Walk to the southern edge of the saddle, and look out across the

*At the ridge crest, Pinnacle Saddle*

Gifford Pinchot National Forest to Mount Adams, the Goat Rocks, Mount St. Helens, Mount Hood, and on really clear days, Mount Jefferson on the far southern horizon.

## --*86*--
## Glacier Vista

| | |
|---:|:---|
| **Rating:** | Easiest |
| **Round trip:** | 3 miles |
| **Hiking time:** | 3 hours |
| **Elevation gain:** | 700 feet |
| **High point:** | 6300 feet |
| **Best season:** | December through early May |
| **Maps:** | Green Trails: Mount Rainier East No. 270, Paradise No. 270S |
| **Who to Contact:** | Mount Rainier National Park |
| | *See map on page 230.* |

Paradise. Close your eyes, and whisper the name. The image that pops into the minds of most folks will be white sand beaches and warm blue waters. But for some of us, Paradise is best served cold. Rather than white sand, we

*Digging a snow cave near Glacier Mountain*

see undulating drifts of cold white snow. Rather than warm blue waters, we see deep sapphire ice. Palm trees are replaced with dark green alpine firs. Paradise, to us, is the alpine landscape of Mount Rainier.

Snowshoers can experience this wintery wonderland at the aptly named Paradise meadows of Mount Rainier National Park. If you want an easy, family-friendly introduction to snowshoeing, there is no better route than the gentle climb through the sprawling meadows above Nisqually Glacier.

To get there, drive east from Tacoma on State Route 7 and bear left onto SR 706 at the town of Elbe. Continue east through the Nisqually Entrance of the park, and proceed up the plowed road to the Paradise Lodge parking area.

From the west end of the parking area, near the Climbers Hut, climb the groomed trail up through the tall snow bank surrounding the parking lot (depending on the snowfall, the snow bank can be upwards of 25 feet high). The trail passes the guide service building, and leads to the groomed sledding run the Park Service maintains in the lower meadows. Stay to the left of these runs, and slowly work your way uphill while drifting west. When you come to the tree line, turn north and follow the edge of the meadow uphill, working around the various drifts and dips that form when the wind whips the snow.

Continuing up the slope about 1 mile, you'll find frequent breaks in the trees on your left. These provide clear views down on the jagged, rock-strewn expanse of the Nisqually Glacier that fills the valley below. At a little more than 1 mile from the parking lot, you'll be in a broad open area known as Glacier Vista, with wonderful views of the whole Nisqually Valley, as well as up to the towering hulk of Mount Rainier. Behind you, the Tatoosh peaks line the southern horizon.

You can return the same way you came, but to vary things a bit, turn right and cross the upper meadow back down to Alta Vista. From the north end of this knoll, look east down into the Edith Creek basin. Then descend along the west side of the hill (the east side of Alta Vista is too steep and slide prone to be safely traversed) to return to the sledding runs and the parking lot.

## --87--
# Panorama Point

**Rating:** Most difficult
**Round trip:** 5 miles
**Hiking time:** 4 hours
**Elevation gain:** 1300 feet
**High point:** 6800 feet
**Best season:** December through early May
**Maps:** Green Trails: Mount Rainier East No. 270, Paradise No. 270S
**Who to Contact:** Mount Rainier National Park

The open snowfields, bowls, and meadows above Paradise draw snow lovers of all kinds, from skiers to snowboarders, but snowshoers have the edge on them all on the way up. Climbing the sometimes steep slopes is best done on a stout pair of snowshoes, and while the skiers and boarders may zip down faster than snowshoers, they blast past the awesome views that snowshoers can admire at their leisure as they slowly descend the mountain's flank. Countless opportunities for snowshoeing can be found in the open areas of Paradise, but heading up toward Panorama Point is the best of the bunch.

To get there, drive east from Tacoma on State Route 7 and bear left onto SR 706 at the town of Elbe. Continue east through the Nisqually Entrance of Mount Rainier National Park, and proceed up the plowed road to the Paradise Lodge parking area.

From the west edge of the parking lot, snowshoe up the steep meadow behind the guide service building, skirt around the left side of the groomed-snow play area, and hike north along the west side of the tree-covered crown of Alta Vista peak. The route rolls uphill through meadows and thin tree cover, with excellent views of the mountain when the weather is clear.

From the small saddle on the north side of Alta Vista, climb along the prominent ridge crest as it leads straight toward Mount Rainier. The route

GUIDE TO ROUTES
Route 86 ------
Route 87 ------

Pebble Creek

To Camp Muir

Panorama Point

Glacier Vista
6336 ft

Route 87

Nisqually Glacier

Edith Creek

Nisqually River

Alta Vista

Myrtle Falls

Route 86

Paradise Park

Paradise Lodge

Guide service

Ranger station

Paradise

N

0          0.25
MILE

Visitor center

parallels the massive finger of Nisqually Glacier, and at 1.5 miles, crosses a flat bench aptly named Glacier Vista. This is the best place to find a panoramic view of the sprawling glacier as it stretches from high on the flank of the mountain nearly to the Road to Paradise. If you are tired from the relentless climbing, turn back here knowing you have experienced some of the best

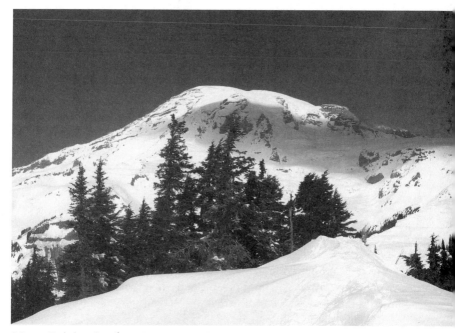

*Mount Rainier view from Panorama Point*

views of the route; or catch your breath while soaking in the scenery, and then continue up to Panorama Point.

From Glacier Vista, the route climbs steeply northeast through open hillside meadows (with a few thin stands of wind-savaged alpine trees) to another broad bench nearly 1 mile farther up the mountain. (The distance varies from 0.6 to 1 mile, depending on how steeply you climb.)

Panorama Point lives up to its name, with grand views of the mighty mountain, its lower flanks, and the serrated ridge line of the Tatoosh Range to the south. On clear, cold days, the rocky spires of the Goat Rocks Wilderness Area as well as the perfect cone of Mount Adams are visible to the southeast.

To return to Paradise, head east across the bench of Panorama Point and descend the wide open slopes of the upper Edith Creek basin. The basin is wide and you can pick your own path once you enter it, but use caution when making the first drop into the basin. For the safest route, hike southeast no less than 0.5 mile from Panorama Point to skirt out and around the steepest slopes, which are always heavily corniced. Once past the obvious cornices and steep drops, head down the slope along Edith Creek and follow it all the way down to Paradise, passing under Alta Vista and entering the upper Paradise Valley to approach the Paradise Lodge and parking area from the east.

## --*88*--

# Mazama Ridge

**Rating:** More difficult
**Round trip:** 6 miles
**Hiking time:** 5 hours
**Elevation gain:** 900 feet
**High point:** 5700 feet
**Best season:** December through early April
**Maps:** Green Trails: Mount Rainier East No. 270, Paradise No. 270S
**Who to Contact:** Mount Rainier National Park

This is a wonderful trail for snowshoers of all tastes. Like to 'shoe where there are great panoramic vistas of mountain peaks? No problem. Like trails with pretty local scenery? This one has some of the finest subalpine meadows and forests in the country, all blanketed in the deepest snow found in Washington. Want to watch other recreationists play? Snowboarders and telemark skiers love this trail, with its many open slopes on which they can practice their turns. Looking for a chance to see wildlife? In addition to the wide variety of avian life—from camp-robber and Stellar's jays to ravens and red-tailed hawks—snowshoe hares, red foxes, and a variety of small, scurrying beasts inhabit the forest fringes.

Snowshoers will also find that they are not bound by a specific trail on this route. Hiking up Mazama Ridge, they can amble off in any direction and pick their own paths through the deep snow of the meadows along the ridge crest. There is no finer place for snowshoers to enjoy the total freedom of movement that their 'shoes afford them.

To get there, drive east from Tacoma on State Route 7 and bear left onto SR 706 at the town of Elbe. Continue east through the Nisqually Entrance of Mount Rainier National Park, and proceed up the plowed road to the Paradise Lodge parking area.

From near the guide service and ranger station buildings, climb the slope above the parking area and head off to the right, staying above Paradise Lodge, to enter the broad open meadows of the upper Paradise Valley. Staying above the roadway, cross Edith Creek on a wide footbridge, just above the ice-cloaked waterfalls. From the bridge, head due east, traversing around the head of Paradise Valley to approach the steep wall of Mazama Ridge at about 0.7 mile.

Start up the ridge, angling right (south) while climbing steeply for 0.5

*View from Mazama Ridge*

mile to attain the ridge crest at 5700 feet. Cross to the eastern side of the crest for great views in that direction. Then turn right and follow the ridge south through thin stands of dwarf trees (their growth stunted by the howling winds that frequently scour this open ridge) and wide open meadows. Looking south, the multiple peaks of the Tatoosh Range—Pinnacle Peak, The Castle, Unicorn, Boundary Peak, and the rest—are visible as a jagged line against the sky. At the southern end of Mazama Ridge, near the 2.5-mile mark, look down onto Reflection and Louise Lakes and east along the deep cut of Stevens Canyon. To the north, Mount Rainier towers over it all.

To return, go north along the western edge of the ridge to meet the tracks you made along the eastern edge on your way in. Turn and follow those tracks back to Paradise.

## --*89*--

# Camp Muir

|  |  |
|---:|:---|
| **Rating:** | Most difficult |
| **Round trip:** | 10 miles |
| **Hiking time:** | 9 hours or 2 days |
| **Elevation gain:** | 4400 feet |
| **High point:** | 10,000 feet |
| **Best season:** | February through early May |
| **Maps:** | Green Trails: Mount Rainier East No. 270, Paradise No. 270S |
| **Who to Contact:** | Mount Rainier National Park |

Camp Muir, named for the legendary naturalist John Muir, is the gate to the summit of Mount Rainier. Virtually every climbing party that heads up from Paradise passes through Camp Muir. But you don't have to be summit bound to enjoy a trip to the camp. And you don't have to camp to visit the camp. The route to Camp Muir is long, strenuous, and very susceptible to poor weather. But it can also be incredibly beautiful, with views that can't be found anywhere else. When the skies are clear and the snow is firm, snowshoers can slog up the long, steep slopes, pausing whenever they need a breather and enjoy endless views south. Mount Adams can be seen beyond the Goat Rocks peaks. Mount St. Helens can be seen on the far side of the Tatoosh Range. Far to the south, Mount Hood stands, and beyond it, far down in central Oregon, Mount Jefferson can sometimes be seen on the hazy horizon.

*View from Camp Muir route*

This long climb is best done late in the winter or better yet, in the spring, when the days are longer so you'll have extra daylight hours to make the long plodding climb. The route should also be reserved for days when the weather forecast calls for clear, stable weather. The long, barren slopes all clad in white can be extremely confusing and dangerous when the clouds blow in. The trek here should be considered an alpine mountaineering experience rather than just a stroll in the snow.

To get there, drive east from Tacoma on State Route 7 and bear left onto SR 706 at the town of Elbe. Continue east through the Nisqually Entrance of Mount Rainier National Park, and proceed up the plowed road to the Paradise Lodge parking area.

From the western side of the parking area, start up through the meadows, following the route to Panorama Point (Route 87). Snowshoe up past the groomed sliding areas populated by families with inner tubes, and continue around the west side of Alta Vista, plodding up the long slope to Panorama Point. Here, you're nearly half way to the camp. Before heading onward and upward, stop and enjoy the views—look south to The Castle, Pinnacle Peak, and Denman Peak in the heart of the Tatoosh Range. You can also see the long, craggy line of the Goat Rocks peaks leading south to Mount Adams. To the southeast, look for the abbreviated top of Mount St. Helens.

From Panorama Point, your route continues north, climbing through the Pebble Creek valley (7200 feet) a bit more than 1 mile from the point. In the valley, you'll find some big drifts that need to be crossed. Be careful with these drifts—some can be 20 or more feet tall and corniced at the top.

Beyond Pebble Creek, you enter the Muir Snowfield and the long, straight shot over the final miles and the last 2800 feet of elevation. You'll see the knob of McClure Rock on your right just after crossing Pebble Creek, and as you approach 9000 feet, you'll see the iron-hard frame of Anvil Rock. The last 0.5 mile, covering nearly 900 feet of elevation, makes you work for that final goal of reaching Camp Muir.

At the camp, though, you can rest and relax. If you're staying, you can relax for as long as you like. (Check with the ranger before heading up the mountain if you want to stay at Camp Muir. You'll need an overnight permit.) If you're day tripping, don't relax too long—you have a long slog back down the slope before nightfall.

## --*90*--
# Silver Falls/Grove of the Patriarchs

**Rating:** More difficult
**Round trip:** 3 miles/5 miles
**Hiking time:** 2 hours/3.5 hours
**Elevation gain:** 200 feet/400 feet
**High point:** 2500 feet
**Best season:** January through early March
**Maps:** Green Trails: Mount Rainier East No. 270, Packwood No. 302
**Who to Contact:** Mount Rainier National Park
*See map on page 240.*

This is an excellent route for snowshoers looking for a quiet forest outing, without the need to struggle with a lot of climbing and routefinding. The trail is generally flat and wide, and it is low enough so that the snow doesn't obscure the trail. The trail is so easy to follow that snowshoers can spend their time enjoying the views around them rather than looking for the path through the trees. The route follows the gorgeous Ohanapecosh River upstream from Ohanapecosh Campground, slicing through lush old forests and passing the beautiful Silver Falls—made even more beautiful by the silver shards of ice that line the rocks around the cascade. The trail continues up the valley to a haunting stand of massive trees on a broad island in the middle of the Ohanapecosh River.

The Grove of the Patriarchs is a beautiful cathedral in summer months,

*Snow-lined creek near the Grove of the Patriarchs, Silver Falls route*

but when the forest floor is blanketed with a white quilt of snow, the enormous trees of the grove are made to seem even larger than they are. The stark contrast of the brilliant white snow and the dark, scaly tree trunks makes the immensity of the cedars, hemlocks, and firs almost incomprehensible.

To get there, from Packwood drive east on U.S. Highway 12 to its junction with State Route 123 and turn left (north). Drive to the Ohanapecosh Campground on the left. (At times, this is the end of the plowed road, although usually the road is plowed another 1.5 miles to the Stevens Canyon entrance of Mount Rainier National Park.) Park in the plowed lot at the campground.

Snowshoe down the road leading into the campground, and just before the road crosses the Ohanapecosh River, turn into the northern loop of campsites. The trail begins at the northernmost end of this loop, just before the loop turns east away from the river.

Start up the trail as it climbs gradually to a bench above the river and rolls north through thin forests between the river and the road. The trail is wide and offers plenty of views of the river while staying well clear of the roadway (which is frequently used by skiers and occasionally by snowmobilers). This trail is generally unused except by other snowshoers, so there is plenty of solitude and quiet time along the way.

The trail crosses the river at 1.5 miles on a wide, rustic bridge with pretty views up the river to the crashing waters of Silver Falls. The bridge is usually slick, but with handrails on both sides, the crossing is easy and the wide deck is spacious enough for you to pause and enjoy the views.

For a closer look at the falls, continue across the bridge and turn right on the trail on the far bank to climb upstream alongside the falls. After snapping a few pictures and admiring the cascade, either turn back and return to Ohanapecosh Campground or continue upstream for another 0.5 mile to Stevens Canyon Road. (Stay right at the junction a few hundred yards above the falls; the left fork leads to Route 91, Olallie Creek.)

Cross the wide road near the tollbooths, and head up the wide, well-signed trail to the Grove of the Patriarchs. The trail skirts along the west bank of the river and, in 0.5 mile (mile 2.5), crosses the river on a narrow suspension bridge. This bridge is usually very slick, so cross with extreme care, making full use of both handrails, and enter the cathedral-like stand of ancient trees that is the Grove of the Patriarchs. After enjoying the scenic splendor of the forest, return the way you came, or follow the Stevens Canyon Road and SR 123 south to Ohanapecosh Campground for a quicker return.

## --91--
# Olallie Creek

**Rating:** Most difficult
**Round trip:** 6.8 miles
**Hiking time:** 7 hours or 2 days
**Elevation gain:** 1800 feet
**High point:** 3800 feet
**Best season:** January through early March
**Maps:** Green Trails: Mount Rainier East No. 270, Packwood No. 302
**Who to Contact:** Mount Rainier National Park

Often overlooked, this trail is overflowing with opportunities for snowshoers looking for solitude along a quiet forest path. The huge, old trees, abundant wildlife, and remarkable sylvan environment of this area, coupled with a general dearth of winter visitors, means this trail is an ideal retreat from the busy schedules of modern life. There are no sweeping panoramas, no drop-dead gorgeous views of peaks, valleys, or rivers. But there are endless small graces along the route—snow-draped ferns, ice-adorned lichens, cathedral-like stands of cedar and fir, tracks of birds and animals to identify, and usually plenty of the birds and animals who laid the tracks.

The trail can be enjoyed as a simple, unhurried day hike or as a multiday snowshoe trek, with many options for an ultimate destination, including a

To Indian
Bar Camp

Olallie
Creek CG  Olallie Creek

Wonderland
Trail

Route
91

Cedar Flats

Grove of the
Patriarchs

Cowlitz Divide

Silver
Falls

Stevens
Canyon
Entrance

Laughingwater
Creek

Route
90

Stevens Canyon Road

Ohanapecosh River

0       1
MILE

N

Ohanapecosh
CG

123

high ridge route that does offer incredible views and picturesque panoramas. But the real beauty of this trail is the quiet forest, and that can be enjoyed by hiking as little as the first mile of the route.

To get there, from Packwood drive east on U.S. Highway 12 to its junction with State Route 123 and turn left (north). Drive to the end of the plowed road at the junction with the Stevens Canyon Entrance to Mount Rainier National Park. Occasionally, the road is plowed only as far as the Ohanapecosh Campground. If that is the case, park in the lot at the campground and snowshoe 1.5 miles along the roadway to the entrance.

Just west of the tollbooths at the Stevens Canyon Entrance, turn left and enter the forest on a wide trail, signed Silver Falls Trail, and hike southwest 0.25 mile to a junction with a trail on the right. Turn right onto this path, signed Olallie Creek, and hike through the forest a few hundred yards, cross the wide Stevens Canyon Road, and reenter the forest on the north side of the road. The trail climbs steadily but not too steeply for the next 2.5 miles, traversing a lush old-growth forest as it ascends the slopes. At 1.7 miles, the trail crosses a small creek and, at 2 miles, climbs a short series of switchbacks before turning west and traversing the slope above Olallie Creek.

The trail levels out near mile 3 and tapers toward the creek in the valley bottom. Near mile 3.4, the trail crosses the stream at Olallie Creek Campground. Enjoy a quiet lunch in this serene forest camp, and then retrace your steps. If you are looking for more adventure, continue up the trail as it ascends the Olallie Creek valley and ends at a junction with the Wonderland Trail at the crest of the Cowlitz Divide. Head north on the Wonderland, and climb a steep ridge to Indian Bar Camp (9.7 miles from the trailhead), with its stunning views of the mountain and all the peaks to the south.

*Along the Olallie Creek route*

## --92--

# Packwood Lake

**Rating:** Most difficult
**Round trip:** 9 miles
**Hiking time:** 7 hours or 2 days
**Elevation gain:** 500 feet
**High point:** 3200 feet
**Best season:** Late January through early March
**Map:** Green Trails: Packwood No. 302
**Who to Contact:** Gifford Pinchot National Forest, Cowlitz Valley Ranger District

This lake is a popular summer destination for family campers, and it is even more impressive when visited in winter. The large lake is just outside the border of the Goat Rocks Wilderness Area, and an old service road slices through the forest alongside a water pipeline all the way to the dam at the lower end of the lake. The hike from the road end to the lake weaves through thick, old forest, and views are limited. But the local scenery makes up for the lack of distant sights.

This road provides easy early-winter access to skiers and snowmobilers. After a few snowstorms, the road is made impassable by avalanches, and snowshoers will find the trail through the young forest silent and seemingly made with them in mind. The trail, though, is in avalanche country too, so snowshoers must know the current avalanche conditions and should avoid this trail when the danger is any higher than moderate.

To get there, from Seattle drive south on Interstate 5 to U.S. Highway 12. Continue east on US 12 to Packwood. Turn right at the Packwood Ranger Station, and continue 6 miles on the Packwood Lake Road to the trailhead. Park at the snow line if you can't get to the official trailhead and start walking from there.

Whether you walk or drive to the official trailhead, you'll want to spend a few minutes there. The view is remarkable because a big, open window in the trees perfectly frames that big snow cone to the north, Mount Rainier.

Upon leaving the trailhead, the trail is fairly wide and easy to follow. It dips immediately into the sparse old forest and enters a shadowy world of green, gray, and white. The trail meanders up and down, gradually gaining elevation over the first 4 miles only to drop more than 200 feet in the last 0.5 mile before rolling out along the lakeshore. In periods of unusually heavy snow, the 4 miles of trail may be stretched by an additional 2 or 3 miles of road walking. But that extra mileage just makes for a more rewarding payoff at camp at day's end.

The snow underfoot is bright against the dull gray fir and cedar tree trunks, while overhead, waxy green boughs and droopy beards of green lichen provide color to this cold sylvan world. But the best of the scenery is not the stationary stuff around you; it's the small gray streaks that flit from tree to tree. These feathery bundles of energy go by many names—whiskey jacks, gray jays, or camp-robbers—but regardless of what you call them, you will enjoy their company.

The south shore of the lake is the safest haven for camp because it is gently graded and well forested, which minimizes the threat of snowslides. It also offers the best views. Plenty of sheltered areas for camps are scattered along the length of the lake, but smart campers will pitch their tents at the far end of the lake so they can enjoy the fiery sunsets that illuminate Mount Rainier to the north. If weather clouds the horizon, though, the views to the south are nearly as stunning—the 7487-foot Johnson Peak looms large at the head of the Packwood Creek valley.

A word of warning: amidst all this beauty, danger lurks close by. The snowy mantle covering the lake looks stable and strong, but this is a big body of water at the relatively low elevation of 2900 feet, so the ice is almost always too thin to bear the weight of heavy bodies tramping across it. Stay off the lake. If you don't, you'll likely end up in the lake, and in winter that means hypothermia.

## --93--

# Sand Lake

|  |  |
|---:|:---|
| Rating: | More difficult |
| Round trip: | 6.6 miles |
| Hiking time: | 5 hours or 2 days |
| Elevation gain: | 900 feet |
| High point: | 5300 feet |
| Best season: | Late December through early March |
| Map: | Green Trails: White Pass No. 303 |
| Who to Contact: | Gifford Pinchot National Forest, Cowlitz Valley Ranger District |

Skirting beautiful high alpine meadows, the Pacific Crest Trail (PCT) rolls north from White Pass on a gentle climb, providing snowshoers with a wonderful opportunity to enjoy the high country of the Cascades in winter without a long slog up a wide logging road. This trail dips into thick old stands of forest, but it is the open meadows, long ridges, and high peaks that make this a special trail. Pass by large circular plains of snow (frozen lakes) and rolling dunes of drifted snow. This trail offers an immersion into the dreamlands of mountain country in winter. Snowshoers of all abilities will find enjoyment here, as the terrain is open and gentle. They can hike as much, or as little, as they desire.

To get there, from Packwood drive east on U.S. Highway 12 to the summit of White Pass. Park on the north (left) side of the highway in the large overnight parking area near the White Pass Ski Area (just west of the large hotel).

*Mount Adams from the Sand Lake route*

The PCT actually crosses US 12 to the east of the ski area, but you can catch it by skirting Leech Lake—which abuts the parking area—on its south shore, staying well to the side of the groomed ski tracks. Follow the curve of the lakeshore to the north for 0.5 mile, and just like that, jump on the PCT.

The trail climbs gently through a thick stand of fir and then open meadow for 1.4 miles to a small creek basin. Stay left here (a trail also leads off to the right, cruising down the creek valley through open forest to Dog Lake in 1.5 miles), and traverse a large meadow at the head of the creek valley, passing the nearly round Deer Lake basin at 2.7 miles. At the lake, the trail turns north once more and rolls gently uphill through meadows broken occasion-

ally by thin stands of wind-gnarled trees. The trail is obliterated by snow in this open country, but the route stays along the broad crest of a shallow ridge as it leads due north.

At 3.3 miles, find Sand Lake on the right (east) side of the ridge. The lake is often obscured because the gentle slope of the banks and the surrounding open country allow the snow to drift in and cover it. So look for an oblong flat surface just below the ridgeline at 5300 feet. This is the place to turn around, unless you plan on pitching camp out in the winter wilderness. For extended exploring, hike on up the trail as it rolls north, pushing through more meadows, forests, and past small alpine lakes.

The Sand Lake basin and the small ridge above it offer nice views of the surrounding peaks, including Cramer Mountain to the north, Spiral Butte to the east, and Round Mountain to the southeast. It's sometimes possible to see the summit of Mount Adams protruding on the southern horizon, too.

## -- 94 --

# Cramer Lake

|  |  |
|---|---|
| **Rating:** | Most difficult |
| **Round trip:** | 9 miles |
| **Hiking time:** | 7 hours |
| **Elevation gain:** | 800 feet |
| **High point:** | 5000 feet |
| **Best season:** | Late December through early March |
| **Map:** | Green Trails: White Pass No. 303 |
| **Who to Contact:** | Wenatchee National Forest, Naches Ranger District |

This route offers terrain and scenery similar to that found along the Pacific Crest Trail on Route 93 to Sand Lake. But far fewer people visit the Cramer Lake Trail, so snowshoers can add solitude to the list of wonders they'll encounter along the route. Starting at the shore of a wide lake basin, this route has views of pretty peaks, meandering creeks—sometimes in old-growth forest settings, sometimes weaving gracefully through open meadows—and long, panoramic views of the South Cascade summits and deep canyons of the eastern foothills.

Although this is a backcountry trail, the route is generally easy to follow with some moderate climbing, so most snowshoers with a solid hiking background will enjoy the workout and the rewards found here.

To get there, from Packwood drive east on U.S. Highway 12 to the summit of White Pass. Continue east 1.5 miles to Dog Lake Campground. Generally a wide pullout is cleared at both the west end of the lake (near the campground) and at the east end (near the highway bridge over the lake's outlet stream). Park in whichever area is available.

From the highway, snowshoe west along the southern edge of the lake and pick up the trail at the north side of Dog Lake Campground. The trail traverses the slope away from the lake, staying above the small feeder stream that pours in from the north. A mile up the trail, cross the creek in a thin stand of trees and begin a moderately steep climb northeast along the slope.

The forest gives way frequently to large, open meadows, and the round top of Spiral Butte dominates the view to the east. At 4800 feet, about 2 miles from the trailhead, the trail turns left and heads straight north across open meadows and thin forest. The trail here is fairly flat and straight, leading to the shores of Cramer Lake at 4.5 miles.

For a variation on the return, start back on the same trail, but just 1 mile south of the lake, veer south-east toward Spiral Butte. Cross a small creek basin, and traverse the flank of the butte at about 4900 feet. A long line of open meadows, separated by thin strands of forest, cover the side of the mountain, and you can work your way down to the 4300-foot level as you continue south around the mountain.

When the Dog Lake basin is in view, drop down into the thin forest at the north end of the lake and cross the flat meadow to get back to the western side of the lake for the final 0.25-mile snowshoe back to the trailhead. Avoid the eastern shore of the lake unless snow conditions are very stable because the lake butts up against a steep avalanche chute.

*On the way to Cramer Lake*

## --95--

# Tieton River Meadows

**Rating:** Easiest
**Round trip:** Up to 10 miles
**Hiking time:** 8 hours
**Elevation gain:** 350 feet
**High point:** 3500 feet
**Best season:** Late December through early March
**Map:** Green Trails: White Pass No. 303
**Who to Contact:** Wenatchee National Forest, Naches Ranger District

Is there anything more serene than snow-flocked pine trees? This route ambles gently up the wide Tieton River valley, rolling through broad meadows and through sun-streaked forests. Elk can often be found browsing amongst the trees, and even if the majestic big beasts are absent, you'll likely encounter lesser critters. Pine martens scurry through the snow, as do weasels, snow-shoe hares, bobcats, cougars, coyotes, foxes, and an array of birds.

To get there, from Packwood drive east on U.S. Highway 12 to the summit

*Parka along the Tieton River trail*

of White Pass. Continue east 7.5 miles to the Clear Lake Road (Forest Road 1200). Turn right and drive 3 miles to the Tieton River Sno-Park at the junction with FR 1207.

Hike up the road as it slides gradually up the Tieton River valley. On either side of you are towering valley walls that at times show vertical rock faces, while at other times they are lined with lush pine forests. The route crosses Hell Creek at about 1 mile, and moves along the base of the north valley wall. Here, the boundary of the Goat Rocks Wilderness is just a snowball's throw away to the right. As you continue up the road, you can enjoy wonderful views of Old Snowy Mountain, which stands like a sentinel at the head of the valley.

At 2.8 miles, the road crosses Miriam Creek, and edges back toward the middle of the valley for the final run to the road's end at 5 miles, at the edge of the wilderness (the road corridor is a 5-mile long peninsula of unprotected land jutting into the wilderness).

Beyond the road end, summer hiking trails continue up the valley, one eventually leading to the very summit of Old Snowy Mountain. But this trail is steep and difficult to follow come winter. Leave that for warm summer days. Instead, stick to the valley road, and if you need further adventures, bust out into the various meadows and clearings along the way to explore those wildlife refuges.

# --*96*--
# Goat Peak

**Rating:** Backcountry
**Round trip:** 5.6 miles
**Hiking time:** 5 hours
**Elevation gain:** 2600 feet
**High point:** 5900 feet
**Best season:** Late December through early March
**Map:** Green Trails: Bumping Lake No. 271
**Who to Contact:** Wenatchee National Forest, Naches Ranger District

This is a winter scramble up a ruthlessly steep trail, but the views and the scenery along the way are unmatched. The route climbs quickly up a steep ridgeline on a narrow hiking trail, and snowshoers won't find much to look for in the first mile as they struggle up the slope. Although the trail may be demanding, it is a route used only by snowshoers. So many of the other trails in this area are dominated by cross-country skiers and snowmobilers that snowshoers will welcome the workout, knowing that they don't have to share the trail with noisy speedsters.

Snowshoers who enjoy wildlife may want to stroll around the meadows in the valley bottom near the Sno-Park before starting up the trail. A large herd of elk roams this valley, and there is always the possibility that they will be browsing near the Hells Crossing area, so give a look for them before starting the climb.

To get there, from Yakima drive west on U.S. Highway 12 to its junction with State Route 410. Turn right (northwest) onto SR 410 and drive 34 miles to the Hells Crossing Sno-Park on the left (south), just opposite the Hells Crossing Campground (closed).

The trail climbs south from the Sno-Park, heading up the east side of a small draw. The route isn't too steep for the first 0.5 mile, and after that it makes a long traverse east around the flank of

*View over the Cascade foothills, Goat Peak route*

the hill to the ridge crest. At 1 mile, the trail turns vertical as it ascends the steep ridge crest, heading south toward the towering summit of Goat Peak. The route is exposed at times, and there are some tricky pitches, especially near 1.2 miles and again at 1.8 to 2 miles. Treeless sections are occasionally scoured by wind.

The trail dips down onto the eastern side of the ridge at 2.5 miles, and the last 0.25 mile is a gentle traverse to the top of American Ridge just before the Goat Peak summit. It is possible to climb to the top of the peak, but the approach on the American Ridge Trail is exposed and heavily corniced at times. It is better to just enjoy the stunning views from the ridge crest at the top of the trail and leave the summiting for a summertime outing.

From the top of American Ridge, the views are outstanding. To the east is the long, open country of the eastern foothills of the Cascades. To the north is Fifes Ridge and 6375-foot Fife Peak. To the south is the expansive William O. Douglas Wilderness and, beyond, the perfect cone of Mount Adams.

## --97--

# Mount St. Helens Summit

|  |  |
|---|---|
| **Rating:** | Backcountry |
| **Round trip:** | 8 miles |
| **Hiking time:** | 9 hours |
| **Elevation gain:** | 5700 feet |
| **High point:** | 8365 feet |
| **Best season:** | Late December through early February |
| **Map:** | Green Trails: Mount St. Helens Northwest No. 364S |
| **Who to Contact:** | Mount St. Helens National Volcanic Monument |

On this climb up Mount St. Helens, snowshoers can simply walk straight up the deep snow piled on the flank of the big volcano, taking a direct approach to the rim of the massive crater. Along the way, they can enjoy sweeping views out over the southern reaches of Washington's Cascades.

Once at the summit, snowshoers can peer cautiously over the edge of the crater rim to see the steaming lava dome building in the crater and look out over the miles of destruction wrought by the May 18, 1980, blast. Snowshoers have an advantage over summer climbers in that permits are not needed for midwinter ascents. From May 15 to October 31 every year, anyone attempting the summit must have one of the limited number of climbing permits (only forty are issued each day). But after the first of November, the mountain is open to anyone who wants to climb its snow-blanketed slopes.

To get there, from Woodland drive east on State Route 503 to the community of Cougar and continue east another 7 miles to a junction with Forest Road 83. Turn left (north) onto FR 83, and drive 5.8 miles to the Marble Mountain Sno-Park at the end of the plowed road.

From the Sno-Park, snowshoe north on Swift Creek Trail No. 244 as it follows the east bank of the creek toward the mountain. The trail climbs gradually, allowing you to loosen up and get into a good swing for the long, steady climb ahead. At 2.2 miles, the trail passes a well-marked side trail on the right leading down to June Lake (also reached via another trail described in Route 98). Stay left and climb northwest, moving above timberline to cross Swift Creek at 2.5 miles.

Once past Swift Creek, continue to traverse to the left (northwest) for another 0.25 mile, and then turn straight up the slope and start the long slog to the top. The idea is to follow the path of least resistance, flowing with the contours of the mountain. If the slope becomes too steep directly above, contour to the left or right until the pitch of the slope lessens somewhat or a more attractive avenue of ascent is found. By maintaining a bearing of nearly due north, with just a bit of correction to the west, you can top out on the ridge near the upper end of Monitor Ridge—the long, high spine to the west of Swift Creek. Monitor Ridge is the route used by summer climbers and leads to the best viewing site on the crater rim, although the true summit is found around to the northwest from the top of Monitor Ridge.

*Snowshoers preparing to go above timber line*

Because the upper slopes of Mount St. Helens are open and treeless, a great deal of wind scours the snowpack up there. This can result in deep drifts of soft snow or sheets of hard-packed snow and ice, depending on the conditions during the storms. Come prepared with snowshoes featuring aggressive mountaineering cleats on both heel and toe and carry—and know how to use—an ice ax for self-arresting in the event of a fall. This is a mountain climb and winter mountaineering skills are required.

## --98--

# June Lake

|  |  |
|---|---|
| **Rating:** | More difficult |
| **Round trip:** | 5 miles |
| **Hiking time:** | 3 hours |
| **Elevation gain:** | 500 feet |
| **High point:** | 3100 feet |
| **Best season:** | Late December through early March |
| **Map:** | Green Trails: Mount St. Helens Northwest No. 364S |
| **Who to Contact:** | Mount St. Helens National Volcanic Monument |

*Along the trail to June Lake*

The June Lake Trail is a beautiful hike any time of year, but exploring the trail on snowshoes, with the deep old forest, wide lake basin, and crashing waterfall all swaddled in a blanket of white, is the only way to enjoy the truly wild nature of the area. The trail is a gentle path through the woods, and snowshoers of all ages and abilities will appreciate and enjoy the remarkable beauty of the route.

Located on the south side of the big volcano, this trail doesn't delve into the blast zone, nor does the scenery make snowshoers think about the volcanic nature of the area. Indeed, if the eruption of 1980 comes to mind, it's usually in the context of "I can't believe an area this beautiful survived such a big eruption." The Mount St. Helens summit is visible along the trail to the lake, but looking up at the south flank of the mountain, with its snowy mantle of winter, it looks like just another big, beautiful peak. And June Lake is such a remarkable setting that it doesn't need the powerful imagery of the eruption to make it a wonderful snowshoeing destination.

To get there, from Woodland drive east on State Route 503 to the community of Cougar and continue east another 7 miles to a junction with Forest Road 83. Turn left (north) onto FR 83, and drive 5.8 miles to the Marble Mountain Sno-Park at the end of the plowed road. Small maps of the local winter trails are generally available in the kiosk inside the warming hut at the Sno-Park.

From the Sno-Park, snowshoe north from the upper parking lot on the well-signed Pine Marten Trail No. 245E. This trail, which is often groomed for skiers, parallels the road, but it is off-limits to snowmobiles. (You can also hike up the road to the June Lake trailhead, but it is often crowded with speeding snowmobiles.) The trail heads north for 0.75 mile, and then hooks right (east) and dips down to join the road at 1 mile. After using the road bridge to cross the wide Lake Creek, turn left and snowshoe into the large parking area of the well-marked June Lake trailhead.

The trail leaves the north end of the broad lot and crosses a large meadow in full view of Mount St. Helens. The open, treeless slopes are painted stark white by the drifting snow, and most weekends when the weather is clear, snowshoers on the June Lake Trail can watch snowshoers and skiers climbing the Monitor Ridge route (see Route 97) to the summit of the volcano.

The trail stays well above Lake Creek as it climbs gradually through a few stands of second-growth forest and open clearcuts before finally crossing into the protected national monument at 2.4 miles. The last few hundred yards of trail dip steeply down to cross the creek on a wide bridge before rolling north to the shore of June Lake. Across the lake, on the right, is a waterfall cascading down through a curtain of interlaced icicles. The wide bench at the lakeshore makes a wonderful picnic spot with its spectacular views.

## --99--
# Worm Flows

| | |
|---:|:---|
| **Rating:** | Backcountry |
| **Round trip:** | 7 miles |
| **Hiking time:** | 4.5 hours |
| **Elevation gain:** | 500 feet |
| **High point:** | 3100 feet |
| **Best season:** | Late December through early March |
| **Map:** | Green Trails: Mount St. Helens Northwest No. 364S |
| **Who to Contact:** | Mount St. Helens National Volcanic Monument |

*See map on page 254.*

The Worm Flows, long rippling lava flows from an eruption eons ago, roll down the southeast flank of Mount St. Helens creating a remarkably unique environment. The flows are somewhat masked by winter's heavy blanket of snow, but the undulating landscape testifies to their existence. The lava flowed and solidified into a roll, and then more lava flowed out over it, only to solidify into another roll. And on, and on, and on. The winter trails here barely touch on the Worm Flows, but they do offer great views of this geologic oddity on the flank of the mountain.

This route also offers an easy snowshoe trek through a chain of open meadows, linked by stands of pretty forest. There are opportunities to look up at the south face of Mount St. Helens or just enjoy the more immediate surroundings of sun-dappled meadows, sparkling woodland streams, and snow-laden evergreens. Look for a variety of birds here, from Stellar's and gray jays to ptarmigan and grouse, as well as small mammals burrowing through, and skittering over, the snow. Martens, weasels (with their winter white coats), coyotes, and raccoons may be seen here—or at least they are evident by the tracks they leave behind.

To get there, from Woodland drive east on State Route 503 to the community of Cougar and continue east another 7 miles to a junction with Forest Road 83. Turn left (north) onto FR 83, and drive 5.8 miles to the Marble Mountain Sno-Park at the end of the plowed road. Small maps of the local winter trails are generally available in the kiosk inside the warming hut at the Sno-Park.

Snowshoe north from the upper parking lot on the well-signed, nonmotorized Pine Marten Trail No. 245E, which parallels the road (open to snowmobilers) for a mile. The road and trail merge briefly at 1 mile so

*On the slope below the Worm Flows*

that snowshoers and skiers can safely cross the frigid waters of Lake Creek. Then the trail climbs to the left and away from the road once more, crosses the trail to June Lake (Route 98), and heads east to its end at mile 1.8. Although the Pine Marten Trail ends here, several other trails begin. A large kiosk/message board is posted here each winter, with a map of the local trails well marked on it.

Several routes are possible, but the one most appropriate for snowshoers is the Middle Sasquatch Trail across the base of the Worm Flows. This trail, No. 236A, is a 3.4-mile loop through meadows, forests, and the Worm Flows. From the end of the Pine Marten Trail and the trail kiosk, go left and snowshoe up a gentle hill between two creek basins. Well-placed blazes on trees and poles mark the route, but if they aren't visible, just stay on a northerly bearing, climbing along an old, faint logging road. (It is sometimes difficult to see the road when the snow is deep or heavily drifted.)

At the top of the ridge, near mile 2.7, find a well-marked trail intersection with a very distinct logging road heading east. This less-prominent trail leads straight ahead through the junction and is the start of the longer loop option, which adds about 2 miles to the total trip distance. For the Middle Trail, though, go right onto the logging road and follow it on a long, gradual drop through open forest for 1 mile to another well-marked trail junction. To the left is the end of the longer loop option, so go right to complete the Middle Trail loop. The trail curves south for 0.25 mile, and then turns abruptly west and completes the loop portion of the hike at 5.2 miles. Follow the Pine Marten Trail back to the Sno-Park from the end of the loop.

## --*100*--

# Table Rock/Squaw Peak

**Rating:** Most difficult/Backcountry
**Round trip:** 22 miles
**Hiking time:** 2 to 3 days
**Elevation gain:** 1800 feet
**High point:** 5900 feet
**Best season:** December through February
**Map:** USGS: Godman Spring, Deadman Peak
**Who to Contact:** Umatilla National Forest, Pomeroy Ranger District

This hike starts out easy and gets progressively more difficult to the end—at which point the views make the whole effort worthwhile. Table Rock is a flat-topped ridge crest that is home to an old, still-used fire lookout tower. Due west of the lookout is the untouched Mill Creek watershed, a deep forested basin that has been protected and placed off-limits to all—this watershed provides the drinking water for the Walla Walla area.

The lookout is accessible by four-wheel-drive vehicles in the summer, but shortly after the first snows fall in late autumn, the road is closed by slides and avalanches. Winter hikers, in fact, have to avoid sections of the road and hike the knife-edged ridges for the last couple of miles.

*Lookout tower on the broad summit of Table Rock*

To get there, from Dayton turn south off U.S. Highway 12 onto Fourth Street (North Touchet Road) and drive south 19.5 miles to the Touchet Corrals Sno-Park. The parking area is on the left.

The parking area was built by volunteer labor from the local snowmobile club back in the late 1970s when the nearby Bluewood Ski Resort was built. Snowmobilers continue to be the primary users of this Sno-Park, but snowshoers and skiers also flock to the area. Most trails begin at the end of a long "expressway" that parallels the road from the Sno-Park for nearly a mile before ducking under the road, through a 6-foot-tall culvert.

On the other side, the trail climbs a steep bank and follows the snow-covered road. Just a couple miles up the road, the trail forks at a registration box. Stop here long enough to sign in, and then continue straight ahead on the main road. In just 0.1 mile, another fork is met. Stay right at this junction, and continue to climb for another 1.5 miles as more and more views greet your eyes. The road you are following was cut into a steep valley wall, but in twenty years of enjoying this area, I have never seen a single avalanche on this section. As you near the head of this valley, the route levels off in a broad open meadow. Most traffic (skiers and snowmobilers) will take off to the left, cutting through the meadow to angle back toward the top of the ski area. Instead, follow the path to the southwest into the trees.

After a long, arcing 0.5 mile, a third junction is encountered. This is where you leave everyone else behind and head for the wild country. Take a left onto this narrow track into the trees and begin climbing a twisting, turning two-track path. This route parallels the boundary of the Wenaha-Tucannon Wilderness Area. If you step twenty paces or so to the left, you are in the wilderness.

This route climbs gradually, occasionally breaking into small open meadows with views into the deep Wenaha Valley. Take a few minutes to study the valley below because you might see elk, or at least their paths worn into the deep snow. At about 8.5 miles, in a shallow saddle, you leave the road. Hike into the deep snow to your right until you reach the top of a small prominence. Bear south once more, sticking to the contour of the ridge top. The ridge grows ever steeper and more narrow until, after about 2 miles, you find yourself looking down into a deep saddle in the ridgeline. The ridge crest is no more than 12 feet wide at this point and at the bottom of the saddle— some 200 feet below.

As you start the final 0.5-mile climb to the lookout tower ahead, the ridge narrows to 6 feet in places. Stick to the middle, and you'll be fine—you're actually walking on rock here. Fierce winds whip up out of the Mill Creek basin on your right and crash down into the Wenaha Valley on your left.

At the top of the final pitch, find the lookout tower—now boarded up

and secured against the bitter winter winds. Enjoy the view, and then move off to the eastern edge of the rocky plateau where an old ranger cabin, stock shed, and corral are found at the edge of the forest. Set up camp on the lee-ward side of these buildings for a quiet night.

If you have any energy left after making camp, follow the road east, down past the cabin, and in just 0.25 mile, you'll encounter the main road (which you abandoned some miles before). Cross this road, and hike to the top of the cone-shaped peak directly ahead. This is Squaw Peak, and it is within the Wenaha-Tucannon Wilderness. It is about the same elevation as Table Rock, but where the view from the lookout is down into the protected Mill Creek watershed, the view from Squaw Peak is down into the protected wilderness area. Looking south, you'll see the Oregon Blue Mountains (just 2 miles as the crow flies) and on clear days, you can make out the jagged peaks of the Seven Devils bordering Hells Canyon, as well as the peaks of the Wallowa Mountains.

# Appendix A
## Contact Information

### WEATHER
**Northwest Weather and Avalanche Center**
7600 Sandpoint Way NE
Seattle, WA 98115
(206) 526-6677
*www.nwac.noaa.gov*

### LAND MANAGERS
**Mount Tahoma Trails Association**
PO Box 206
Ashford, WA 98304
*www.skimtta.com*

### *Washington State Parks*
*www.parks.wa.gov*

**Mount Pilchuck State Park**
c/o Washington State Parks Northwest Region
220 Walnut Street, Box 487
Burlington, WA 98233
(360) 755-9231

### *National Park Service*
**Mount Rainier National Park**
Headquarters
Tahoma Woods, Star Route
Ashford, WA 98104
(360) 569-2211
*www.nps.gov/mora*

**Mount St. Helens National Volcanic Monument**
Headquarters
42218 NE Yale Bridge Road
Amboy, WA 98601
(360) 247-3900
*www.fs.fed.us/gpnf/mshnvm*

**Olympic National Park**
Visitor Center and Wilderness Information Center
600 East Park Avenue
Port Angeles, WA 98362
(360) 565-3130 and (360) 565-3100
*www.nps.gov/olym*

### *Gifford Pinchot National Forest*
*www.fs.fed.us/gpnf*

Cowlitz Valley Ranger District
10024 U.S. Highway 12
Randle, WA 98377-9105
(360) 497-1100

### *Mount Baker–Snoqualmie National Forest*
*www.fs.fed.us/r6/mbs*

Darrington Ranger District
1405 Emmens Street
Darrington, WA 98241
(360) 436-1155

Mount Baker Ranger District
810 State Route 20
Sedro-Woolley, WA 98284
(360) 856-5700

Skykomish Ranger District
74920 NE Stevens Pass Highway
Skykomish, WA 98288
(360) 677-2414

Snoqualmie Ranger District
Enumclaw Office
450 Roosevelt Avenue E
Enumclaw, WA 98022
(360) 825-6585

North Bend Office
42404 SE North Bend Way
North Bend, WA 98045
(425) 888-1421

## Okanogan National Forest
*www.fs.fed.us/r6/oka*

### Methow Valley Ranger District
Twisp Office
502 Glover
Twisp, WA 98856
(509) 997-2131

Winthrop Office
24 West Chewuch Road
Winthrop, WA 98862
(509) 996-4000

## Olympic National Forest
*www.fs.fed.us/r6/olympic*

### Hood Canal Ranger District
Quilcene Office
295142 U.S. Highway 101
Quilcene, WA 98376
(360) 765-2200

## Umatilla National Forest
*www.fs.fed.us/r6/uma*

### Pomeroy Ranger District
71 West Main
Pomeroy, WA 99347
(509) 843-1891

## Wenatchee National Forest
*www.fs.fed.us/wenatchee*

### Cle Elum Ranger District
803 West Second Street
Cle Elum, WA 98922
(509) 674-4411

### Lake Wenatchee Ranger District
22976 State Route 207
Leavenworth, WA 98826
(509) 763-3103

### Leavenworth Ranger District
600 Sherbourne Street
Leavenworth, WA 98826
(509) 548-6977

### Naches Ranger District
10061 U.S. Highway 12
Naches, WA 98937
(509) 653-2205

# Appendix B

## Quick Reference to the Trails

| | Trail Name | Rating | Best Season | Hiking time | Elevation gain (feet) | Family friendly | Panoramic views | Wildlife viewing |
|---|---|---|---|---|---|---|---|---|
| 1 | Hurricane Hill | Easiest+ | Dec-March | 4 hrs | 800 | X | X | |
| 2 | Mount Angeles | Backcountry | Dec-March | 6 hrs | 600 | | X | X |
| 3 | Eagle Point | Most Difficult | Dec-March | 7 hr+ | 2500 | | X | X |
| 4 | Klahhane Ridge | More Difficult | Jan-March | 6 hrs | 1500 | X | X | X |
| 5 | Blue Mountain / Deer Park | More Difficult | Jan-March | 6 hrs+ | 2500 | | X | X |
| 6 | Mount Townsend | Most Difficult | Dec-March | 7 hrs + | 2500 | | X | X |
| 7 | Lena Lake/ Valley of Silent Men | Backcountry | Jan-Feb | 6 hrs | 2000 | X | | X |
| 8 | Coal Pass | More Difficult | Jan-March | 6 hrs | 2400 | X | X | |
| 9 | Coleman Glacier | Backcountry | Jan-Feb | 1-2 days | 4500 | | X | X |
| 10 | White Salmon Creek | Easiest | Dec-March | 6 hrs | 300 | X | | |
| 11 | Artist Point | More Difficult | Dec-April | 4 hrs | 1200 | X | X | |
| 12 | Middle Fork Nooksack | Backcountry | Dec-Feb | 5 hrs | 900 | X | | X |
| 13 | Schriebers Meadow | More Difficult | Jan-March | 1-2 days | 1200 | X | X | X |
| 14 | Sauk Mountain | Backcountry | Dec-Feb | 8 hrs | 3500 | | X | X |
| 15 | Iron Mountain | Backcountry | Jan-March | 8 hrs | 1800 | | X | X |
| 16 | Segelsen Ridge | Easiest+ | Jan-Feb | 6 hrs+ | 2500 | X | X | X |
| 17 | Rat Trap Pass | More Difficult | Dec-Feb | 6 hrs | 1900 | | X | X |
| 18 | Crystal Lake | Backcountry | Jan-Feb | 1-2 days | 2800 | | X | X |
| 19 | Kennedy Hot Springs | Backcountry | Jan-Feb | 1-2 days | 1050 | | | X |
| 20 | Mount Pilchuck | Easiest+ | Jan-Feb | 10 hrs | 2600 | | X | |
| 21 | Heather Lake | More Difficult | Jan-Feb | 4 hrs | 1100 | X | X | X |
| 22 | Lake Twentytwo | Backcountry | Jan-Feb | 4 hrs | 1200 | | X | X |
| 23 | Boardman Lake | More Difficult | Dec-Feb | 1-2 days | 1800 | | | X |
| 24 | Bear Lake | More Difficult | Jan-Feb | 6 hrs | 1400 | X | | X |
| 25 | Mallardy Ridge | More Difficult | Jan-March | 6 hrs | 1900 | | X | X |
| 26 | Marten Creek | Backcountry | Dec-Feb | 5 hrs | 1300 | X | | X |

| | Trail Name | Rating | Best Season | Hiking time | Elevation gain (feet) | Family friendly | Panoramic views | Wildlife viewing |
|---|---|---|---|---|---|---|---|---|
| 27 | Kelcema Lake | More Difficult | Jan-Feb | 6 hrs | 1600 | X | | X |
| 28 | Coal Creek | More Difficult | Jan-March | 4 hrs | 900 | X | | |
| 29 | Big Four Ice Caves Viewpoint | Easiest | Jan-March | 3.5 hrs | 250 | X | | |
| 30 | Silver Star View | More Difficult | Dec-March | 3 hrs+ | 700 | X | | |
| 31 | Upper River Run | Easiest | Dec-March | 4 hrs | 500 | X | | X |
| 32 | Cedar Falls | More Difficult | Dec-March | 5 hrs | 800 | X | | X |
| 33 | Paul Mountain | Easiest+ | Jan-March | 5 hrs | 1500 | X | | |
| 34 | Buck Mountain | More Difficult | Dec-March | 6.5 hrs | 2500 | | X | X |
| 35 | Lookout Mountain | More Difficult | Dec-March | 5 hrs | 2100 | X | X | |
| 36 | Eagle Creek | Backcountry | Jan-March | 4 hrs+ | 4900 | | X | X |
| 37 | East Fork Foss River | More Difficult | Dec-April | 1-2 days | 1200 | | | X |
| 38 | Tonga Ridge | Easiest | Nov-Dec | 5 hrs | 1400 | X | X | |
| 39 | Surprise Lake | Backcountry | Dec-April | 6 hrs | 2300 | | X | X |
| 40 | Lake Susan Jane | More Difficult | Dec-April | 3.5 hrs | 1200 | X | | |
| 41 | Skyline Lake | More Difficult | Dec-April | 2 hrs | 1100 | | | |
| 42 | Lake Valhalla | More Difficult | Dec-March | 5.5 hrs | 1700 | X | | X |
| 43 | Lanham Lake | More Difficult | Dec-March | 3 hrs | 1100 | X | | X |
| 44 | Wenatchee Ridge | Easiest+ | Jan-Feb | 7 hrs | 2000 | X | X | |
| 45 | Chiwaukum Creek | More Difficult | Dec-March | 6 hrs+ | 1200 | | | X |
| 46 | Eightmile Creek | Backcountry | Dec-March | 1-2 days | 2600 | | X | X |
| 47 | Talapus Lake | Most Difficult | Jan-March | 7 hrs | 1600 | | X | |
| 48 | Granite Mountain | Backcountry | Dec-March | 8 hrs | 3750 | | X | |
| 49 | Source Lake | More Difficult | Jan-March | 5 hrs | 1000 | X | | |
| 50 | Snow Lake | More Difficult | Jan-March | 7 hrs + | 2000 | | X | X |
| 51 | Commonwealth Basin | Backcountry | Jan-March | 7 hrs | 2300 | | | X |
| 52 | Kendall Peak Lakes | Most Difficult | Jan-March | 7 hrs | 1700 | | X | |
| 53 | Lower Gold Creek Basin | Easiest+ | Dec-Feb | 4 hrs | 400 | X | | |
| 54 | Alaska Lake | Easiest+ | Jan-March | 8 hrs+ | 1600 | X | | |
| 55 | Mount Margaret | Easiest+ | Dec-Feb | 6 hrs | 2800 | X | | X |
| 56 | Keechelus Ridge | More Difficult | Jan-Feb | 5 hrs | 2100 | | X | |
| 57 | Amabilis Mountain | Most Difficult | Jan-Feb | 6 hrs | 2100 | | X | |
| 58 | Twin Lakes | Easiest | Dec-Feb | 5 hrs | 400 | X | | |
| 59 | Windy Pass/ Mount Catherine | Most Difficult | Dec-Feb | 8 hrs | 2300 | X | | |
| 60 | Keechelus Lake/ John Wayne | Easiest | Dec-Feb | 3 hrs | 200 | X | | |
| 61 | Hex Mountain | More Difficult | Dec-March | 6 hrs | 2600 | | X | |
| 62 | Sasse Ridge | Backcountry | Dec-March | 2 days | 2700 | | X | X |
| 63 | Thorp Mountain | Backcountry | Dec-March | 2 days | 2800 | | X | X |

| | Trail Name | Rating | Best Season | Hiking time | Elevation gain (feet) | Family friendly | Panoramic views | Wildlife viewing |
|---|---|---|---|---|---|---|---|---|
| 64 | Salmon la Sac Creek | Most Difficult | Dec-March | 5 hrs | 1300 | | | X |
| 65 | Cooper River | More Difficult | Dec-March | 6 hrs | 400 | X | | |
| 66 | Indian Creek | Easiest+ | Dec-March | 2-10 hrs | 1300 | X | X | X |
| 67 | Swauk Forest Discovery Trail | Easiest | Dec-March | 2 hrs | 450 | X | | X |
| 68 | Diamond Head | More Difficult | Dec-March | 7 hrs | 1800 | X | X | X |
| 69 | Haney Meadow Loop | More Difficult | Dec-March | 8 hrs+ | 1600 | X | | X |
| 70 | Wenatchee Crest | Easiest | Dec-March | 5 hrs | 400 | X | | |
| 71 | Sun Top | More Difficult | Jan-Feb | 7.5 hrs | 3000 | | X | |
| 72 | Bullion Basin | Backcountry | Dec-March | 4 hrs | 1500 | | X | X |
| 73 | White River | Easiest | Dec-Feb | 3 hrs | 400 | X | | |
| 74 | Mowich Lake | Easiest | Dec-March | 6 hrs+ | 1400 | X | | |
| 75 | Paul Peak | Most Difficult | Dec-March | 6.5 hrs | 1800 | | | X |
| 76 | Copper Creek Hut | More Difficult | Dec-April | 5 hrs | 1000 | X | | |
| 77 | Busywild Overlook | Easiest | Dec-March | 4 hrs | 900 | X | X | |
| 78 | Snow Bowl Hut | More Difficult | Dec-April | 7 hrs + | 2000 | X | X | |
| 79 | High Hut | More Difficult | Dec-April | 7 hrs + | 2400 | X | X | |
| 80 | Kautz Creek | More Difficult | Jan-March | 7 hrs | 2800 | | | X |
| 81 | Eagle and Chutla Peaks Trail | Most Difficult | Jan-March | 6 hrs | 2900 | | X | X |
| 82 | Rampart Ridge | More Difficult | Jan-March | 5 hrs | 1200 | X | X | X |
| 83 | Wonderland Trail | Easiest | Dec-April | 5 hrs | 1300 | X | | X |
| 84 | Reflection and Louise Lakes | More Difficult | Dec-May | 4 hrs+ | 560 | | X | X |
| 85 | Pinnacle Saddle | Most Difficult | Dec-May | 5 hrs | 1400 | | X | X |
| 86 | Glacier Vista | Easiest | Dec-May | 3 hrs | 700 | X | X | |
| 87 | Panorama Point | Most Difficult | Dec-May | 4 hrs | 1300 | | X | |
| 88 | Mazama Ridge | More Difficult | Dec-April | 5 hrs | 900 | X | X | X |
| 89 | Camp Muir | Most Difficult | Feb-May | 9 hrs+ | 4400 | | X | |
| 90 | Silver Falls/Grove of the Patriarchs | More Difficult | Jan-March | 3.5 hrs | 400 | X | | X |
| 91 | Olallie Creek | Most Difficult | Jan-March | 7 hrs + | 1800 | | | X |
| 92 | Packwood Lake | Most Difficult | Jan-March | 7 hrs + | 500 | X | | X |
| 93 | Sand Lake | More Difficult | Dec-March | 5 hrs | 900 | X | | |
| 94 | Cramer Lake | Most Difficult | Dec-March | 7 hrs | 800 | X | | X |
| 95 | Tieton River Meadows | Easiest | Dec-March | 8 hrs | 350 | X | | X |
| 96 | Goat Peak | Backcountry | Dec-March | 5 hrs | 2600 | | X | X |
| 97 | Mount St. Helens Summit | Backcountry | Dec-Feb | 9 hrs | 5700 | | X | |
| 98 | June Lake | More Difficult | Dec-March | 3 hrs | 500 | X | | |
| 99 | Worm Flows | Backcountry | Dec-March | 4.5 hrs | 500 | | | X |
| 100 | Table Rock/Squaw Peak | Backcountry | Dec-Feb | 2-3 days | 1800 | | X | X |

# Index

# About the Author

----------------------------------------------------

DAN NELSON considers himself an outdoor enthusiast. After eleven years as the editor of *Washington Trails* magazine, and as the current editor of *Hang Gliding & Paragliding* magazine, he works and plays in the backcountry of Washington on a daily basis. He is an avid hiker, backpacker and paraglider pilot. If he is not out enjoying the backcountry, he is indoors writing about it. In addition to his work as editor of *Hang Gliding & Paragliding*, Dan contributes to *The Seattle Times* and *BACKPACKER* magazine, specializing in Northwest destinations and outdoor equipment reviews. He is also author or editor of four other guide books (*Best of the Pacific Crest Trail: Washington; Best Loop Hikes: Washington; Accessible Trails in Washington* and co-author with Ron Judd of *Pacific Northwest Hiking: The Complete Guide*); and one book of wildlife essays (*Predators at Risk in the Pacific Northwest*).

Dan was born in Ripon, Wisconsin, but his family moved to Dayton, near the Blue Mountains of southeast Washington, when he was just three years old. His family soon began to spend summers camping in the Blues, and Dan grew up hunting, fishing, hiking and skiing throughout those mountains and the nearby Snake River plateau. He moved to Puyallup in 1989 after graduating from Washington State University, and has been living there ever since.

THE MOUNTAINEERS, founded in 1906, is a nonprofit outdoor activity and conservation club, whose mission is "to explore, study, preserve, and enjoy the natural beauty of the outdoors . . . ." Based in Seattle, Washington, the club is now the third-largest such organization in the United States, with 15,000 members and five branches throughout Washington State.

The Mountaineers sponsors both classes and year-round outdoor activities in the Pacific Northwest, which include hiking, mountain climbing, ski-touring, snowshoeing, bicycling, camping, kayaking and canoeing, nature study, sailing, and adventure travel. The club's conservation division supports environmental causes through educational activities, sponsoring legislation, and presenting informational programs. All club activities are led by skilled, experienced volunteers, who are dedicated to promoting safe and responsible enjoyment and preservation of the outdoors.

If you would like to participate in these organized outdoor activities or the club's programs, consider a membership in The Mountaineers. For information and an application, write or call The Mountaineers, Club Headquarters, 300 Third Avenue West, Seattle, WA 98119; 206-284-6310.

The Mountaineers Books, an active, nonprofit publishing program of the club, produces guidebooks, instructional texts, historical works, natural history guides, and works on environmental conservation. All books produced by The Mountaineers Books fulfill the club's mission.

*Send or call for our catalog of more than 500 outdoor titles:*

The Mountaineers Books
1001 SW Klickitat Way, Suite 201
Seattle, WA 98134
800-553-4453
mbooks@mountaineersbooks.org
www.mountaineersbooks.org

The Mountaineers Books is proud to be a corporate sponsor of Leave No Trace, whose mission is to promote and inspire responsible outdoor recreation through education, research, and partnerships. The Leave No Trace program is focused specifically on human-powered (nonmotorized) recreation.

Leave No Trace strives to educate visitors about the nature of their recreational impacts, as well as offer techniques to prevent and minimize such impacts. Leave No Trace is best understood as an educational and ethical program, not as a set of rules and regulations.

For more information, visit *www.LNT.org*, or call 800-332-4100.